MW00353852

THREAT to DEMOCRACY

THE APPEAL OF AUTHORITARIANISM IN AN AN AGE OF UNCERTAINTY

FATHALI M. MOGHADDAM

American Psychological Association
Washington, DC

Published by
American Psychological Association
750 First Street, NE
Washington, DC 20002
https://www.apa.org

Order Department
https://www.apa.org/pubs/books
order@apa.org

In the U.K., Europe, Africa, and the Middle East, copies may be ordered from Eurospan
https://www.eurospanbookstore.com/apa
info@eurospangroup.com

Typeset in Meridien and Ortodoxa by Circle Graphics, Inc., Reisterstown, MD

Printer: Maple Press, York, PA
Cover Designer: Naylor Design, Washington, DC

Library of Congress Cataloging-in-Publication Data

Names: Moghaddam, Fathali M., author.
Title: Threat to democracy : the appeal of authoritarianism in an age of uncertainty / by Fathali M. Moghaddam.
Description: First edition. | Washington, DC : American Psychological Association, [2019] | Includes bibliographical references and index.
Identifiers: LCCN 2018054610 (print) | LCCN 2019009225 (ebook) | ISBN 9781433831089 (eBook) | ISBN 1433831082 (eBook) | ISBN 9781433830709 (hardcover) | ISBN 1433830701 (hardcover)
Subjects: LCSH: Authoritarianism—Psychological aspects. | Dictatorship—Psychological aspects. | Democracy.
Classification: LCC JC480 (ebook) | LCC JC480 .M64 2019 (print) | DDC 320.5301/9—dc23
LC record available at https://lccn.loc.gov/2018054610

http://dx.doi.org/10.1037/0000142-000

Printed in the United States of America

10 9 8 7 6 5 4 3 2 1

This book is dedicated to Muzafer Sherif, Stanley Milgram, and Philip Zimbardo, for their seminal research illuminating the power of context to shape behavior.

CONTENTS

PREFACE

I wrote this book because of the urgent need to gain a deeper understanding of the widespread decline of democracy and the unnerving movement toward dictatorship in the 21st century. We are confronted by serious and unexpected challenges to our freedoms and human rights. By the end of this century, the United States, the European Union, and other societies that are at present relatively open may be overtaken economically and militarily by China and other dictatorships. Closed societies might well become the dominant global powers and the ones that set the norms around the world.

Open societies are not only facing threats from the outside. The election of Donald Trump and the rise of populist far-right "strongmen" (leaders who use threat, intimidation, displacement of aggression onto minorities, and various other tactics that undermine democracy) movements in a number of countries signal threats to open societies from the inside.[1] The recent history of authoritarian strongmen, including Hitler (1889–1945) and Mussolini (1883–1945), who for a time enjoyed wildly popular support, is not promising in terms of preserving open societies. Of course, as Federico Finchelstein[2] pointed out, the fascism of the 1930s is different from the populism of the 21st century, just as the strongmen of the 1930s are in some respects different from Trump and other 21st-century strongmen. However, 1930s fascism and 21st-century populism have in common the direct threat to the free press, rule of law, and democracy.

We need to gain a deeper understanding of threats to democracy in the context of *globalization*, the increasing economic and cultural integration of societies around the world, and the international populist backlash that is sweeping across national boundaries. No doubt, the threat to democracy is to some degree linked to the excesses of free-market capitalism, as Karl Polyani[3] (1886–1964) and a number of more recent authors[4] have argued. However, the irrationalist dimension of 21st-century populist antidemocracy movements is of the greatest importance and also requires analysis, and I argue that psychological science is a necessary and fruitful foundation for understanding the plight of contemporary democracy.

The puzzle of how to explain and combat populist support for authoritarian leadership became central to my life when I returned to Iran in early 1979. The 1979 revolution in Iran toppled the dictator Shah but soon after brought to power the dictator Khomeini through populist support. What explains this populist enthusiasm for authoritarian rule? The psychological literature presents possible answers, with psychoanalytic explanations and Erich Fromm's "escape from freedom"[5] thesis being widely influential. Fromm's analysis concludes that freedom in the modern world is associated with anxiety, alienation, and other painful experiences from which people want to escape.

My focus on Fromm's analysis is justified by its high level of historic and continued influence. At the time of the publication of this book, Fromm's seminal work, *Escape From Freedom,* had been cited about 7,000 times, and the number of citations it had received increased from between 100 and 200 each year in the first decade of the 21st century to more than 300 citations each year in the second decade, indicating rising influence. Although my ideas as expressed in this book have been influenced by a variety of perspectives, including cognitive psychology, cognitive neuroscience, social psychology, and political psychology, I pay particular attention to Fromm because of his continued and global influence. *Escape From Freedom* has been translated into numerous languages, and I have witnessed Fromm's ideas being discussed in various non-Western societies, including in Iran, where the book is available in Farsi.

But Fromm's explanation is unconvincing in many ways. From my own research in Iran immediately after the revolution, it was clear that most Iranians followed Khomeini not to escape from freedom but to enjoy the freedoms and the "better life" he promised. The problem is that most Iranians were misled because at that time few understood Khomeini's real plans and motives. The Shah's censors had made sure that Khomeini's highly backward views about women, democracy, and human rights had remained hidden. As I discuss in later chapters, this proved to be a foolish policy, with terrible consequences for Iranian society. Second, from about 1977, a group of Western-educated and relatively liberal Muslims surrounded Khomeini and filtered his communications, so he (misleadingly) came across as being in support of openness, freedom, and democracy (after he became dictator, Khomeini actually had most of these liberal Muslims killed or sidelined in other ways). Most Iranians who supported Khomeini did so because they believed he was leading them on a path to greater liberation and glory, not to an escape from freedom.

The same is true in other cases of populist support for authoritarian strongmen, including in the United States. To label Trump supporters as "deplorables" is to neglect their deeper motivations. Supporters of Donald Trump see him as "Making America Great Again" and as leading them to greater freedom and glory, not escaping from freedom and glory.

The target audience for this book includes (a) the lay public and academics interested in better understanding the psychology of dictatorship and threats to democracy in the United States and around the world and (b) students and teachers in courses on politics, government, and political psychology.

ACKNOWLEDGMENTS

I am deeply grateful to Rom Harré, David Lightfoot, Donald Taylor, Philip Moore, Bill Bryson, Jonathan Cobb, Duncan Wu, and other colleagues for rich conversations through which I have gained valuable insights. A number of anonymous reviewers and students (particularly Sierra Campbell) provided feedback on earlier drafts of this book. Christopher Kelaher of the American Psychological Association played an important role in the launching of this project, and I am grateful to him for his insights and support. Katherine Lenz provided insightful editorial guidance in the final stages of the project, and I am grateful for her input.

ENDNOTES

1. As Jon Stone (2018) reports, far right populists are surging in influence across Europe.
2. Finchelstein (2017).
3. Polyani (1944).
4. For example, see Kuttner (2018).
5. Fromm (1941).

THREAT to DEMOCRACY

Introduction

ESCAPE

Mehrabad Airport, Tehran, Iran. November 1983. I was trying not to show signs of emotion, but my heart was racing even faster than my mind. We had just watched security guards triumphantly confiscate the passport of a middle-aged Iranian woman immediately in front of me in the winding line of people fearfully waiting to get through customs and security, and finally out of Iran. The security guards had discovered a dozen or so small diamonds hidden in the lining of her suitcase and gleefully held up the jewels for all to see, while snatching away her passport. Having lost her chance of leaving Iran legally, she collapsed to the floor begging for mercy. Now her only option would be to pay smugglers who could slip her across the border into Turkey or Pakistan, or rob her and slit her throat.

We had all become truly desperate. I was part of a flood of people frantic to escape the growing despotism, postrevolution turmoil, and utterly senseless war plaguing Iran in the wake of the despotic shah's fall.[1] Everyone felt compelled to try to hide something of high monetary value in their luggage—gold coins, jewelry, small antiques—anything that could be sold to support oneself outside Iran, now suffering under Khomeini's dogmatism and ruthlessness. Getting through airport security was only the first step, and we all knew it was essential to have some money to restart our lives wherever we could find shelter in the world outside Iran.

http://dx.doi.org/10.1037/0000142-001
Threat to Democracy: The Appeal of Authoritarianism in an Age of Uncertainty,
by F. M. Moghaddam

How dramatically my life had changed in just 5 years. As I stood watching the guards feverishly tear apart my luggage, the two small cases I would eventually leave with, I recalled myself as a younger, more idealistic person, eager to rejoin and serve Iranian society. I had been a student in England as the anti-shah movement gained momentum in the 1970s and when the revolution erupted and the shah's corrupt American-backed dictatorship collapsed in 1978–1979. Eager to help build a democratic Iranian society, I had rushed back to the country of my birth. I had driven overland from London to Tehran in a caravan of cars filled with Western-educated Iranians, all of us hopeful for the future of Iran and the Middle East. We believed that the growth of Iranian democracy would ignite reforms and launch peace movements in the surrounding societies of the Islamic world and the entire region would make huge progress. We dared to dream that the democratization of the Islamic world would improve Arab–Israeli relations.

As soon as I arrived in Tehran I began teaching at universities, writing and speaking out about social issues and democracy for a broader audience, reveling in the political and cultural freedoms that we now enjoyed. In the 1979 Spring of Revolution, one could taste freedom on the jubilant streets of Tehran. We were young, wildly enthusiastic, and idealistic.

Women were experiencing exhilarating improvements in their lives—free to actually decide for themselves whether they wanted to wear the Islamic *hijab* (veil), liberated to play a larger public role in the wider society. The shah's father, the founder of the Pahlavi dynasty, had forced women to remove the veil; now Islamic extremists wanted to force women to wear the full hijab, but in the giddy revolutionary atmosphere of early 1979, no one had the power to force them to do anything. Women became far more active in the political and cultural life of Iran, almost as publicly visible as men. Along with women, all manner of religious, political, and ethnic minorities had burst into the public arena. In 1979, everything seemed to point to Iran becoming a more open, tolerant, and democratic society. But that proved to be a tragic and costly mirage, both for Iranian society and for me personally.

FREEDOM FOUND, FREEDOM LOST

Iranians had moved from the sterile stability of the shah's regime to a more exciting and unpredictable situation. A people who were used to being ordered what to do and what to think suddenly found themselves with new possibilities. This was an exciting and exhilarating experience for many people, as we looked with wonder and hope at the power vacuum that had opened up. But we failed to recognize that Khomeini and his followers were preparing to use whatever means necessary to take charge and fill that power vacuum. Their vision of the ideal Islamic society did not involve openness, freedom of expression, minority rights, or even basic human rights for the general population.

Khomeini used a two-pronged approach to end freedoms and reinstate dictatorship, this time with himself instead of the shah as absolute dictator. First, he presented himself as the champion of freedom and justice for all, the leader who would safeguard their aspirations for liberation and collective glory. He told the people that they were superior to the West because they had Islam. They did not need to copy the West because Islam had given them an authentic identity, one that would liberate them from the yoke of Western oppression. They would find their freedom, justice, glory, and authenticity through Islam. This message was consistently broadcast in 1978 and 1979.

The second prong of Khomeini's strategy consisted of brute force, ruthlessly applied. Particularly since 9/11, I have heard people claim that "terrorism does not work." They are wrong: Sometimes it can be incredibly effective. In 1979, terrorist tactics were effectively used in Iran by a fanatical religious minority, determined to capture all power and gain absolute control of the country. The Islamic fanatics following Khomeini used bombings, assassinations, kidnappings—an array of violence to terrorize the Iranian population into submission, to enable them to reinstate a dictatorship, this time with extremist mullahs controlling the reins of power. The shah's regime had evaporated, but now we faced Islamic dictatorship and quickly learned how easy it is for religious fanatics to kill "with God on their side." Instead of freedom, we were now experiencing the bitter taste of terror on the streets under the new dictator Khomeini.

By early 1980, it had become a chaotic, dangerous time to live in Tehran. The Hostage Crisis at the American Embassy (which began November 4, 1979, and ended January 20, 1981) was still in its infancy, but it had already brought a feverish atmosphere to the city; freedom was methodically being suffocated. Khomeini's fanatical followers used the Hostage Crisis to monopolize attention and resources, as they branded their political competitors as "spies" and "enemies of Islam." Several secular political groups were also still active in 1980, but they now struggled to survive, while Islamic extremists fought to suppress any challenge to their monopoly of power. Car bombs, sudden disappearances, and assassinations became routine, and amid the bloody confusion, Iranian women were pressured to return to the Islamic veil and get out of public life. Those "immoral" women who had become *be-hijab* (without the veil) were forced to "mend their ways," sometimes by having acid hurled at their faces. The Islamic extremists were adamant that women should be driven back to their traditional role inside the home–even those millions of women who had been educated in universities, many with advanced degrees from elite Iranian and Western universities.

To consolidate his power, in 1980 Khomeini directed his fanatical followers, who claimed that God had placed the image of his face on the moon, to launch a so-called Cultural Revolution. The specific targets of the Cultural Revolution were the universities, which were the last bastion of resistance against the reinstatement of dictatorship.[2] I was teaching at both Tehran University and the National University at that time and was a witness to Khomeini's brutal attack on universities. He sent in mobs wielding clubs, chains, and knives to shut down the institutions; students and faculty who resisted were violently attacked. Khomeini accused those professors who dared oppose him of being un-Islamic traitors who had sold out to the West and who had "rotten brains." Some faculty and students were imprisoned or killed.

Soon the prisons, which had recently been joyfully emptied during the anti-shah revolution, were brimming once again with brutalized political prisoners—all "in the name of God!" As in the case of the Bolsheviks in the 1917 revolution in Russia,[3] in Iran a fanatical minority used ruthless aggression to opportunistically grab power in the postrevolution turmoil. The focused, categorically thinking, unquestioning determination of would-be dictators, such as Khomeini, gives them a huge advantage over the "wishy-washy" open-minded democratic opposition. We are reminded here of Alan Bullock's insight that "like Hitler, Stalin could afford to be an opportunist because, unlike his opponents, he was clear about his aims."[4]

I was thinking about Tehran's rapidly expanding Evin Prison with its alarming number of new political prisoners when the security guards gave up searching my suitcases and grudgingly waved me through to the airport departure area. Tears filled my eyes. Although almost free, I was leaving my mother behind. I would see her only briefly again before she died in Iran 16 years later.

Should I have known Iran would move from the shah's dictatorship to the even more brutal dictatorship of Khomeini and the mullahs? Had I been too naive and overly optimistic? Did we supporters of democracy use the wrong tactics; could we have prevented the Islamic dictatorship in Iran? As I slowly and tortuously rebuilt my life in the West, first in Canada and then in the United States, I have continued to anguish over these questions. Recent experiences, from the ill-fated, poorly planned, and disastrously implemented attempt to export democracy to Afghanistan (2001) and Iraq (2003) to the disappointing outcome of the Arab Spring (2010–2012), reinforce the idea that we were too naive in imagining that we could transform Iran from a dictatorship to democracy in a matter of months or even a few years. The prodemocratic forces in Iran proved incapable of changing individual and collective behavior fast enough to achieve a more open society.

I had individually escaped from the dictatorship of the mullahs, but Iranian society had returned to suffocate in the clutches of another dictatorship, just as so many other societies have found themselves trapped in a new, different type of dictatorship after what was imagined to be a successful antidictatorship revolution. I had reached the relative freedom of Western societies, but collective escape from dictatorship has proved far more difficult for Iran as a nation. I argue that limits on *political plasticity*, the ability to change (or not to change) social relations when structures change,[5] mean that the road from dictatorship to democracy is a long one, for all nations.

The concept of political plasticity leads us to explore how fast and in what ways political behavior can be changed, at the individual and collective levels. For example, moving societies away from dictatorship toward democracy requires changes in styles of leadership and changes in leader–follower relations. Dictatorial leadership involves decision-making and power being concentrated in the hands of the dictator, whereas in democratic societies decision-making is less centralized and involves participation and input from ordinary people.

Plasticity in this domain refers to the question of how fast a society used to dictatorial leader–follower relations and decision-making can successfully move to a democratic style leader–follower relations and decision-making. As I discuss in later chapters, what happens after revolutions suggests that the style of leader–follower relations is slow to change: The general trend has been for revolutions that topple a dictatorship to be followed by another dictatorship. This suggests that at least in some domains, there is low behavioral plasticity in the domain of politics.

THE DICTATORSHIP-DEMOCRACY CONTINUUM

We can conceptualize Iran and all major societies as lying on a continuum, with one end represented by *absolute dictatorship*, in which a dictator has absolute power over a population with no room for resistance or self-expression, and the other by what I have termed *actualized democracy*, in which there is "full, informed, equal participation in wide aspects of political, economic, and cultural decision-making independent of financial investment and resources"[6] (see Figure 1). Historically, movement along this continuum has tended to be away from absolute dictatorship toward democracy. However, movement is not always from dictatorship to democracy; in certain historical periods, movement is "backward" from democracy to dictatorship, as in the case of Germany in the 1930s and Turkey, Venezuela, and some other countries early in the 21st century (discussed in more depth later in this book). Also, at present, there are no absolute dictatorships or actualized democracies.

I believe actualized democracy is the ideal goal for all societies. This is because in actualized societies, citizens have been educated to achieve the psychological characteristics necessary to participate fully in decision-making as free and independent individuals (for more in-depth discussions, see the critical debates on actualized in *The Road to Actualized* Democracy[7]). Also, individual freedom can be maximized in actualized democracy. Although contemporary societies, including those in North America and the European Union, are still far from becoming actualized societies, it is important to articulate such an ideal from the perspective of psychological science and to examine the psychological characteristics citizens and leaders need to acquire to be able to achieve and sustain actualized democracies.[8]

Historical development along the dictatorship–democracy continuum has been in four main overlapping stages[9]: (a) primitive dictatorship (e.g., Iran, North Korea), (b) transitional dictatorship (China, Russia), (c) semideveloped democracy (United States, European Union countries), and (d) actualized democracy (not yet achieved by any country). These broad, overlapping

FIGURE 1. The Dictatorship-Democracy Continuum

Absolute Dictatorship -- Actualized Democracy categories, discussed in more depth in what follows, help us to better understand the big picture regarding changes from dictatorship to democracy. Although any proposal that political development takes place in "stages" can be criticized as simplistic, even when the overlapping nature of such stages is emphasized, I believe this conceptualization serves a useful purpose as a framework for analysis.

THE FOUR OVERLAPPING STAGES OF POLITICAL DEVELOPMENT

There are no absolute dictatorships, but unfortunately there are still many primitive dictatorships.

Stage 1: Primitive dictatorships are unsophisticated, brutal, and widely recognized for what they are. North Korea, Iran, Saudi Arabia—these regimes that are dogmatic, corrupt, and brutal in their ideologies and methods of repression against their own people. Political opposition to authority is punished in these regimes by imprisonment, torture, and sometimes death.[10] They adopt modern technology mainly to keep control of the population and to strictly instill their particular ideology.[11] In the case of North Korea, technological advancement in missile and nuclear technology has been rapid relative to advancement in political and social domains.[12] The ideology of primitive dictatorships can be religious, such as versions of fundamentalist Islam, or secular, such as versions of Marxism or nationalism. Irrespective of the characteristics of the ideology used by the regime, in primitive dictatorships, this ideology is rigidly enforced and used to maintain a high level of obedience and conformity in both elites and the masses. In important respects, this is how all dictatorships used to function before some of them evolved to become more sophisticated.

In primitive dictatorships, ideology is used like a sledgehammer against potential or actual opponents of the regime, including in areas that do not seem directly to touch on politics, such as social relationships, fashion, and the arts. Gender roles are rigidly enforced through ideology. For example, in Islamic dictatorships such as Iran and Saudi Arabia, there is a heavy emphasis on the enforcement of hijab for women and the separation of men and women in physical spaces. One of the favorite government tactics is to displace aggression onto women and hit hard at their "immoral behavior" as a way of distracting attention from larger political and economic issues and as a strategy for mobilizing support from traditionalist men with low education. This group of men feel particularly threatened by liberated women with advanced university degrees and are eager to help the government keep women "in their place."[13]

The threat felt by traditional, low-education men in Islamic primitive dictatorships has intensified in part by the increasing success of women in higher education. For example, in Iran, despite systematic government policies to thwart progressive gender roles, women outnumber men among students gaining entrance to universities.[14] The Iranian government counters this by ensuring that there are major obstacles confronting women in the employment market, so no matter how well women do in education, after graduation, they are confronted by numerous dead-ends. Iranian women can shine outside but not inside Iran, as did Maryam Mirzakhani when, in 2014 as a professor in the United States, she became the first woman in history (and the first Iranian) to win the Fields Medal (the equivalent of the Nobel Prize) in mathematics.

Because of their rigid adherence to backward ideologies, primitive dictatorships remain stunted economically, although they invest heavily in their militaries.[15] For example, North Korea remains behind economically[16] and in human rights,[17] despite its advances in weapons technology. Because Iran and Saudi Arabia exclude at least 50% of the brainpower of their societies (i.e., women!) from constructively contributing to the workforce, they remain at a disadvantage in the economic competition between nations, despite their enormous oil and gas reserves.[18] (Saudi Arabia made "advances" in 2018 by permitting women to drive cars, under certain conditions!)

Stage 2: Transitional dictatorships, the most important examples being China and Russia, involve a monopoly of power by an individual or a clique but do not rigidly enforce a uniform ideology. For example, in China, there are still posters of Chairman Mao and Karl Marx in public places, and the Communist Party monopolizes power but does not enforce communist ideology—far from it. The main goal of the regime is simply to maintain a power monopoly, without worrying about the paradox of a Marxist state having huge group-based inequalities and so many billionaires. Similarly, in Russia, the main ideology pushed by the Putin regime is associated with nationalism, the Russian Orthodox Church, and the cult of President Putin. Anyone who is a threat to Putin's power is attacked and neutralized, irrespective of their ideology.[19] Internationally, transitional dictatorships, and Russia in particular, use varieties of direct and indirect tactics, including the use of sophisticated electronic communications and *lawfare,* the use of law to accomplish military goals, to fight democracy.[20]

The transitional dictatorships are becoming subtler in their use of propaganda and economic incentives, but they still use brutal policies toward dissenters. Anyone who poses a serious threat to the regime is hammered into oblivion, sometimes even after escaping abroad. For example, in April 2018 Russian agents poisoned Russian defector Sergei Skripal and his daughter Yulia in Salisbury, England, where they had taken refuge.[21]

However, social life, social relationships, and gender roles are more flexible in transitional dictatorships. Women have a great deal more freedom in how they appear in public, the careers they pursue, and their relationships with men. As long as women support the dictator individual or cult, they are given room to develop their talents, make progress in the private sector, and even enter politics. Nonetheless, in transitional dictatorships, there are still taboos against LGBTQ people, and attempts are made to rigidly enforce traditional gender roles.[22] There are also some restrictions on the arts, particularly when artists attempt to use their creations as a way to criticize the central authority, such as the case of the all-female rock band Pussy Riot, whose members were arrested after playing in Savior Cathedral in Moscow on February 21, 2012, in protest against the Russian Orthodox Church's support of Vladimir Putin's reelection. If they had not attacked Putin through protest songs such as "Holy Shit," band members could have continued their careers as punk musicians in Russia. What got them into trouble was their attacks on centralized power, not their "devious" music. The Putin government gives a lot of freedom to artists, and to the general public in social life more broadly, as long as Putin's power is not challenged.

Transitional democracies can move forward toward democracy, but also backward toward dictatorship. There is a group of countries, including Turkey, Venezuela, Poland, and Hungary, that, by the end of the 20th century, seemed to be emerging from being transitional dictatorships and moving closer to democracy, but at the start of the 21st century, they are sinking back toward primitive dictatorship. These countries are in a transition, and it will become clear in the next few decades whether they sink back completely to primitive dictatorships or move forward to becoming more open societies. A lot will depend on their leaders, such as Recep Tayyip Erdogan of Turkey. Unfortunately, for such countries, the "success" of Erdogan and other strongman leaders means increased monopoly of power in the leader's hands, corresponding to backward political movement for their countries (see the discussion of Turkey in Chapter 2, this volume).

Stage 3: Semideveloped democracies comprise the countries of North America, the European Union, and all the other countries typically labeled *democratic*. Again, we must not assume that semideveloped democracies only experience forward movement toward greater openness and stronger democracy. There are warning signs that some semideveloped democracies could slip back toward dictatorship in the 21st century.

A danger in semideveloped democracies is the increasing dislocation of power and rifts between the elites and the masses.[23] Backward movement can arise when ruling elites that are interconnected across political, financial, industrial, military, educational, mass media, show business, and other key sectors of society manage to gain popular support, but then use this support to create a more closed, less democratic society. For example, Donald Trump has used populist support to attack the free press and flout the rule of law.[24]

In Trump's case, electoral success was achieved through a merging of show business and politics, so that his political rallies, which have continued during his tenure in the White House, were intended primarily to entertain and to rally his base, rather than to serve as critical, informed discussions or provide correct factual information about his policies. The tax and health care changes Trump brought about after his 2016 election success have provided enormous financial benefits for the ultra-rich[25] but have decreased government tax revenues and harmed the living standard of the poor.[26] The danger is that in the next few decades, social services and welfare programs for the lower and middle classes will be cut to pay for the decrease in government tax revenues and the resulting trillion dollar government annual budget deficits. Throughout the 2016 election campaign and since, Trump has ignored the issues of wealth inequalities and redistribution. Despite this, support for Trump has continued among his core supporters,[27] most of whom are lower and middle-income and will in the longer term suffer from his economic policies because the government services they rely on will be reduced to pay for tax cuts.

Research suggests that Trump owes his success in part to *displacement of aggression*,[28] that is, action intended to harm others by a person who feels provoked against a third-party target who is not responsible for the provocation. Trump has channeled discontent onto Hispanics, African Americans, women, and other minorities seen by many right-wing voters as "getting an unfair break."[29] Although the exact role of education in support for Trump is disputed,[30] clearly his supporters negatively target ethnic minorities, women, immigrants (whom he has repeatedly referred to using derogatory language[31]) and those whom they see as upsetting what they believe to be a meritocratic America.[32] Trump also channels displaced aggression onto elites and the "rigged system," which he claims only he can fix.[33]

Trump represents a serious danger of backward movement in the United States and other semideveloped democracies. This backward movement may lead to the evolution of a new type of dictatorship, in which, paradoxically, freedom (misleadingly) seems to be limitless, information boundless, and possibilities for enterprise endless. But within this "open" system, there are actually strong limitations, in part arising out of tensions in globalization. Dani Rodrik[34] identified one such important tension, which seems to question basic ideas in Adam Smith's free trade thesis.[35] For supporters of free trade, open-door economic policies would increase wealth, make nations more interdependent and peaceful, and improve lives for everyone. But Rodrik argued that globalization is leading to a "trilemma": national sovereignty, democracy, and global economic integration cannot all take place at the same time. Any two of them can exist together, but the three are incompatible. This becomes clear when we consider that globalization and economic integration requires free trade and the elimination of transaction costs, including import tariffs. But nation states rely on transaction costs and increased nationalism is usually associated with trade barriers and "putting up walls" of all kinds, as reflected in Donald Trump's Make America Great Again campaign, with increased tariffs, trade wars, and actual or proposed walls against outsiders.

This "trilemma" leads to new tensions, contradictions, and movements, such as the populist "antiglobalization" movements that have led to the rise of Trump and other right-wing nationalists. Another aspect of the trilemma is that globalization and economic integration is seen by some as weakening local democracy, putting power in the hands of powerful decision-makers far removed from ordinary people. An example is the centralization of power in Brussels, the capital of the European Union, far away from locals in countries such as the United Kingdom. The outcome for many people in the United Kingdom was a feeling of being "taken over" by undemocratic powers in Europe, with Brexit being a solution to return to national sovereignty. Of course, national sovereignty and a "make us great again" sentiment leave the door open for strongman leaders with antidemocratic tendencies. These developments imply that we should pay close attention to the conditions in which backward movement could take place toward dictatorship.

According to the *springboard model of dictatorship*,[36] dictatorship arises when two conditions are met: First, the springboard to dictatorship comes about;

second, there is available a potential dictator motivated to use the springboard to rise to power. The springboard is a particularized context that is optimally suited to the rise of a dictator. Among the key elements of the springboard are people in a society experiencing a high level of subjective threat (e.g., the threat of attack from external or internal forces), economic insecurity, low levels of trust, collective helplessness, and fear of impending decline. Contextual factors that increase the probability of dictatorship include the presence of elites who try to use the dictator to further their own interests (e.g., changing tax laws and other regulations to benefit themselves).

Under these conditions, a potential dictator is helped to power through crisis incidents. Hitler created a crisis and a "justification" for ending civil liberties from a simple incident, a left-wing radical setting fire to a government building.[37] Khomeini used the "hostage crisis" (involving the 1979 invasion of the U.S. Embassy in Tehran and the taking of the 52 American diplomats as hostages) to monopolize power and wipe out his competitors in Iran. Similarly, crisis incidents in Western countries, such as major terrorist attacks in the United States or war between the United States and a nuclear power such as North Korea, could help dictators come to power in Western societies.

Stage 4: *Actualized democracy*, a fully developed democracy,[38] has not yet been achieved. The Scandinavian countries and Switzerland are probably closest to this ideal. These are relatively small societies, ranging between 5 million and 10 million in population. Organizing democracy in these small, affluent societies has proven to be more feasible.[39]

THE ROLE OF POPULISM AND THE STAGES OF POLITICAL DEVELOPMENT

The term *populism* is notoriously difficult to define,[40] although there is general agreement that at the start of the 21st century what Cas Mudde called a "populist *zeitgeist*" has emerged[41] and there is now more fertile soil for the growth of populist movements internationally, with support from the American ultra-right[42] (Eric Oliver and Wendy Rahn have shown[43] that Trump used more populist language, such as antielite slogans, than all other candidates in the 2016 presidential U.S. election, including Bernie Sanders). For the purposes of this discussion, I identify five main features shared by the different populist movements. First, populism is based on the belief that the people have the right to rule society directly and without restrictions. This involves a rejection of checks and balances on the "will of the people." Second, the people are seen as the "silent majority" who know what is right and what should be done. The people instinctively sense what is right, without having to rely on science and "elite learning." Third, populism involves antagonism toward the elite, who are seen as not just aloof but also "immoral" and a threat to the sovereignty of the people. Political parties, government functionaries, elite "representatives," and other forms of intermediaries between the people and political power are rejected. Fourth, another group that threatens the interests of "the people" are "the others," those who are different and devious, those who do not belong to the people. These include minority ethnic and religious groups, immigrants and refugees, criminals, and those who are seen to act as "leeches" on society and threaten the interests of the people. A final characteristic of all populist movements is faith in a strong leader who is "from the people," an individual who fights the elites, attacks the dissimilar "others," and protects the true interests of the people.

Populist leaders succeed by reinforcing and propagating a tribal view of the world. This view depicts the in group, "us," "our people," "our kind," "our blood," "we the honest, law-abiding, good, virtuous," "we who belong on this land, the land of our fathers," against those "others," they who are "animals," "outsiders," "invaders," "devious," "false," "foreign," "profiting from us," and "taking what rightly belongs to us." The populist leader positions the elite as conspirators against the people, in collaboration with the others, the aliens, the outsiders who are invading our land. Who will save the people? Only the populist leader can save them; only he can protect them against the threats from the inside and outside.

Populist movements play an important role in determining progress along the stages of political development. The impact of populist movements is to push society away from democracy and the higher stages of political development, toward dictatorship and the lower stages. This is because populist movements reject rule of law, constitutionalism, checks and balances, political parties, representative democracy, pluralism, minority rights, and other important pillars of the open society. The overwhelming priority of populist movements is the interests of "our own tribe," and a strong leader who represents "our" interests to the exclusion of others. The rise of populism in the 21st century has coincided with the weakening of the open society and the emergence of a populist form of democracy.[44]

MESSAGE OF THIS BOOK

I argue that the failure to achieve actualized democracy and the continued pull of dictatorship arise for two main reasons. First, under certain historical conditions, people support potential or actual dictators, populist "strongmen," because they see them as the best avenue for protecting their freedoms and *sacred groups*, the nation-state, ethnicity, religion, and other groups to which people have the strongest attachments and for which they are willing to make the highest sacrifices; sacred groups are the groups with the strongest social identities. They are not escaping freedom; rather, they are attempting to safeguard their freedom and (albeit mistakenly) see the strongman dictator as their savior. However, there are different kinds of freedoms (a topic discussed in detail in Chapter 4), and those who support the strongman tend to give priority to what I have termed *attached freedom*, glory and liberation achieved through membership in a positively evaluated sacred group, such as a "superior" nation-state or race, or a "God-favored" religion. Attached freedom is very different from *detached freedom,* which celebrates the independent, mobile individual. From the perspective of the populist masses, the strongman dictatorial leader provides the best path for achieving attached freedom, and so they enthusiastically elect him, eventually to discover that his promises are utterly false.

To recognize how this kind of situation can arise, consider the enormous popular support for Adolf Hitler[45] and various other authoritarian strongmen in recent history. In his monumental work on Hitler and Josef Stalin (1878–1953), Alan Bullock pointed out that in the late 1930s, Hitler had developed a popular image of being a "man of the people . . . as providing Germany, for the first time since Bismarck, with the authoritarian leadership that many Germans in all classes regarded as authentic German political tradition." [46] Hitler's supporters saw him as leading them to attached freedom and glory.

The dictator uses the promise of individual empowerment through collective strength to lure supporters and get them to buy into his schemes and narratives. Individuals sense that they are far stronger and more capable as part of a sacred group; the psychological research on empowerment also reflects the far greater capabilities of individuals in collectives.[47] Identification with the sacred group inspires and directs individuals to achieve higher level performances. The dictator harnesses this collective energy to achieve his own goals, which inevitably involve giving himself more power and eliminating his competitors.

Second, achieving fully developed democracy has proven to be extremely difficult because the changes necessary in people's psychological characteristics to move societies away from dictatorship toward actualized democracy are extremely slow and difficult to achieve, even under favorable conditions. Almost all of the research focus has been on the process of revolution and the overthrow of dictatorship. Too little attention has been given to what happens after the defeat of a dictatorship and specifically on the changes in cognition and action that need to take place for a society to move toward a more democratic system of government. In practice, these changes have been difficult and slow to achieve, a topic I discuss later in more depth.

The escape back to dictatorship under conditions of threat, particularly the endangerment of sacred groups, is reflected in the emergence of a number of national leaders with extraordinary talent for opportunistically facilitating and strengthening dictatorships, both within their own national borders and around the world. Vladimir Putin of Russia is the most prominent of these leaders, but Xi Jinping of China will prove to be more globally influential in the long term, even though he is less flamboyant. Putin and Xi Jinping are leading a global effort to strengthen movement toward dictatorial rather than democratic governance. In terms of personality characteristics, Donald Trump naturally fits with this global movement away from democracy, and internationally his relations are with the leaders of dictatorships (e.g., Russia, North Korea) rather than with democracies (e.g., Canada, the EU countries). However, within the United States, he is constrained by institutions, primarily the U.S. Supreme Court and the U.S. Congress. But as *The Global Risks Report* of the World Economic Forum[48] pointed out, an impending global danger is the rise of "charismatic strongman politics," spearheaded by Putin of Russia, Xi Jinping of China, and now Trump of the United States.

After 2,500 years of struggle, democracy continues to be fragile and underdeveloped, including in Western societies. The progress necessary to bring about actualized democracy requires psychological changes—transformations in how people behave, how they interact with others, and how they problem-solve. But are we humans capable of making the necessary changes at the collective level? We know that many individuals can make the necessary psychological changes, but such individuals might be exceptional. The larger question is about the changes needed in the masses of ordinary people: How plastic, how malleable is our behavior at the collective level?

In postrevolution Iran, I learned that the behavioral plasticity of ordinary people is at the heart of progress toward democracy. If we want to move from dictatorship to democracy, it is not enough to topple a dictatorship, write a new constitution, and adopt slogans about freedom and independence. We need to change the way the ordinary masses think and act, from thought and action supportive of dictatorship to thinking and action supportive of democracy. It proved to be impossible to make this change fast enough in Iran, just as it has proven to be impossible to make this change fast enough after most major revolutions.

Two and a half centuries after the American Revolution and the birth of the United States, democracy in America remains seriously underdeveloped, and the United States is failing to serve as the flag bearer for democracy. The rise of China is presenting the world with an alternative, nondemocratic path to economic prosperity. As things stand, it is not clear whether the democratic or the dictatorial tendencies will win out and become dominant across the globe at the end of the 21st century. For those who desire and work for a victory for democracy, it is essential that we more fully understand the conditions that have resulted in weakening of democracies and a swing in favor of dictatorships.

PLAN OF THE BOOK

Part I follows this Introduction; Chapter 1 explores patterns of change in history, contrasting images of historical change as linear with images of historical change as cyclical. I point out the different psychological foundations of change as linear and change as cyclical. The continuation of dictatorships in different guises supports a cyclical view of historical changes. The case of Turkey is examined in Chapter 2, as an illustrative example of how "backward" movement can take place away from democracy and toward dictatorship. The four chapters in Part II explore the relationship between freedom and dictatorship. The overall message of Part II is that dictators gain support by seeming to safeguard attached freedom gained through membership in sacred groups. Chapter 3 puts forward an alternative to the traditional psychoanalytic explanation of the enigma of the "immortal dictator." Dictatorship does not come about because of a need to "escape freedom"; rather, support for dictators is a misguided path to safeguard attached freedom. In Chapter 4, attached freedom is further distinguished from detached freedom, which envisages freedom as realized when an individual is a self-regulating, self-directed entity, and acts independently from collectives. In Chapter 5, attached freedom is examined in relation to *sacred groups*, such as the nation-state, for which people are ready to sacrifice and die. Chapter 6, the final chapter in Part II, further explores the concept of political plasticity and the malleability of behavior in political contexts.

The two chapters in Part III explore the relationship between globalization and dictatorships. A perfect storm is being created for the development of dictatorships through 21st-century conditions. We are entering a new phase in which the dictator's personality is in harmony with the opportunities made available to grab power. Globalization in the 21st century is "fractured," the main characteristics of *fractured globalization* being the following:

1. Technological and economic forces are pushing us toward greater global integration and transformation into "one world." However, our identity needs are still pulling us to remain local and attached to the nation-state, our religion, and other sacred groups.[49] The slogan "global economy, local identity" captures this pull in opposite directions.

2. These oppositional forces are associated with dangerous collective identity threats, and people feeling, in particular, that their sacred national and religious groups are under attack from "invaders." In Western societies, these invaders are seen to be refugees, illegal immigrants, "radical Muslims," and other "outsiders." In non-Western societies, the invaders are seen as Western corporations and military powers, but also "Hollywood culture" and Western values.[50]

3. The appeal of the local and particularly nationalism feeds populist anti-globalist sentiments. Potential dictators thrive in this climate of severe collective identity threats to sacred groups.

The dictator takes advantage of conditions created by globalization (discussed in Chapter 7) and the "springboard to dictatorship" to spring to power. The symbiotic relationship between dictators and their core followers is explored in Chapter 8. In some cases, the availability of a potential dictator and the springboard to dictatorship enables the reversing of political development (as in the example of Turkey under Erdogan, discussed in Chapter 2).

In Part IV, two chapters explore future trends. The factors that continue to pull us toward dictatorship are examined in Chapter 9. The vast majority of middle and lower class people around the world, including in Western societies, are already feeling humongous economic pressures. More and more of the wealth in their societies has flowed into the hands of fewer and fewer people. The middle classes read about this huge wealth concentration in best-selling books such as *Capital in the 21st Century* by Thomas Piketty,[51] among others,[52] but they feel helpless to do anything about it. They feel depressed upon reading

Walter Scheidel's[53] thesis that, historically, war has served as the "great leveler" and provided the most effective remedy to the trend of increasing income inequality—surely rational policies should be able to do better than war at leveling the playing field? But not so far in human history, it seems. This sense of collective helplessness is exasperated by the rapid, "out-of-control" pace of technological change, which pushes particularly the middle class to adapt and work harder but has not brought increases in their standard of living or productivity.[54]

Those who attempt to reform the system are confronted by enormous bureaucracies, which can hide officeholders from responsibility and nurture *authoritarianism*, the strict obedience to authority and the abandonment of personal freedoms. A second seemingly neutral trend that helps authoritarianism, and eventually dictatorship, is the failure of mass education to include robust civic training. Even in the healthiest democracies, many citizens do not participate in politics; those who vote tend to be richer, Whiter, and older, and the knowledge base of many citizens is poor[55] (to varying degrees, similar problems exist in all Western democracies[56]). Only one in four U.S. high school seniors is at least "proficient" in civic knowledge and skills.[57] Education for the elites is in the process of abandoning the goal of educating the "whole person," despite some resistance from supporters of liberal arts education. Instead, elite education is moving toward training specialists in narrower and narrower fields of expertise.[58]

Received wisdom tells us that the computer revolution, together with the World Wide Web, Facebook, Twitter, Google, and other related innovations, should help better inform and educate people. After all, we can now interact with so many other people, and seek information and ideas from so many sources. Surely these trends will help democracy around the world? But with their current training, people tend to use the Internet in ways that endorse their existing worldviews and biases, exchanging information and ideas in echo chambers with like-minded others.[59]

Another factor is the use of the Internet by Putin and other dictators as part of their schemes to strengthen authoritarianism around the world.[60] These trends influence the evolution of what I call *global authoritarian integration*, the increased tendency for authoritarian forces to connect with and support one another and act as an integrated force across national borders. This is a case of similarity attraction, such as Russian and Chinese dictatorships supporting the Iranian dictatorship, with both Russia and Iran supporting the Syrian dictatorship, and China and Iran supporting the North Korean dictatorship.

This perfect storm creating the springboard to dictatorship includes a fusion of show business, politics, business, and sport, erasing traditional boundaries. It is not new that people can move from show business to politics; Ronald Reagan did that very successfully in the 1980s. The change today is far more radical: Now politics *is* show business, just as show business *is* politics, and so is sport, and so is business, and so are Facebook and Twitter. This complete fusion has meant that persuasion and success in politics can now come about almost completely through appeals to emotions and identity, to how people feel about things and the groups they identify with, rather than based on facts and logic.[61] "Alternative facts" matter more than real facts. Politics as show business, as exemplified in Trump's America, means that make-believe and fiction can be even more persuasive than cold facts and science.

In the final chapter, I explore solutions to the current global trends away from democracy. We have to fight hard and be persistent to prevent further decline of democratic freedoms around the world, to safeguard the openness that we already enjoy, and we must fight even harder to move societies forward to achieve actualized democracies.[62] The program for resilience and fighting back must be based on reforming the education system, starting with schools but including higher education. Civic education and civic engagement must become central to education. The pro-democracy movement has gained renewed energy and has "fire in the belly," so the future looks more hopeful in the fight against dictatorship. This book is part of the democratic renewal.

ENDNOTES

1. Abbas Milani (2011) has written the seminal work on the last shah.
2. Khomeini targeted the universities and raged against Iranian intellectuals whom he saw as thinking outside the Islamic framework; see http://www.merip.org/mer/mer88/khomeini-we-shall-confront-world-our-ideology.
3. See Marples (2000).
4. Bullock (1993, p. 459).
5. Moghaddam (2018c); Moghaddam and Howard (2017).
6. Moghaddam (2016b, p. 4).
7. Wagoner, de Luna, and Glaveanu (2018).
8. Researchers need to give far more attention to the characteristics of the ideal society from a psychological perspective (Moghaddam, 2016b).
9. I developed this four-stage model after studying the research on political development. A very good source is the series of books published by Princeton University Press, starting with Pye (1963).
10. I am not suggesting that torture and the mistreatment of government opponents only takes place in primitive dictatorships; see Donnelly and Whelan (2017) for a discussion of torture and the misuse of power in global context.
11. Marguleas (2017).
12. For an assessment of North Korean advancement in the nuclear domain and Western engagement strategies, see Cha and Kang (2018).
13. A number of authors have pointed out the threat traditional Muslim men feel from educated women; for example, see Hanif (2012).
14. See Salehi-Isfahani (2008). Also, in 2014, there were 18,481 women out of a total of 43,544 faculty members https://www.msrt.ir/en/page/20/statistics#Graduates.
15. For a critical discussion of Saudi Arabian society and economy, see Al-Rasheed (2018). A great deal has been published on revolutionary Iran; for example, see Axworthy (2016). However, a "conspiratorial" approach has been taken by some authors, focusing on the ways in which the U.S. government has misrepresented Iran to the American public and attempted to manipulate events inside Iran; see Benjamin (2018) and Crist (2013).
16. Kim (2017).
17. Yeo and Chubb (2018).

18. The growth failure of oil economies such as Iran and Saudi Arabia have been discussed from different angles (e.g., Nili & Rastad, 2007), but the bottom line is that the governments in Iran, Saudi Arabia, and other oil-producing countries have remained corrupt and removed from the needs of the people.
19. For discussions of Putin's Russia, see Gel'Man (2015), Laqueur (2015), Van Herpen (2013, 2014), and Wegren (2016). For a view that gives Putin more credit, see Sakwa (2014).
20. See Orde Kittrie's (2016) highly insightful and timely examination of how law is increasingly being used as a weapon of war. Also, Sanger, Sullivan, and Kirkpatrick (2018) revealed how Russia targets its critics abroad.
21. Swinford (2018).
22. For example, see Scher (2018) regarding LGBTQ Russians.
23. Shipman, Edmunds, and Turner (2018) reflect a new focus by authors on the increasing chasm between the elite and nonelite.
24. Particularly since 2016, the mainstream media routinely reports on Trump's attacks on the free press and his flouting of the rule of law; for example, see Toobin (2018).
25. Sorkin (2017).
26. As Robert Shapiro (2018) has convincingly argued, the poor are worse off under Trump.
27. Silver (2018).
28. See Moghaddam (2013, pp. 107–110), and N. Miller, Pederson, Earlywine, and Pollock (2003).
29. See D. N. Smith and Hanley (2018).
30. Manza and Crowley (2017) provided evidence that casts doubt on the general image of Trump supporters as low in education.
31. Foley (2018).
32. Cech (2017).
33. Sinclair, Smith, and Tucker (2018).
34. Rodrick wrote about the inescapable "trilemma of the world economy" in specialized papers earlier, but the most accessible discussion is in his 2011 book *The Globalization Paradox*.
35. A. Smith (1776/2017).
36. I developed this "interactional" model based on the idea that both the context and the individual are essential components of how dictatorship evolves, as opposed to models that only focus on the personality of the dictator (Moghaddam, 2013).
37. See Moghaddam (2013) for a further discussion of the use dictators make of "crisis incidents."
38. See Moghaddam (2016b) for an in-depth discussion.
39. Lipset (1959).
40. For discussions of populism and its definitions, see Albertazzi and McDonnell (2008), Judis (2016), and Mudde (2007).
41. Mudde (2004, p. 542).
42. For example, Steve Bannon, who helped Trump become president, has helped strengthen networks of European ultra-right populists (Horowitz, 2018).
43. J. E. Oliver and Rahn (2016).
44. For a discussion of populist forms of democracy, see Pappas (2014).
45. See Chapter 3 in Crew (1994).
46. Bullock (1993, p. 451).
47. There is a wide range of research on individual empowerment through collective processes; for examples, see Saab, Tausch, and Cheung (2015); Voegtlin, Boehm, and Bruch (2015).
48. World Economic Forum (2018).
49. Moghaddam (2008b).

50. Moghaddam (2008a, 2010).
51. Piketty (2014).
52. Dorling (2014) and Atkinson (2015) are particularly good on documenting the rise of inequality. However, Scheidel (2017) also provided excellent evidence on this; see particularly Table 15.1.
53. Scheidel (2017).
54. Gordon (2016) presented convincing evidence that the productivity leap achieved in 1870–1970 was special and perhaps unique, and since the 1970s, productivity has been relatively stagnant.
55. See Coley and Sum (2012); Galston (2004); Kahne and Sporte (2008); Sherrod, Torney-Purta, and Flanagan (2010); U.S. Department of Education (2012); and also Moghaddam (2016b, pp. 111–112)
56. Banks (2015).
57. Robelen (2011).
58. Moghaddam (1997).
59. The intuitive idea that there is an echo chamber is now backed by some empirical evidence; see Goldie, Linick, Jabbar, and Lubienski (2014).
60. For a broader review of control in dictatorships, see discussions in Corner and Lim (2016).
61. The role of emotions in persuasion has been experimentally studied by social psychologists at least since the mid-20th century but in recent decades most successfully through the elaboration likelihood model; see Petty, Cacioppo, and Kasmer (2015); Petty, Cacioppo, and Schumann (1983).
62. For more detailed discussions of actualized democracy, see readings in Wagoner, de Luna, and Glaveanu (2018).

POLITICAL PATTERNS AND REVERSALS TO DICTATORSHIP

Trust ye?
With every minute you do change a mind,
And call him noble, that was now your hate;
Him vild, that was your garland.

—WILLIAM SHAKESPEARE, *CORIOLANUS* (I.i.181–184)

In Shakespeare's play *Coriolanus,* the title character describes the masses as fickle and constantly shifting in their allegiances; one minute they hate a leader, but the next minute they treat him as a darling. Is Coriolanus correct in his negative views of the masses? Is he correct when he says about the masses, "Who deserves greatness/Deserves your hate"? (I.i.176–177). I argue that the masses and "popular will" do not have fixed, unchanging characteristics, just as development in human societies does not take place according to a fixed, predetermined formula. Both the characteristics of "the masses" and the direction of societal change are flexible and open to influence in important ways. In Chapters 1 and 2, I further develop this argument through illustrative examples.

In Chapter 1, I examine different conceptions of societal change. A first view is that societal change necessarily involves progress, according to a preset plan. Both the political left and political right have argued for the inevitability of progress, toward some preset outcome, such as the classless society or democratic capitalism. I contrast this with a cyclical view of societal change, which argues for inevitable cycles of elite rule, counter-elite mobilization, revolution, the toppling of the old elite and the coming to power of a new elite, leading to another cycle of elite rule and counter-elite revolution. My argument is that humans can influence the ways in which their societies change or do not change; there is no inevitable pattern or destination for change in human societies. For example, societies do not inevitably move from being less open and dictatorial to being more open and democratic.

As an illustrative example of how there is not an inevitable unidirectional movement from dictatorship to democracy, in Chapter 2, I address the case of Turkey. I could have examined other societies (e.g., Iran, Russia, Venezuela, Brazil) to show how the promise of democracy can rise and then decline. However, I selected the illustrative example of Turkey because of the enormous promise this country seemed to have for making progress toward becoming more democratic. Over the past half century, Turkish economic, political, and cultural progress seemed impressive. This progress was reflected in official statistics indicating societal change, but I also experienced it personally during my repeated visits to the country. It seemed that Turkey would eventually join the European Union as another democratic nation. However, in the 21st century, the characteristics of both the context and the leadership in Turkey changed toward dictatorship rather than democracy. What looked like "inevitable" movement toward greater openness and democracy at the end of the 20th century has turned toward harsh antidemocratic change in the 21st century.

Just as societal change is not inevitable and predetermined in any particular direction, the characteristics of the masses and "popular will" are in some important respects flexible. Civic education, prodemocracy information campaigns through both traditional mass media and new forms of social media communications, these are some of the many ways in which the public can become better informed and more constructively engaged in politics, negating the views expressed by Coriolanus.

1

Repeating Patterns of Political Behavior

The idea of progress holds that mankind has advanced in the past—from some aboriginal condition of primitiveness, barbarism, or even nullity—is now advancing, and will continue to advance through the foreseeable future.

—ROBERT NISBET, *HISTORY OF THE IDEA OF PROGRESS*

As Robert Nisbet persuasively argued in his book *History of the Idea of Progress*,[1] quoted above, a central dogma in Western civilization has been the inevitability of progress. Change is envisaged as involving linear movement from relatively primitive stages of development to more advanced stages, including from dictatorship to democracy. The assumption of progress and associated psychological changes in people is central to both Marxist and capitalist models of political development.

The Marxist model predicts a steady progress with predictable steps: Just as capitalism evolved from feudalism, socialism will evolve from capitalism.[2] Changes in economic systems are assumed to lead to changes in the psychological characteristics of people. The change from capitalism to socialism will take place as the proletariat repeatedly clash with the capitalist class and eventually gain class-consciousness, recognizing that their own class interests are opposed to the class interests of capitalists (this is a foundational psychological change in perceptions). Class-consciousness eventually enables the proletariat to mobilize as a distinct class through the leadership of a revolutionary vanguard, overthrow the capitalist class, and seize power. This

http://dx.doi.org/10.1037/0000142-002
Threat to Democracy: The Appeal of Authoritarianism in an Age of Uncertainty,
by F. M. Moghaddam

leads to the establishment of the proletariat dictatorship, in which a small group governs on behalf of the proletariat and in their interests.

The proletariat dictatorship gradually transforms the psychological characteristics of everyone in society, so that private ownership, individual profit incentives, the urge to accumulate wealth and to consume more and more, and other features of capitalism are no longer needed in or positively evaluated by society. Citizens are transformed psychologically and become motivated to work for the collective good, rather than for personal profit (psychological research might be used to argue that such a change goes against "human nature"[3]). In these new societal conditions with collective incentives and collective ownership, social classes gradually disappear and a classless society eventually takes shape. According to Marx, central governments dissolve in classless societies because the function of governments is to protect the interests of the ruling class, and when there are no social classes and no ruling class, there is no longer a need for a central government.

The idea of progress also underlies the capitalist version of political development, but instead of a classless society, the "end of history" in the capitalist schema is assumed to be a free-market capitalist state. Other political systems, based on communist, religious, or other ideologies, are assumed to fall by the wayside as they fail to compete with the efficiencies of free-market capitalism. These "efficiencies" arise because the "natural" tendency is for people to produce better when they are motivated by individual incentives, a perspective reflected in the works of economists such as Milton Friedman (1912–2006).[4] Because free-market capitalism provides everyone freedom to innovate and be entrepreneurial, individual talents will flower and bloom. Individuals such as Bill Gates will be able to innovate and create wealth, liberated from the shackles of government regulations, and through their creativity and productivity, these "genius" individuals will also create jobs and wealth for the rest of society.

In the capitalist ideal, freedom in all its different manifestations is the key to continued progress. At the international level, there must be free trade and the free flow of all resources, so that the free market will establish the most competitive prices for all goods, services, and labor. Similarly, at the national level, governments, labor unions, and other such forces should stay out of the marketplace, so that prices for everything, including labor, are set by supply and demand. The closer a society is to this free-market model, the more efficient it will be and the higher the standard of living people will enjoy. The triumph of the United States over the Soviet Union is taken to be proof of the validity of this viewpoint. Eventually, only societies close to the free-market model will be efficient enough to survive. As Milton Friedman triumphantly declared after the fall of the Soviet Union,

> By now, many countries in Latin America and Asia, and even a few in Africa have adopted a market-oriented approach and a smaller role for government. Many of the former Soviet satellites have done the same. In all these cases . . . increases in economic freedom have gone hand in hand with increases in political and civil freedom and have led to increased prosperity; competitive capitalism and freedom have been inseparable.[5]

Thus, there is a widely held assumption on both the political left and right that earlier, "primitive" stages of political development will lead to more advanced stages, until the ideal society is achieved: The classless society in the case of Marxism and a free-market state in the case of capitalism. In both the Marxist and capitalist ideal end states, people are free, and the central government has a minimal role. This idea of progress also underlies the assumption that change will be unidirectional, from dictatorship to an ideal state, from closed to open societies. There may be temporary stoppages, but the overall pattern of change will be toward the ideal, open society.

THE ALTERNATIVE CYCLICAL VIEW

This idealistic view of political development is seriously challenged by an alternative, realist, cyclical model proposed by the Italian thinker Vilfredo Pareto (1848–1923). This cyclical view is based on a different psychological foundation. Pareto is well known in economics,[6] but his less known contributions to social psychological theory are also seminal and highly persuasive. Like his countryman Niccolò Machiavelli (1469–1527), Pareto adopts a realist rather than idealist model in that he attempts to portray how he believes humans actually behave rather than how they ideally should behave—what human psychological characteristics actually are, rather than what they should be. Insofar as Marx is a realist, Pareto is in agreement with him. But at a certain point, Marx parts from realism and goes down an idealist path and an imagined classless society, while Pareto stays with realism (his critics might say cynicism) and the idea of perpetual group-based inequalities.

While Marx uses the terms *capitalist* and *proletariat,* Pareto uses the terms *elite* and *nonelite* to depict those who rule and enjoy greater power and resources, and those who are governed and are poor in terms of power and resources. Pareto agrees with Marx that elites use ideologies to camouflage their resource monopoly and grip on power and mislead the nonelite masses by instilling in them false consciousness, resulting in a misleading worldview that misrepresents the true nature of social classes and the diametrically opposite interests of the elite and the nonelite. Irrespective of whether socialism, capitalism, Islam, or some other ideology is used as a justification and "front," the real goal of the ruling elite is to continue to rule and to keep the nonelite masses confused and subservient; in this, Pareto agrees with Marx. The main difference between the two thinkers becomes clear when we consider their predictions for what group-based inequalities lead to: Pareto and other elite theorists see rule by the elite as inevitable, perpetual, and universal in all of human history and in all societies. As Gaetano Mosca (1858–1941), another leading elite theorist, explained,

> In all societies . . . two classes of people appear—a class that rules and a class that is ruled. The first class, always the less numerous, monopolizes power and enjoys the advantages that power brings, whereas the second, the more numerous class, is directed and controlled by the first.[7]

Pareto proceeds to propose a cyclical pattern to change, starting with the idea that every elite sows the seeds of its own destruction by becoming corrupt and inefficient. This situation comes about because every elite "closes up" and fails to allow the circulation of talent. Some talented individuals from the nonelite masses will attempt to rise up to join the elite, and it is actually in the interests of the elite to allow these talented "stars" to rise and join them, and also to allow those who enjoy elite status but lack the required talent to fall from the elite and join lower status groups. This circulation of talent will safeguard the political system and maintain the rule of the current elite.

Pareto also describes history as a "graveyard of aristocracies"[8] because every elite eventually closes up and refuses to allow talented nonelite individuals to rise up and join the elite or individuals lacking talent to exit from the elite and join lower status groups. Cronyism and other forms of corruption gradually weaken the talent pool in the elite and strengthen the growth of a talented counter-elite intent on overthrowing the ruling elite. The ruling elite becomes increasingly corrupt and ineffective, lacking the talent and motivation to maintain power. (More than 2,000 years earlier, Plato explored this topic in *The Republic* and made similar observations about the essential role of elite circulation.[9] Plato and Pareto also agree that some elite offspring will lack talent to perform at the elite level, just as the nonelite will have some offspring who have the necessary talent to move up and perform as part of the elite.) The talented counter-elite eventually mobilizes the nonelite masses and topples the regime: The revolution has succeeded!

Whereas for many theorists the revolution is the start of consequential political change, reform, and linear movement forward, for Pareto, the revolution is part of a cycle that repeats itself without changing the political system. The successful counter-elite simply takes over the power, the privileges, and the top position of the former elite, and the nonelite masses are maneuvered back into their lower status position to suffer false consciousness in another form. Elite rule continues, but with a new elite and often with a new ideology. Thus, in Iran in 1979, the mullahs took over from the shah but with a new "Islamic" ideology: The masses were now sacrificing for Allah, rather than for the shah. Similarly, in Russia in 1917, Lenin, Stalin, and other "revolutionaries" took over from the tsar but with a new communist ideology: The masses were now supposedly sacrificing for and showing loyalty to "the people," rather than the tsar. Pareto warns that we should not be fooled by the rhetoric of the "revolutionary government": At a deeper level, revolutions are simply the replacement of one elite by another, with the nonelite masses continuing in their subservient position.

Pareto sees the cyclical nature of human history as an inevitable outcome of human psychology. In all human groups and in all fields of activity, some individuals are more talented, motivated, and hardworking than the rest. This "elite" group of talented individuals inevitably rises to the top and inevitably accumulates more power and resources for themselves. But because of human selfishness, the elite misuse their power, refuse to allow circulation of talent, and a counter-elite inevitably leads another revolution.

From Pareto's perspective, then, historical change is cyclical. The rhetoric and camouflage used by different ruling elites and "revolutionary" counter-elites differs across time and place, but elite rule continues. Pareto claims that when we delve beneath the surface, we recognize that elite rule is present in all of history and in all societies. He argues that this cyclical trend will inevitably continue into the future in all human history.

The true intention of the counter-elite is to take the place of the old elite, but if this were discovered, "no one would come to its assistance. . . . On the contrary, it appears to be asking nothing for itself, well knowing that without asking anything in advance it will obtain what it wants as a consequence of its victory."[10] Pareto warns that ruling elites' rhetoric should not mislead us. Such rhetoric will describe the political system using labels such as *free market*, or *socialist*, or *Islamic Republic*, or *democracy*, and always *in the interests of "the people,"* but in practice, all elites rule in their own minority interests. The gap between the elite and nonelite continues, although the elite and its rhetoric changes over time and across revolutions.

EXPLAINING REPEATED BEHAVIORAL PATTERNS

Pareto's cyclical model of elite rule is compelling. This model proposes that stratification and inequalities will continue and that the elite will always enjoy more power, economic resources, social status, and advantages in general. The elite will use revolutions, elections, and other strategies to give the impression that the nonelite share political power and shape outcomes, that the government reflects the "will of the people," but in practice, the elite continues to monopolize power and resources. Pareto's views seem to be endorsed by well-documented recent trends, reflecting increased concentration of wealth in fewer and fewer hands around the world. [11] Irrespective of the rhetorical "front" put forward by the elite, whether it is communism in China, nationalism in Russia, Islam in Iran and Saudi Arabia, or some other front, the concentration of wealth in elite hands has continued. This is part of a picture involving predictable and repeated patterns of behavior.

Patterned Behavior

In the domain of human behavior, there are contextual conditions that make certain behavioral outcomes more probable; in this sense, psychology is a probabilistic science. To arrive at a realistic estimation of the probability of an event taking place, we need to consider that most human behavior is normatively regulated rather than causally determined.[12] That is, in most situations, people look to local ideas about "correct behavior" as guides to how they should think and act, and mostly follow such guides. Our conceptions of what is "correct" behavior in any given situation is taught to us through the family, school, and other agents of socialization. We have some measure of freedom to conform or not to conform, but most of the time, we tend to conform to what we believe to be the "correct" way to behave.

In some cases, our behavior is causally determined, where *X* necessarily always leads us to do *Y*. This is referred to as *efficient causation*, but little human behavior falls under this category.[13] For example, if I fall from my bicycle, hit my head, and suffer memory loss, this is efficient causation: The knock on the head resulted in my memory loss. In efficient causation, the relationship between cause and effect, does not involve human intentionality or any measure of free will. The probability of an outcome is 100%.

But some measure of free will plays a role in much of human behavior, and the probability of us carrying out a particular action involves some choice. How we choose to behave depends a great deal on the norms for correct behavior. Although most of our behavior is normatively regulated, we can still make good estimations of the probability of certain behaviors under given conditions. For example, research by the brilliant social psychologist Stanley Milgram shows that under certain conditions, even most people with normal personality profiles will obey orders from an authority figure to inflict serious harm on others.[14] In practice, this means people are more likely to obey orders to do harm to others in certain conditions that can come about in societies as varied as Nazi Germany, North Korea, and U.S.-occupied Iraq, where soon after the 2003 U.S. led invasion of Iraq "ordinary Americans" tortured Iraqi prisoners in the Abu Ghraib prison.[15]

Circumstances in the 21st century are helping to create a perfect storm and make more probable the conditions necessary for the rise of authoritarianism and dictatorship around the world. This is a fairly predictable pattern of events we experienced in the 20th century—with terrible consequences.

In the 1930s, Germany and much of the industrialized world experienced a terrifying storm, leading to the rise of authoritarianism and dictatorships. In this era, fascism was on the rise across many societies, and dictatorships used their strongholds in Germany, Italy, and Japan to cast their hideous shadows across the world.[16] The consequence of unified aggression by this brutal antidemocratic force was highly destructive, as German, Japanese, and Italian dictatorships together with their allies overwhelmed almost all of continental Europe and much of the Far East. From 1938, when Germany invaded Austria, European democracies were crushed one by one, until by late 1941 Great Britain was the only engaged fighting nation standing in the way of total fascist domination. The Japanese attack against the United States fleet at Pearl Harbor on December 7, 1941, resulted in the United States entering the war and eventually tipping the scales in favor of the Allies.

But not all the countries fighting on the side of the Allies were democracies, and at the end of the Second World War, democracy only developed in some of the regions freed by the Allied powers. The Soviet Union, ruled by the brutal dictator Josef Stalin (1878–1953), fought on the side of the Allies—Stalin and Hitler both fanatically craved absolute power, and the world proved to be too small for both of them.[17] Immediately after the defeat of Hitler and the end of World War II, the Soviet Union squashed freedoms and established dictatorships in all of the territories it had overrun during the war, including Eastern Europe. What Winston Churchill (1874–1965) referred to as an Iron Curtain came crashing down, separating the two worlds of dictatorship and democracy. The Cold War had begun.

After the collapse of the Soviet Empire and the end of the Cold War in the 1990s, there was great optimism that the "end of history" had been reached and all societies would become capitalist democracies.[18] Some assumed freedom and open societies would spread. But this optimistic expectation about linear historical progress proved to be naive and incorrect. In the past few decades, we have experienced a dramatic turn toward authoritarianism and dictatorship, and now 21st-century globalization is creating conditions for the strengthening of new, powerful, and dangerous antidemocratic trends.

Repeated Patterns of Dictatorship

The turn away from open societies and toward dictatorship at the start of the 21st century should be seen as part of a larger pattern of repeated return to dictatorship. The development of open, democratic societies requires changes in political behavior in both leaders and followers, and this requirement has proven to be a major stumbling block.

The challenge of bringing about change in political behavior, and the important role of political plasticity,[19] is highlighted in major revolutions, which typically result in a return to former patterns of behavior and the reestablishment of dictatorship, rather than achieving a change from one system to another.[20] The French Revolution (1789) led to the execution of the king and numerous aristocrats, but Napoleon crowned himself emperor, set up his own family as kings and queens around Europe, and perpetuated the monarchy. The Russian Revolution (1917) wiped out the tsar and his immediate family, but an entire string of new "tsars" came to power, from Stalin to Putin. Similarly, the "communist" system of China established from the 1950s has brought into power "new emperors" and an elite with enormous private wealth in so-called communist China. Revolutions in Iran (1979) and the Arab Spring (2011–2013) have replaced one dictatorship with another and reinforced the same idea: Under most conditions, patterns of political behavior are difficult to change in a matter of a few years, or even decades.

Again and again in history, we see a return to dictatorship even after societies have achieved and enjoyed some measure of openness. This return to dictatorship takes place in two major ways. First, even after monumental prodemocracy revolutions, there is typically a change from one form of dictatorship to another, rather than a transition from dictatorship to democracy. Typical of this is the experience of Iran in 1979–1980, when I personally participated in a society that found and then tragically lost freedom. A second form of return to dictatorship takes place when there is a gradual decline in democratic culture and dictatorship reemerges through the efforts of a potential dictator who "springs to power" and becomes an actual dictator. The situation in Germany in the 1920s and 1930s serves as an example here, and the United States faces this same challenge of potential return to dictatorship in the 21st century. Both the first and second forms of a return to dictatorship are influenced by the characteristics of the potential dictator: the mental outlook and personality of the individual who springs forward at a critical time to reestablish dictatorship.

THE "NATURAL" GRAVITATION TOWARD DICTATORSHIP

Movement toward democracy is not inevitable but comes about only through continuous vigilance, hard work, and efficient organization on the part of prodemocracy individuals and groups. Experience has shown that without persistent, organized, large-scale effort to move society toward greater democracy, the tendency will be backward movement toward dictatorship. Why is this?

There are two related reasons: the first top-down and the second bottom-up. First, in times of turmoil, people prefer dominant, aggressive leaders. Second, antidemocracy and prodictatorship leadership emerges during times of collective threat, political turmoil, and crisis. This is particularly when sacred national, ethnic, or religious groups are threatened. Typically, the leaders who spring forward in such circumstances are power-hungry, ruthless, and willing to do whatever it takes to grab and monopolize power. They are the ones willing to order their followers to "smash!" and "annihilate!" the opposition, just as Lenin did in 1917 and Khomeini did in 1979. The only major exceptions to this have been George Washington and Nelson Mandela, who voluntarily set and abided by term limits to their political leadership. All other major leaders who came to power through revolution remained in power until they died, sometimes naturally. In postrevolution situations, moderate, mild, middle-of-the-road, peaceful, prodemocracy leaders do not stand a chance against the ruthlessness of the Stalins and Khomeinis of the world—despots who insist on clutching the reins of power until their last breath.

The ruthlessness of the kind of leadership that typically emerges through revolutions is reflected in the saying "Revolutions eat their own children," which I saw in action during the revolution in Iran. One by one, even during the first year of the revolution, the more moderate individuals and groups were killed, imprisoned, or driven into exile and hiding abroad. This included those who had been closest to Khomeini during the revolution, such as Abolhassan Bani Sadre, Mehdi Bazargan, Sadegh Ghotbzadeh, and Ebrahim Yazdi. Even other ayatollahs who dared to disagree with Khomeini were hounded, "demoted," and banished, including Grand Ayatollah Mohammad Kazem Shariatmadari and Grand Ayatollah Hussein-Ali Montazeri. Nobody who in any way disobeyed Khomeini was allowed to survive; even if there was a slight hint of disobedience, they were in one way or another eliminated.

The ruthless rise of Khomeini after the 1979 revolution demonstrates a clear pattern in history: Dictators rise to grab power because they are willing to act mercilessly and to eliminate the opposition: "Obey me or be killed!" Moderate and prodemocracy leaders are not ruthless in the same way, and they become victims of violence themselves. They become the "children" who are eaten by the revolution. In this way, the "natural" trend is for dictatorships to return;

whenever there is a "crisis" or major "threat" to sacred groups, the rise of dictatorship increases again.

But the threat of resurgent dictatorship is not confined to Iran and other non-Western societies. The case of Germany in the 1930s demonstrates that the most scientifically and industrially advanced nations can sink back into dictatorship. This backward movement is more likely to happen during times of insecurity and perceived threat to the sacred groups, which certainly arose after the 1929 financial crash and the economic and political instability that followed. We must keep in mind that the rise of fascism during the 1930s was not isolated to Germany, Italy, and other Axis powers. Hitler and the Nazi movement had a great deal of support among the British aristocracy and the elite of Western societies during the 1930s.[21] King Edward VIII of Britain, who abdicated and became Duke of Windsor, was profascist. Sir Oswald Mosely, who established the British Union of Fascists, used to lead the Blackshirts, the equivalent of Hitler's Brownshirts, in huge and widely supported political marches in London during the 1930s. Some major American industrialists and politicians also supported Hitler[22] before America joined the fighting in World War II and it became impossible for anyone in America to publicly support Hitler.

Just as the unstable and threatening conditions of the 1920s and 1930s led to support for Hitler and the fascist movement in Western societies, including the United States and Great Britain, the conditions created by 21st-century globalization are leading to a resurgence of authoritarianism and dictatorships around the world. This is indicated by measures used by Freedom House[23] and other credible sources, showing a decline in democracies, including a decline in American democracy, in the first decades of the 21st century. Reporters Without Borders has reported on a recent decline in press freedom around the world, including in the United States.[24] This is in large part because Donald Trump has led a full-frontal "populist" assault on the American press, and the "press freedom" ranking of the United States has declined to 45th in the world. As with the popular support shown for Hitler and Mussolini in the 1930s, populist support for antidemocratic leaders in the West is a highly dangerous trend associated with rising authoritarianism internationally.

CONCLUDING COMMENT

The predictions put forward by Marx, Pareto, and their followers are similar in the sense that both thinkers see historical development following a predictable path. For Marx, the inevitable path is that of the development of class-consciousness, leading to the proletariat revolution, the dictatorship of the proletariat, and eventually the classless society. For Pareto, the inevitable path is from one counter-elite revolution to the next, with every revolution being followed by the rise of a new ruling elite who abandon, exploit, and rule over the nonelite. Thus, both Marx and Pareto see a static and inevitable pattern for change. But both thinkers are wrong, because actual historical development is more flexible, as events have shown.

Human history is not inevitably moving according to any one, predetermined pattern; we humans are capable of shaping and reshaping our own historical development to some degree. Also, new developments in genetics, cell growth, and medical sciences generally are opening up entirely new possibilities for how we shape the human organism.[25] We could decide to develop our bodies in dramatically different ways, with enormous implications for social and political transformations. This is not to suggest that we will go down such a path or that the possibilities for change are not limited in some respects, but that we could change in new ways—we have choices to make in shaping our future(s). At the same time, the future is not completely malleable, and some outcomes have been shown to be more likely than others.

One of the fairly rigid patterns of behavior we see repeated in different societies is the development of the springboard to dictatorship, the rise of populism, and the springing forward of a "strongman" to take advantage and move society back toward dictatorship. We have seen this pattern repeated in the early 21st century, with Putin, Khomeini, Erdogan, and other strongmen taking the lead. The rise of populism in the European Union and the United States will test the ability of democratic institutions to control the antidemocratic tendencies of Trump and other strongmen.

In the next Chapter, I examine the case of Turkey as an example of how movement on the dictatorship–democracy continuum can be backward toward dictatorship, and not necessarily always forward toward democracy.

ENDNOTES

1. Nisbet (1980, pp. 4–5)
2. See Marx (1867/1976, 1852/1979), Marx and Engels (1848/1967), and S. A. Smith (2014).
3. The conditions in which groups can become more than the sum of their individual members have been explored by Baumeister, Ainsworth, and Vohs (2016).
4. M. Friedman (1962/2002).
5. M. Friedman (1962/2002, p. ix).
6. See Wood and McLure (1999).
7. Mosca (1939, p. 50).
8. Pareto (1935, III, p. 1430).
9. Plato (1987).
10. Pareto (1971, p. 92).
11. Piketty (2014).
12. See Chapter 2 in Moghaddam (2013).
13. Harré and Moghaddam (2016).
14. The best account of the original studies is in Milgram (1974). I have discussed Milgram's studies in the context of dictatorship (Moghaddam, 2013, pp. 132–134). Because of ethical concerns, in recent years, the classic Milgram obedience study could only be tested partially, but the partial replication did validate the original results (Burger, 2009).

15. A detailed and critical discussion of the psychology of events in Abu Ghraib prison was provided by Zimbardo (2008).
16. For a discussion of the historical background to the rise of fascism in Europe, see Blum (1998).
17. See Bullock's (1993) seminal work on Hitler and Stalin.
18. For example, Fukuyama (1992).
19. See Moghaddam (2018c).
20. See Moghaddam (2013, 2016b).
21. See Pool and Pool (1979).
22. See Pool and Pool (1979).
23. See http://www.voanews.com/a/freedom-house-democracy-scores-decline-many-countries/3796130.html.
24. See https://rsf.org/en/2017-world-press-freedom-index-tipping-point.
25. There is an explosion of research on machines and their future in relation to humans; for example, see Katz (2017).

2

Reversals From Democracy to Dictatorship

On May 16, 2013, a completely unplanned and unexpected event took place in Washington DC, during which I had a brief encounter with Mrs. Emine Erdogan, the wife of the Turkish president, Recep Tayyip Erdogan, making me momentarily famous in the eyes of some and infamous in the eyes of others.

I had already become intrigued with Mr. Erdogan in the course of my political psychology research because he was consolidating and monopolizing power in Turkey in a style similar to that of President Putin in Russia. Erdogan and Putin have both used populist nationalist support, as well as the religious establishment (Sunni Islam in Turkey and Russian Christian Orthodox in Russia), to maneuver between the positions of prime minister and president, eventually settling into the position of president with a weak "rubber-stamp" cabinet of their own choosing and a manipulated constitution that, in revision, extended their own power monopoly. In essence, Erdogan and Putin have used the mechanisms of democracy to defeat democracy and establish themselves as the new sultan[1] and tsar, respectively. Instead of discussing Turkey as an example of a "reversal" from democracy toward dictatorship, we could discuss Hungary, Poland, Venezuela, or a number of other countries around the world where democracy has been seriously weakened at the start of the 21st century. The turn away from democracy is taking place across many nations and regions, and I use Turkey here as an important illustrative example.

http://dx.doi.org/10.1037/0000142-003
Threat to Democracy: The Appeal of Authoritarianism in an Age of Uncertainty,
by F. M. Moghaddam

On the afternoon of May 16, 2013, a small conference, "The Role of Businesswomen in Peace-building and Development," was held at the Mayflower Renaissance Hotel in Washington, DC. This is one of the most well-known hotels that serve as a venue for official functions in the city, bringing together politicians and businesspeople, with academics sometimes playing a role as well. This particular conference coincided with Mr. Erdogan's visit to the United States and was cosponsored by the Turkish Businesswomen's Association. Another cosponsor was the Georgetown University Conflict Resolution Program, for which I served as director.

While her husband was engaged in other diplomatic business, Mrs. Erdogan attended the conference and made a brief speech. Because of my role as director of the Georgetown University Conflict Resolution Program, I was asked to walk on stage and present Mrs. Erdogan with a gift at the end of her speech. The gift was actually a number of small objects in a box. One of my books had been placed in the box. The book was not particularly noticeable among the other gifts.

After I walked onto the small stage and presented the gift box to Mrs. Erdogan, she unexpectedly looked inside the box and noticed the book. To my surprise, she took the book out and asked the interpreter about it. When the interpreter explained that it was one of my books, Mrs. Erdogan smiled and said the two of us should take a picture with the book, which we did. The entire event took less than a minute and was not memorable in any way—except that the book was *The Psychology of Dictatorship*![2]

An hour later, I had returned to my Georgetown University office when the barrage began. Large numbers of people, mostly Turks, started contacting me about the book gifted to Mrs. Erdogan. Many congratulated me for having "declared to the world Erdogan is a dictator!" Some attacked me for "insulting our dear president!" Some asked conspiratorial questions, such as "Was the U.S. government behind you giving the book? Was it the CIA?" The Turkish media was eager to interview me. The photograph of me "presenting the book to Mrs. Erdogan" sped around the world, and I became instantly famous in the eyes of some but infamous in the eyes of others. *The Psychology of Dictatorship* was quickly translated into Turkish and published in Turkey, and articles about the book appeared in the Turkish mass media, with photographs of me, the book cover, and Mrs. Erdogan.

THE NEW GLOBAL CONTEXT OF 21ST-CENTURY DICTATORSHIP

The reaction I experienced to the photograph of Mrs. Erdogan, my book cover, and me, being flashed around the world could only have happened in this era of 21st-century globalization. The world has shrunk, so that we all now live in a small fishbowl. Everything we do can become instantly known and commented on by countless others. A small-scale incident in a Washington, DC, hotel can suddenly become the center of a tempest in a teacup. This is particularly the case when people feel that their sacred groups are in some ways being threatened.[3]

Identity Needs in Turkey

Globalization has created new collective identity threats and brought to the forefront collective identity needs, particularly in nations undergoing seismic changes, such as Turkey.[4] The rapid growth of the Turkish economy from the 1990s expanded the middle class and sped up urbanization and modernization. But these rapid and expansive changes also led to traditionalists feeling threatened, particularly pious Islamic men confronted with the rise of university-educated "liberated" Turkish women.[5] The tensions and strains in Turkish society resulted in the springboard to dictatorship coming to life, giving potential dictators the opportunity to spring to power.

The unexpected incident involving Mrs. Erdogan having her picture taken with my "dictatorship book" sped up a process that had already started in my mind: studying Turkey as an example of how change can take place away from democracy toward dictatorship and Mr. Erdogan as a case study on how a potential dictator transforms toward becoming an actual dictator. Recep Tayyip Erdogan was born in 1954 into a religious family in one of Istanbul's overcrowded working-class neighborhoods. Growing up, he had to struggle because of not only financial poverty, but also the prejudices the secular elite showed against religion.[6] From the time of modern Turkey's founder Mustafa Kamal Ataturk (1881–1938), elite Turks looked to copy Western secularism as the path to modernization and success. However, copying the West has deep psychological shortcomings (which I discuss next), clearly experienced by many traditional Turks outside the country's elite.

The Good Copy Problem in Turkey

Turkey and other Islamic societies are confronted with what I have termed the *good copy problem*.[7] I could see this clearly in Iran during the 1970s, as the last shah attempted to move Iranian society to become a "good copy" of Western societies. "We can become the Switzerland of the Middle East" was the shah's message. But despite the money flooding into Iran from enormous oil, gas, and mineral exports, Iranians instinctively felt that they could at best become "good copies" of the West; they could not become authentically Western. They could learn English and other Western languages and mimic Western ways, but they could not become the "real thing."

Turks were having similar troubled experiences in developing their national identity in the post–World War II era. On the one hand, Turkey joined NATO in 1952 and was considered a steadfast anticommunist military ally for the West. On the other hand, Turkey, an Islamic society, is not considered Western culturally, and Turkish efforts to join the European Union have been rebuffed repeatedly. Ataturk had placed an iron dividing line between politics and religion,[8] but traditional Turks refused to keep Islam separated from politics as they searched for an authentic modern Turkish national identity. Islam became a key ingredient of a national Turkish identity that signaled authenticity and did not merely attempt to mold Turkey as a "good copy" of the West.

Received wisdom tells us that the Turkish military has been the authentic and stalwart defender of Ataturk's secular legacy, but this received wisdom is utterly misleading. Left-wing political groups grew in strength in Turkey during the 1970s and 1980s. This was seen as a very serious threat by the Turkish military, as well as the United States and NATO. Communism was sweeping across the entire Near and Middle East regions. The Soviet Union invaded Afghanistan in 1979, and in Iran the Soviet-backed Tudeh Party was a dangerous threat to the shah's regime—a regime that was teetering and completely collapsed in 1979. The antidote to communism was seen to be political Islam.

The United States and other Western countries nurtured political Islam in the fight against the spread of communism in the Near and Middle East.[9] In Afghanistan, Islamic fundamentalists received support from Western powers and eventually managed to drive Soviet forces out of Afghanistan. In Pakistan, neighbor to Afghanistan and Iran, General Muhammad Zia-ul-Haq (1924–1988), with direct and indirect Western backing, put an end to the Soviet threat by establishing an Islamic dictatorship in 1978 and ruling until his mysterious death in a helicopter accident in 1988. In Iran, an Islamic regime replaced the shah and ruthlessly wiped out the Soviet-backed Tudeh Party, as well other left-leaning political groups. In Turkey, communists and left-leaning groups were stopped in their tracks by the 1980 military coup, which through the leadership of General Kenan Evren (1917–2015), shattered the division between Islam and government. Secularism was still talked about in Turkey, but after 1980, the government energized Islamic movements and pushed Islam back into every corner of Turkish society,

The coup leader and subsequent president, General Evren, delivered public speeches with the Koran in one hand. The new constitution made education in the tenets of Sunni Islam compulsory in elementary schools (it was already compulsory at the high school level). The expansion of *imam hatip* schools (government-financed and operated clerical training schools), which began in the 1970s, accelerated. The government oversaw a frenzy of mosque-building; with 85,000 state-operated mosques, nominally secular Turkey has more mosques than any other country.[10]

If the goal of the United States and other Western powers was to democratize Turkey, the main focus should have been on keeping Islam out of government. The main threat to democracy in Turkey in recent decades has been dictatorship through political Islam, not through the military or communist rule. It is ironic that Western powers, and particularly the United States, had supported fundamentalist Islam to defeat communism, only to have the Islamic fundamentalists in the Near and Middle East, and even in Europe and North America, turn around and attack the West.

The rise of Erdogan is integral to a purposeful turning back to Islamic identity in Turkey. Until his final year in high school, Erdogan attended an *imam hatip* institution, giving him a religious training that limited him to becoming a cleric or studying theology at university. But Erdogan was determined to enter politics, so he enrolled in a secular public school in his final high school year and went on to study at a business and management school in Istanbul.[11]

Despite his "secular" university training, Erdogan developed his political identity first and foremost as a conservative Sunni Muslim, opposed to the Westernized secular elites who had ruled Turkey since the time of Ataturk.

SPRINGING TO DICTATORSHIP

A study of Erdogan from the time of his becoming the mayor of Istanbul in 1994 to the changes he instigated in the Turkish constitution in 2017, which could keep him in power until 2029 and beyond,[12] shows that he has repeatedly and ruthlessly mobilized support from conservative Turkish Muslims to crush his political opposition. But unlike the Islamists who have entered mainstream politics in Iran, Egypt, and some other countries, Erdogan does not present himself in traditional Islamic clothing or with a beard. He wears expensively tailored suits, sports a trim moustache, and keeps a slim athletic figure from his soccer playing days. Particularly in the earlier days of his political campaigns in the 1990s and early 2000s, he attempted to widen his appeal and to attract "even" women who do not wear the hijab, as well as secular men.

But while presenting a moderate front, Erdogan has changed Turkey to enable the penetration of his brand of Sunni Islam into all corners of society. Most important, he has created conditions to ensure the rapid expansion of both religious *imam hatip* schools and religious instruction in so-called secular schools. Erdogan's explicit goal is to raise a pious generation.[13]

There are strong similarities between Erdogan's methods in Turkey and those of Khomeini and his followers in Iran to achieve the Islamization of society. Both Erdogan and Khomeini have achieved their goal through complete control of two institutions: the school and the mosque. In both cases, first the personnel in schools and mosques were changed—through expulsions of educators and imams who were deemed uncooperative with the regime and the changing of employment rules so new educators and imams friendly to the regime could be hired, even though they did not qualify according to the old rules of employment.[14] Second, there has been a rapid increase in religious instruction (Shi'a Islam in Iran and Sunni Islam in Turkey) in schools and universities as well as a huge expansion of the role of the mosque and imams in everyday life and so-called secular organizations.

The criticism that unqualified personnel have been hired in schools and mosques simply because of their loyalty to Erdogan could be extended to other domains, such as the foreign ministry and Turkish embassies.[15] I focus on schools and mosques because they have enabled the Erdogan regime to have deep penetration of everyday lives of ordinary people.

Personality Factors

In terms of personality characteristics, Erdogan is a potential dictator and has taken giant steps toward becoming an actual dictator. He sees the world as a threatening place, where certain dangerous individuals and groups with national and international ties are conspiring against him.[16] His high level of Machiavellianism and paranoia means that he feels justified in attacking his perceived enemies and stripping them of power, before (as he sees it) they have a chance to attack and destroy him. He positions himself as being from the masses and representing the "common people," and his opponents as representing the elites and Turkey's international enemies.

A clumsy coup attempt against Erdogan on July 15, 2016, served as a vitally important "crisis incident," providing him with new opportunities to diminish civil liberties and tighten his control.[17] A section of the Turkish military attempted to topple the Erdogan government. Turkish Air Force fighter jets took to the skies over Ankara and dropped bombs on the Turkish Parliament, while in Istanbul tanks took to the streets and stopped traffic on key bridges linking the European and Asian parts of the city. Other strategically important centers in Ankara and Istanbul were targeted for takeover. But there was a reaction against the coup from thousands of civilians, who were assisted by loyal sections of the Turkish military. As more and more people became aware of the coup and poured onto the streets, a call went out from tens of thousands of mosques around the country urging people to defeat the coup. By the morning of July 16, 2016, it was clear that the coup had failed. Tragically, during the coup attempt 241 people were killed, and almost 3,000 were seriously injured.

The bungled 2016 coup validated Erdogan's conspiratorial view of the world, heightened his paranoia, and gave him the justification he needed to further destroy his political opposition, severely restrict freedom of expression and rule of law, and achieve power monopoly. Turkey has a history of military coups over the last half century, and the Turkish military prides itself as having stepped into the political domain to "save the nation" when civilian politicians "make a mess." But the 2016 coup attempt was extremely amateurish and poorly managed, leading some critics to believe that either there was no real coup attempt or that Erdogan became aware of the coup attempt early on and allowed the plotters to proceed for a while to have an excuse to end basic freedoms in Turkey (I do not in this book delve into the different scenarios put forward concerning motivations behind the coup but note that this topic has received critical attention[18]). In the crackdown that followed the coup, most of the last remnants of democracy in Turkey were severely weakened.

Erdogan "miraculously" escaped being killed during the coup, and after he and his supporters regained full control of the situation, they set about eliminating not only known but also imagined opposition groups and individuals.[19] Hundreds of thousands of government employees, academics, judges, teachers, journalists, politicians, and others suspected of being opposed to Erdogan were kicked out of their jobs and, in many cases, jailed. Hundreds of news sources were closed down, and the mass media in Turkey was muzzled. As a consequence, "The World Justice Index placed Turkey 99th out of 113 countries in its rule of law ranking, behind Iran and Myanmar."[20] This means that the application of law in Turkish society tends to be arbitrary and inconsistent.

The tens of millions of prodemocracy Turks who opposed both the supposed coup attempt and Erdogan's authoritarian rule, who did not want either a military dictatorship or an Erdogan dictatorship, found themselves trapped. After the failed 2016 coup, Erdogan sprang to monopolize power, established himself as dictator of Turkey, and set about enforcing his views in a wide range of area. He declared alcohol to be the mother of all evil,[21] condemned coed dormitories,[22] proposed that Turkish families should have four children,[23] restricted Internet access in times of opposition uprising and banned Twitter,[24] and declared that Muslim families should not use birth control or family planning in general.[25]

There is a heavy cost to these monopolistic tactics by Erdogan. As commentators have pointed out, "Turkey cannot be a real democratic society when scores of its journalists languish behind bars."[26] There is now a greater lack of government accountability in Turkey, and the government is dealing with rising corruption by further monopolizing power and attacking the political opposition.

More "Trickle-Down Corruption"

"I have only this ring as an asset. If you hear that I have assets more than this, you can call me a thief." This is what Erdogan said in the early part of his political career.[27] But like many others before him who came to achieve power monopoly, Erdogan succumbed to the lure of wealth. He, his family, and his associates used their power to accumulate riches. Along the way, Erdogan gained more political enemies, and attempts were made by pro-democracy activists to publicly reveal the real Erdogan behind the facade of "I only have this ring as an asset."

In 2013, a police sting operation caught Erdogan on the telephone instructing his son, Bilal, to hide large amounts of cash at several family homes to evade the authorities making anticorruption raids. Over the course of several telephone conversations, it became clear that there were still 30 million euros in cash that Bilal was having difficulty hiding. Father and son agreed to use the cash to purchase luxury apartments.[28] According to Erdogan's own words, he is now a thief. Once again, power has brought corruption, and a politician who espoused lofty aspirations for honesty has found it impossible to remain true to his words.

The evidence against Erdogan and his family is overwhelming: They have engaged in large-scale corruption and enriched themselves. The young Erdogan who promised to clean up politics in Turkey and govern with honesty and efficiency has found the lure of gold too strong to resist. However, in true Machiavellian fashion, he has also turned the tables on his accusers and hunted down and jailed many of the government officials who gathered evidence to bring to light his corruption. Erdogan's political power monopoly has meant that instead of being forced to face the evidence against him in a court of law, he has counterattacked and destroyed the police and judicial personnel who tried to bring him to justice,

> Within a week, the regulations concerning the rights of law enforcement officers were changed in such a way that the security forces would have to inform their seniors of their actions at all times . . . several police officers working on this investigation and prosecutors who tried to continue the legal process were removed from their positions. . . . All of these positions have been filled by people close to Erdogan.[29]

The judges who were hoping to bring Erdogan to justice now found themselves kicked out of the courtroom. One critic summed up the situation in this way: "Corruption for Tayyip Erdogan was a way to reward family and friends, undermine opponents, and consolidate his power. His concentration of power is another form of corruption."[30]

Erdogan's concentration of power has included tighter control of the mass media, achieved by closing independent news outlets, arresting and harassing independent journalists, and creating an atmosphere of fear for anyone daring to be critical of him and his circle. Specifically, Erdogan and his supporters have responded to their critics by using a number of frames. For example, the *smear campaign frame* attempts to "discredit the corruption scandal as an attempt to damage the reputation of the government, or even to be a coup attempt."[31] The *sinister powers* frame focuses on "the presence of secretly operating national or international powers that seek to bring the country into turmoil."[32]

Crisis Incidents and the Springboard to Dictatorship

The springboard model of dictatorship[33] identifies a "crisis incident" as one of the key preconditions for the emergence of a springboard that a potential dictator can use to spring to power. For example, in 1933, the "Reichstag fire," when a young communist attempted to set government building on fire in Berlin, Germany, gave Hitler the excuse and opportunity to end most civil liberties and establish a one-party system. Another important example is the "hostage-taking crisis," when fanatical followers of Khomeini invaded the U.S. Embassy in Tehran in 1979, took American diplomats as hostages, and created a "siege" atmosphere in which all political opposition to Khomeini was wiped out and a brutal dictatorship was reestablished in Iran, this time under the mullahs. For Erdogan, the attempted 2016 coup served as the key "crisis incident" that has given him the excuse to establish dictatorship in Turkey. Anyone who questions the authenticity of the coup is treated by the Erdogan government as likely having had a role in it.[34]

Independent assessments from outside Turkey, including by Transparency International and the European Union,[35] have judged Turkey to have become less transparent and more corrupt since Erdogan increased his stranglehold on power in the second decade of the 21st century: "The coup provided Erdogan the opportunity to introduce the executive, presidential system he has long craved."[36]

The Role of External Threat

"Turkey is prepared to take its fight against Kurdish forces in northern Syria as far as Iraq, President Recep Tayyip Erdogan has said."[37] Erdogan's role as "strongman" and "savior" for Turkish nationalism has been helped by the influx into Turkey of about three million refugees from Syria,[38] as well as the movements to achieve independence for Kurds in Iraq and Syria. The Kurdish independence movements in Iraq and Syria, two countries neighboring Turkey, have raised the threat level from the perspective of Turkish nationalists who are already worried that the Kurdish independence movement in Turkey could fragment their nation. Both the Syrian refugees and the Kurdish independence movements have sharply raised perceived threat levels in Turkey.

The Syrian refugees flooding into Turkey initially enjoyed a great deal of sympathy among the Turkish population. Like their Turkish hosts, the Syrian refugees are Sunni Muslims, and in Syria they are persecuted by the brutal Shia Muslim regime led by the dictator Bashar al-Assad (backed by Iran and Russia). However, a number of psychological theories of intergroup relations predict that the sudden influx of millions of people into a region would create intense competition for scarce resource (such as jobs), which in turn would result in more negative intergroup attitudes, perhaps resulting in open conflict.[39] Unfortunately, events proceeded in line with this dire prediction, as reported in *The Washington Post*, "Turkey opened its doors to Syrian refugees. . . . More than 3 million Syrians accepted that welcome. . . . Now. . . . The Turkish public has soured on their presence, citing cultural differences and competition for jobs."[40] Erdogan has also at various times created tensions between Turkey and various Western powers, with the goal of mobilizing his core supporters. *The Washington Examiner*'s analysis as to why Erdogan threatens Israel is also valid for why he threatens the United States, the European Union, and also Russia:

> President Recep Tayyip Erdogan is threatening Israel in order to galvanize his base and strengthen his populist-Muslim appeal. . . . In part, this is an effort for Erdogan to consolidate the religious-populists in his AK party. Those voters revel in Erdogan's increasingly authoritarian approach to fostering political Islam in Turkish society.[41]

Thus, Erdogan has helped to create and taken advantage of the springboard to dictatorship in 21st-century Turkey. In this endeavor, he has been supported by conservative Muslims and ultra-nationalists. Erdogan has put a halt to the liberalization of Turkey and to the progress of Turkish women toward an equal role in Turkish society.

CONCLUDING COMMENT

"Worldwide we see two opposing trends: Globalization is making the world increasingly international, yet at the same time nationalist sentiments are growing stronger."[42] János Kornai's discussion of the "U-turn" away from democracy in Hungary reminds us of two important points. First, across many nations and regions, we are witnessing the rise of strongmen and the turn away from democracy; Ziya Öniş described the situation as a democratic stagnation across both the Global North and Global South.[43] I have focused on Turkey as an important illustrative example, but unfortunately (from a pro-democracy perspective), there are other similar cases. Second, Kornai referred to what I have termed *fractured globalization*,[44] the simultaneous economic, cultural, and other kinds of integration across the world, as well as increasing local separatism and nationalism. The tensions and collective identity threats arising from globalization are playing an important role in creating the springboard to dictatorship, giving strongmen in different societies new opportunities to try to stifle democracy and spring to power as full-fledged dictators.

ENDNOTES

1. Cagaptay (2017).
2. Moghaddam (2013).
3. Kinnvall (2004); Moghaddam (2008a).
4. For economic changes, see readings in Aysan, Babacan, Gur, and Karahan (2018). For a broader review of the background to changes in Turkey, see Kezer (2015).
5. See Shukri and Hossain (2017) on the Islamic rhetoric increasingly adopted by Erdogan's Justice and Development Party (AKP).
6. Cagaptay (2017) provided an introductory biography of Erdogan. No doubt more detailed in-depth biographies will follow Erdogan's departure, after scholars have had more opportunities to assess his record.
7. Moghaddam (2005b).
8. See Mango's (2000) biography of Ataturk.
9. Andrew Hartman (2002) provided a detailed analysis of the U.S. policy to support Islamic fundamentalists as a way of fighting the Soviets in Afghanistan.
10. Cornell (2017, p. S-22).
11. Cagaptay (2017, p. 37).
12. Paul and Seyreck (2017).
13. Cornell (2017, p. S-31).
14. Cornell (2017, p. S-30–S-32).
15. See the discussion of patronage ties by Coşkun (2017, p. 331).
16. Erdogan highlighted supposed threats against him at every turn, such as when on a visit to Bosnia, he claimed he was there despite assassination threats (Stockholm Center for Freedom, 2018). Depicting the world as full of threats against him, justified him striking out first against "enemies."
17. Esen and Gumuscu (2017).
18. Yavuz (2018).
19. Cagaptay (2017).
20. Phillips (2017, p. 171).
21. Waldman and Caliskan (2017, p. 73).
22. Waldman and Caliskan (2017, p. 73).
23. Waldman and Caliskan (2017, p. 73).
24. Waldman and Caliskan (2017, p. 139).
25. Waldman and Caliskan (2017, p. 74).
26. Waldman and Caliskan (2017, p. 231).
27. Phillips (2017, p. 46).
28. Phillips (2017, p. 47).
29. Coşkun (2017, p. 332).
30. Phillips (2017, p. 54).
31. Panayırcı, Işeri, and Şekercioğlu (2016, p. 554).
32. Panayırcı et al. (2016, p. 554).
33. Moghaddam (2013).
34. Bekdil (2017).
35. European Commission (2016).
36. Bekdil (2017, p. 9).
37. BBC News (2018, January 26).

38. Baban and Rygiel (2017); Memisoglu (2017).
39. See the discussion of realistic conflict theory and other materialist theories in Chapter 4 of Moghaddam (2008b).
40. Cunningham and Zakaria (2018).
41. Rogan (2017).
42. Kornai (2015, p. 43).
43. Öniş (2016).
44. Moghaddam (2008a, 2008b).

II

FREEDOM AND DICTATORSHIP

Mayor: *See where his Grace stands, 'tween two clergymen.*
Buckingham: *Two props of virtue for a Christian prince,*
To stay him from the fall of vanity;
And, see, a book of prayer in his hand,
True ornaments to know a holy man.

—WILLIAM SHAKESPEARE, *RICHARD III* (III.vii.96–100)

In Shakespeare's play *Richard III*, the ruthless and Machiavellian Richard takes advantage of circumstances and also creates opportunities for himself to become king, mainly by killing those ahead of him in line for the throne. To orchestrate an appropriate setting for the people to "plead for him to become king," he persuades the Duke of Buckingham and some others, who are opportunistic, gullible, or both, to lead a few hapless citizens to publicly "urge him" to be king. When Buckingham and the others arrive, they see Richard (apparently) "deep in prayer," with a priest on either side of him (the "two props of virtue," mentioned in the preceding quote). In this way, Richard presents himself as virtuous and "Godly," using religion as a cover to hide his murderous, corrupt, and vile personality. The story of Richard III highlights the combination of contextual and dispositional factors that are involved in the establishment and continuation of dictatorship.

As in the case of Richard III, all dictatorships rely on the gullibility of at least some others. The four chapters in Part II explore different aspects of this gullibility and argue that a major reason people support potential or actual dictators is the false belief that the dictator will lead them, through their sacred group, to freedom and glory. In short, people support the dictator because they are fooled by his false promises. Just like the villainous Richard III standing between two priests to position himself as "Godly," the dictator gets popular support by presenting a false picture of himself as a savior, the only one who can ensure the greatness of the sacred group.

3

Understanding the Immortal Dictator

When I left Iran in December 1983, my entire life boiled down to one question: Where in the world would I make my new life?

Academics are natural global nomads. Because academic research is international, academic networks are able to cross most national boundaries, enabling the cross-border movement of not only ideas but also people. Even dictatorships are unable to completely stop the flow of ideas and researchers. I left Iran in December 1983, and in early 1984 I found refuge and work at McGill University in Canada, and then in 1990 I moved to Georgetown University in the United States. Since the early 20th century, American universities have served as a magnet for scholars from around the world, attracted to the United States by the greater freedom and resources available for research. This trend slowed down, but did not end, after Donald Trump became president.[1]

THE RESILIENCE OF DICTATORS

During more than 3 decades of research and teaching in the West since my exit from Khomeini's dictatorship, I have been haunted by questions about the resilience of dictators in human history and the enormous difficulty of establishing democracies. The first serious experiments in democracy began in Athens about 2,500 years ago, but progress toward a democratic world has been painfully slow, and we remain far from the ideal of actualized democracy.

http://dx.doi.org/10.1037/0000142-004
Threat to Democracy: The Appeal of Authoritarianism in an Age of Uncertainty,
by F. M. Moghaddam

The "great revolutions" have contributed in limited ways to democratic progress, but their actual contribution is grossly exaggerated. For example, 2,500 years ago in Athens, free men born in Athens, not women or slaves, could vote. Approximately 2,200 years later, the American Revolution gave rise to a new republic, the United States, in which free men, not women or slaves, could vote. In this sense, the American Revolution only advanced the United States to similar levels of democracy enjoyed in ancient Athens. It was not until 1920 that women gained the right to vote in the United States, and, in practice, it was not until after the Civil Rights Act of 1964 and the improved status of minorities that African Americans and other minority group members could actually cast votes in significant numbers and in relative safety.[2]

But in practice, democracy in the United States still works according to the idea that those who have more money have a larger stake in the nation and that they should therefore have more say in how things are decided. In a seminal empirical study of how important policy decisions are made in America, the Princeton researchers Martin Gilens and Benjamin Page concluded: "In the United States, our findings indicate, the majority does not rule—at least not in the causal sense of actually determining policy outcomes. When the majority of citizens disagrees with economic elites or with organized interests, they generally lose."[3] Wolfgang Streeck described a kind of sickness in Western capitalist democracies:

> a condition of acquired inconsequence, of inflicted as well as self-inflicted irrelevance, of contracted insignificance of democratic politics in relation to the capitalist economy, a condition in which democracy has lost its egalitarian-redistributive capacity, so that it makes no difference any more who is voted into office in what may or may not continue to be more or less competitive elections.[4]

Far-right political movements have swept through numerous democratic societies in the second decade of the 21st century. In Austria, the Austrian Freedom Party gained the presidency and political dominance; in Germany, the Alternative for Deutschland has gained political ground at the expense of moderates such as Angela Merkel; in France, the far-right National Front led by Marine Le Pen made substantial electoral gains, as did the Party for Freedom led by Geert Wilders in the Netherlands, the Golden Dawn in Greece, and the Jobbik in Hungary. The 2018 elections in Italy brought the populist far right to the center of power, with some extremist groups celebrating the fascist dictator Mussolini as a hero.[5] Even Sweden and Slovakia are not immune from this right-wing surge: The Sweden Democrats and Our Slovakia have gained serious political ground. Common to all these far-right movements is opposition to immigration, popular support for a (usually charismatic) "strongman," support for strong national borders and focus on the "purity" of "our people," usually envisioned in terms of a mythical and incorrect idea of "race."[6] The country that has moved farthest along this path is Poland, where the governing Law and Justice party has severely weakened the separation of powers and the rule of law.[7]

Populist movements (as discussed in the Introduction to this volume) have fermented *illiberal democracy*, in which various elements of democracy (e.g., elections) are manipulated to achieve nondemocratic ends. Illustrative of this trend, populist far-right leaders are maneuvering a number of Eastern European "democracies," Poland, Czech Republic, Hungary, and Slovakia, away from openness. A more severe turn toward dictatorship has taken place in Turkey and Venezuela, countries that at the end of the 20th century seemed assured of a more democratic future (the case of Turkey was discussed in Chapter 2). Populist ultra-right leaders such as Jair Bolsonaro of Brazil are gaining influence, in a "Trumpification" sweeping South America.[8] India, the world's largest democracy, suffers from high levels of corruption and inefficiency.[9] China, the world's rising power, is firmly in the grips of elite dictatorial rule. An elite clique ruled China until about the second decade of the 21st century, but now President Xi Jinping has firmly taken monopoly control as "dictator for life" and become the most dominant ruler since Chairman Mao. Other strongmen in the same region—Rodrigo Duterte of the Philippines, Hun Sen of Cambodia, and the military junta (with Aung San Suu Kyi looking on) in Myanmar—have also turned sharply away from democracy. Cambodia, Laos, Thailand, and Vietnam continue as dark dictatorships, while freedom flickers dimly in Indonesia, Malaysia, and Singapore. In Russia, the reign of President Vladimir Putin is supreme in the tradition of the prerevolution tsars. The active emulation of "big dictators" takes place by strongmen in smaller countries, such as Duterte in the Philippines, General Prayuth Chan-Ocha in Thailand, and Abdel Fattah el-Sisi in Egypt.

In short, democracy is in retreat in many countries,[10] but why? I first consider trends in the United States, then return to consider this question in a global context.

THE UPS AND DOWNS OF AMERICAN DEMOCRACY

A high level of academic freedom is one of the invaluable blessings still found in America, but academic freedom is fragile and can be crushed under certain conditions. During the anticommunist campaigns of the 1950s, popularly known as "McCarthyism," universities came under intense political pressure, and many academics lost their jobs as censorship was enforced to prevent the spread of "dangerous ideas" in American universities.[11] McCarthyism is a reminder that American democracy is also fragile and could disappear.[12]

The U.S. presidential elections of 2016 shattered any illusions people had about America's being safe from the danger of dictatorship. Many people take comfort in the belief that "the arc of the moral universe is long, but it bends toward justice," as brilliantly phrased by Dr. Martin Luther King (1929–1968). Some changes seem to celebrate the promise of a more democratic future: the transition to democracy in 30 countries from 1974 to 1990,[13] the collapse of the Soviet empire in 1991, the movement toward democracy in former Eastern bloc countries during the 1990s, the end of apartheid in South Africa in 1994. But the global retreat of democracy in the early 21st century and the coming to power of Donald Trump in the United States has shattered forecasts of an inevitable victory for democracy.

To understand these trends, it is imperative that we focus primarily on the context that gives rise to opportunities for potential dictators to spring to power. Critics have contended that Donald Trump is a potential dictator who tramples on human rights,[14] but the democratic institutions of the United States have held firm and controlled his antidemocratic instincts.[15] In terms of personality characteristics, Trump has charisma (attractiveness than can inspire devotion in at least a core group of supporters), craving for centralized power (wanting to monopolize power in one's own hands), illusions of control (wrongly believing that one controls events and people), Machiavellianism (being cunning and deceptive in relations with others), narcissism (engrossed in oneself and one's own interests), paranoia (suffering delusions of persecution and self-aggrandizement), and self-glorification (exaggerated estimates of one's own importance). In addition to this (from the point of view of democratic values) toxic package of personality traits, Trump is motivated and skilled at displacing aggression onto minorities and "dissimilar others"; he is aggressive and vindictive toward anyone who criticizes or even disagrees with him but very positively biased toward those who show unquestioning obedience to him. Most important, Trump has a troubling disregard for democratic norms; he is a despot waiting for an opportunity to spring to absolute power.[16]

The psychiatrist Allen Frances researched Trump's behavioral style and proposed that he is in important ways similar to Adolf Hitler.[17] For example, Frances pointed out that

> Hitler, like Trump, was despised and underestimated by the political establishment, who felt he could be used and manipulated for their own purposes . . . defied the political establishment and remained true (only) to himself . . . felt disrespected and treated unfairly, and had many scores to settle . . . exploited the fear, anger, and resentments of his people . . . promoted tribalism and reviled minorities as dangerous vermin.[18]

Trump's leadership style also marks him as a potential dictator. He aggressively and overtly attacks the free press, and it is probable that if he had the power, he would severely limit freedom of expression in the United States. This is clear from his repeated depiction of the mainstream press as the enemy of the people and his support for only the jingoistic sector of the media that fawningly applaud him. The Trump White House victimizes and shuns media critics and gives special privileges and access to media supporters. Despite the pressure to buckle under pressure from the Trump White House, the mainstream media has so far continued to report on blatant violations, as when *The Washington Post* reported that Trump administration officials attempted to ban the use of certain "objectionable" terms in government documents, including "evidence based" and "science based."[19] As I discuss in Chapter 8, research since the mid-20th century has shown those high on authoritarianism to be antiscience.

Trump's dismissal of democratic procedures; his dislike for checks and balances, due process, and genuine exchanges of views; and his tendency to see himself as all-knowing, the one who should hold all decision-making power, mean that by being in the leadership position, he necessarily weakens democracy in the United States and around the world. Trump's behavioral style is crystalized in his disdain for anyone or any source critical of him, particularly the free press.[20] In this, he is following the pattern of behavior that is typical for dictators.

In 1979, I was in Tehran during the "Spring of Revolution" when Khomeini launched his attack on the fragile free press that had sprung roots in the post-revolution era in Iran. He denounced those who would not absolutely obey him as the "enemies of the people" and as the sources of what Trump in the 21st century has called "fake news." In 2016, I was in Washington, DC, when Trump attacked the free press as "enemies of the people" and fabricated his own version of reality. Both Khomeini and Trump have used lies and deception and relied on the support of an unswerving group of loyal supporters as well as a rich group of business moguls who pursued policies they believed to be the most profitable—for themselves. *The Economist* noted about the Trump leadership style that

> the organizing principle of Mr. Trump's Republican Party is loyalty. Not, as with the best presidents, loyalty to an ideal, a vision or a legislative program, but to just one man—Donald J. Trump—and to the prejudice and rage which consume the voter base that, on occasion, even he struggles to control."[21]

Trump's strong preference for loyalty over expertise in hiring for key positions exactly parallels the policies of all authoritarian leaders, including Khomeini and Khamenei in Iran.[22]

Of course there are differences: Checks and balances do not constrain the power of Khomeini and other dictators, whereas the U.S. Congress and the U.S. Supreme Court could constrain Trump's power. Khomeini and other dictators rule as long as they live, whereas Trump has to abide by term limits. But common to leaders such as Khomeini and Trump is the insistence on blind obedience and the absolute compliance of their underlings.[23] This has made leadership style in the United States, the reigning superpower, similar to leadership style in China, the rising and future superpower,

> The Trump adviser Kellyanne Conway's February tweet about serving "at the pleasure of @POTUS. His message is my message. His goals are my goals," echoes a notorious remark by Mao Zedong's wife, Jiang Qing: "I was Chairman Mao's dog," Jiang said at her 1980 trial. "Whomever he told me to bite, I bit." And Trump's attacks on the media . . . from calling the mainstream American media "the enemy of the American People" to his recurring attacks on accurate but critical reporting as "fake news"—stems from a strong desire to have only positive press coverage of himself: the only type of press coverage the Chinese media offers on the Chinese leader Xi.[24]

The coming to power of Donald Trump has been accompanied by a surge in right-wing attacks on the mainstream media, with *The New York Times, The Washington Post,* and CNN being prime targets. A 2017 survey of Americans showed that 70% of Republicans trusted Donald Trump more than any of these three media sources.[25] Remarkably, 54% of Republicans said they trusted Donald Trump more than even Fox News—Trump's preferred news source.

The same survey showed almost half of Republicans were in favor of shutting down news media outlets for publishing or broadcasting (what they deemed to be) biased and inaccurate stories. This is a remarkably high level of intolerance for critical voices in the "Land of the Free."

A Gallup/Knight Foundation survey of more than 19,000 adult Americans, *Trust, Media and Democracy*, showed a general concern about "fake news,"[26] but there were divisions between people with different political orientations: 42% of Republicans and only 17% of Democrats reported that accurate news stories that cast a politician or political group in a negative light are always "fake news."[27] Political orientation also made a difference in how problematic people saw it is to select news sources with similar views to one's own: This was seen as a major problem by 68% of "very liberal" respondents but only 48% of very conservative respondents.[28]

The surge of extremist, antidemocratic right-wing populism is evident around the world, as dictatorships gain influence and flex their muscles. Recent events in the United States have strengthened this antidemocratic trend; as a headline in *The Washington Post* explained, "Trump is delighting dictators everywhere."[29] By attacking the free press; dismissing as "fake" any facts, reports, or criticisms he does not like; and ignoring human rights violations, Trump has used and endorsed the tactics of both major (Putin of Russia) and minor (Khameini of Iran) dictators around the world.

What is the use of discussing Trump's personality and tactics? I am certainly not assuming that such discussions will change the views of Trump's supporters; such arguments will not influence them. But there is another important purpose to discussing Trump's personality and behavioral style. First, it is essential that at least both Republicans and Democrats who are more open-minded and tending toward critical thinking be provided with more opportunities to rethink the political turn toward authoritarianism in the United States. Trump is just one part of this wider authoritarian trend (and many principled Republicans oppose him). Second, the discussion of Trump's personality and behavioral style leads us to discussions of solutions to dictatorship, discussed in detail in Chapter 10. A central feature of the solutions discussed is the development of prodemocracy citizens, with personality and behavioral characteristics that are supportive of democracy rather than dictatorship.

Of course, democracy in the United States has been through difficult times before. For example, Barry Weingast noted that "in the 1790s, the Federalist Alien and Sedition Acts explicitly denied the political rights of the Jeffersonian opposition in a manner associated more with the troubled democracies of modern Latin America than with modern America,"[30] and he documented major shortcomings in American democracy during the Civil War. In the 20th century, the *National Origins Act* of 1924 (which attempted to shape the future U.S. population to remain as Western European as possible) was clearly discriminatory against certain minorities and ignored basic tenets of democracy.[31] The era of McCarthyism was the most challenging for the survival of U.S. democracy in recent history,[32] at a time when the rise of the totalitarian Soviet Union cast a large shadow across the world and provided a "justification" for the U.S. government clamping down on dissent at home. In the 21st century, the rise of far-right political movements across the world, as well as the surging global influence of Chinese and Russian dictatorships, is in line with the rise of Trump in America.

EXPLAINING THE TURN TOWARD DICTATORSHIP

How can we explain the turn toward dictatorship? This "prodictatorship turn" in the 21st century is mild, so far, compared with the rise of support for dictatorships in Germany and Italy in the 1930s, which included support for the Nazis among some influential circles, including in the United States and the United Kingdom, before the start of World War II.[33] The most prominent psychological approach to this question has been psychoanalytic, reflected in works such as Gustav Bychowski's *Dictators and Disciples From Caesar to Stalin: A Psychoanalytic Interpretation of History*[34] and Daniel Rancour-Laferriere's *The Mind of Stalin: A Psychoanalytic Study.*[35] The most influential work in this tradition is Erich Fromm's volume *Escape From Freedom.*[36] As I discussed in the Preface to this book, *Escape From Freedom* continues to be the most highly cited psychological work on dictatorship. The global influence of Fromm's psychological explanation of dictatorship is unparalleled and increasing (as reflected by rising annual citations). For this reason, I pay particular attention to *Escape From Freedom.* Like other psychoanalytical works, it has a focus on irrationality as understood from a Freudian perspective.[37]

The psychoanalytic interpretation of irrationality focuses on the unconscious nature of motives, desires, fears, and other psychological factors that influence human behavior, without people being aware of this influence.[38] The unconscious evolves through an intense conflict within the child during the process of socialization; Freud depicted "becoming civilized" as the bringing under control of inborn tendencies, particularly in the areas of sex and aggression, through the imposition of "accepted" morality.[39] The infant personality is first dominated by the *Id*, driven by the *pleasure principle*, demanding instant gratification. But soon after birth, the practical limitations of the real world, including societal norms, start to inhibit the behavior of the infant, and an *ego* develops shaped by the *reality principle*. The child gradually internalizes the morality of the larger society, and a *superego*, which functions as a conscience, takes shape and guides behavior. However, the ego and superego only manage to repress, not eliminate, the basic desires, motives, and other psychological factors that are taboo in society. This repressed material is pushed into an unconscious, which increases in size, until it is the greater part of the largely submerged iceberg, with conscious experience being the tip of the iceberg visible above water.

Ignorance of the main "unconscious" factors that influence their behavior does not prevent people from rationalizing their behavior. Research suggests humans are brilliant at rationalizing. For example, in a study on rhetoric used to justify nations going to war, the warring sides were shown to provide a broad range of justifications that fall under the umbrella of "we are fighting for peace" and "we fight to end wars."[40] The most startling among such rationalizations is still probably a slogan from the First World War, which encouraged people to fight in "The war to end all wars." After all, who would not be motivated to fight in a war to end all wars?

In Fromm's analysis, irrationality in the modern industrialized world meant that humans were unaware of the underlying forces leading them to support the rise of dictatorships in Germany and other countries in the 1920s and 1930s. Industrialization, urbanization, and other features of modernization have led to the "unconscious suffering of the average automatized person . . . the readiness to accept any ideology and any leader, if only he promises excitement and offers a political structure and symbols which allegedly give meaning and order to an individual's life."[41] The modern conditions meant that

> modern man . . . has been freed from traditional authorities and has become an "individual," but . . . at the same time he has become isolated, powerless, and an instrument of purposes outside of himself, alienated from himself and others . . . this state undermines his self, weakens and frightens him, and makes him ready for submission to new kinds of bondage."[42]

Thus, the psychoanalytic interpretation depicts humans as ready to submit to dictatorial authority as an escape from alienation, isolation, meaninglessness, and particularly an escape from freedom—a freedom that has cut traditional relationships and ties of authority and left individuals alienated and alone.

In this and other chapters, I critically reassess different features of Fromm's thesis.

Toward a Better Explanation

The psychoanalytic perspective has served a useful purpose, but it has major shortcomings in the context of the 21st century. First, there are limitations in the psychoanalytic interpretation—even in the basic idea of an unconscious arising through repression. Certainly, there is ample evidence that in many situations, humans are not conscious of the main factors that influence their behavior,[43] but little evidence showing this lack of awareness arises because of repression of material into an unconscious. Second, there have developed in the past few decades powerful alternative research perspectives from which to interpret the lack of awareness among people regarding what influences their behavior. These alternative perspectives include research literature in cognitive science, behavioral economics, political psychology, sociobiology, and neuroscience broadly, providing a much deeper understanding of *implicit cognitive processes*: when memories, knowledge, and other psychological phenomena influence a person's behavior without the person being aware of this influence.

Thus, according to the traditional psychoanalytic view, humans are unaware of the factors influencing their behavior, because of repression of material into the unconscious. But according to the new science of implicit cognition, people have evolved to process information in ways that result in, on the one hand, explicit cognition about which we are conscious and, on the other hand, implicit cognition about which we are not conscious.[44] These two types of thinking have evolved through long-term evolutionary processes; they have both played essential roles in our survival, and they both continue to influence our behavior. From this evolutionary perspective, we are not always aware of the factors that influence our behavior, because we do not need to be from an adaptive perspective. Just as we do not need to be conscious of our heartbeat, breathing, heat regulation, or many other features of our functioning, we do not need to be conscious of all the factors that shape how we think and act.

Fractured Globalization and New Threats

Similarly, at the collective level, we do not need to be, and often are not, conscious of many of the factors that shape group and intergroup behavior. For example, as soon as we are placed in a group, even if the basis for group membership is objectively trivial, we show bias in favor of "our side" (this topic is discussed in more depth in Chapter 6). When our group is threatened, we tend to show more support for strong aggressive group leadership and less support for civil liberties and the rights of minorities (psychological threat and its consequences are also discussed in more depth in Chapter 6). Cognitively, we tend to perceive outgroups as more similar to one another and a "mass" ("they all look the same to me") and our own group as being more variable.[45]

Similarity plays a complex, subtle, and largely implicit role in our group and intergroup behavior.[46] Despite the plots of Hollywood movies that show people who are very different starting out hating each other but magically falling in love by the end of the movie, as a general rule, similarity rather than dissimilarity leads to attraction in both interpersonal and intergroup relations. People tend to be more positively disposed toward the members of groups who are more similar to their ingroups. The research findings[47] are in line with everyday experiences: For example, the arrival in Europe of millions of "dissimilar" refugees from Syria and other parts of Asia and Africa has resulted in backlash and the growth of antiimmigration political movements.

The involuntary and voluntary movement of people on a massive scale across nations and regions is only one part of the enormous changes brought about by what I have termed *fractured globalization*.[48] On the one hand, rapid and vast technological and economic integration is forcing people around the world to become objectively more similar to one another. People around the world are increasingly adopting more similar goods and services, clothing, transportation, films and music, educational systems, basic science, and communications systems. This trend is most striking among the young and the university educated. On the other hand, the need for a distinct collective identity has resulted in people insisting that their group is authentically different, dissimilar to out-groups, and in need of independence. This "authenticity need" has been asserted in particular by groups that have felt most threatened and in danger of decline, such as White men in the United States.

CONCLUDING COMMENT

The dictator has proven to be extremely resilient throughout known human history. Even when societies have made some advances toward being open and democratic, potential dictators have worked hard to help create the springboard to dictatorship, and to successfully spring to power as dictator—as happened in Germany in the 20th century and is happening in Russia and Turkey in the 21st century. Even when societies undergo gigantic antidictatorship revolutions and topple dictators, the postrevolution "opportunity bubble"[49] is most often usurped by another strongman who springs to power and reestablishes dictatorship using another ideological "front." For example, the ideological front of monarchy is replaced by Marxism, Islamism, Republicanism, or some other label, but the dictatorship continues.

The resiliency of the dictator is explained in large part by his extraordinary talent for persuading the masses that only he is able to lead them to freedom and glory, only he can defend their sacred group, and only he can be trusted with power to make them great again. The strongman uses popular support to attack the free press, to silence the intellectual elite, and to destroy rule of law. But the kind of freedom he promises to deliver the masses is attached freedom, rather than detached freedom. This topic is explored further in the next chapter.

ENDNOTES

1. One indication of the slowdown is a decline in the number of foreign science graduate students coming to continue their education the United States (Beeler, 2018).
2. African Americans have continued to face resistance and voter suppression after the 1960s; see Andrews (1997).
3. Gilens and Page (2014, p. 576).
4. Streeck (2017, p. 188).
5. Jones (2018).
6. What Meloni (2016) called a "hard" hereditary viewpoint is now being overtaken by a "soft" hereditarian viewpoint, with epigenetics leading to a greater role being given to the environment in shaping human characteristics. The relationship between biology and politics has a complicated modern history (Meloni, 2016), but clearly the racial views of the Nazis and various other fascist and far-right groups are not just politically unacceptable but scientifically incorrect.
7. Human Rights Watch (2017).
8. Encarnacion (2018).
9. Miklian and Carney (2013).
10. The retreat of democracy is widely noted but examined in an in-depth manner by Kurlantzick (2013).
11. See Holmes (1989).
12. For a broader view of McCarthysim, see Deer and Schrecker (2016).
13. See Huntington's (1991) discussion of the "Third Wave" of democratization.
14. For example, see Gurtov (2018).
15. Albright (2018) has insightfully recognized Trump as the most antidemocratic U.S. president of the modern era.
16. See the extensive discussion of the springboard model of dictatorship in Moghaddam (2013).

17. See in particular Chapter 5 in Frances (2017).
18. Frances (2017, p. 155).
19. Milbank (2017).
20. William McGurn (2018) is among those who have correctly pointed out anti-democratic actions by those opposing Trump. However, showing that others are also engaging in antidemocratic activities does not justify Trump's strong anti-democratic tendencies.
21. "What has become of the Republican Party?" (2018).
22. See Osnos (2018).
23. The common characteristics of strongmen such as Khomeini and Trump are described in Moghaddam (2013).
24. Fish (2017).
25. "Fox Populi," (2017).
26. See Gallup/Knight (2017).
27. Gallup/Knight (2017, p. 29).
28. Gallup/Knight (2017, p. 36).
29. Gerson (2017).
30. Weingast (1998, p. 148).
31. For more details, see https://history.state.gov/milestones/1921-1936/immigration-act.
32. Schrecker (1998).
33. See Moghaddam (2013) and Pool and Pool (1979).
34. Bychowski (1969).
35. Rancour-Laferriere (1988).
36. Fromm (1941).
37. Freud (1953–1974).
38. The nature of the unconscious, and its relation to overt behavior, continues to be explored and contested in modern empirical research; for example, see Biderman and Mudrik (2018).
39. See Chapter 4 in Moghaddam (2005a).
40. Vance-Cheng, Rooney, Moghaddam, and Harré (2013).
41. Fromm (1941, p. 256).
42. Fromm (1941, p. 270).
43. See the discussions of System 1 thinking in Kahneman (2011).
44. There are several well-known ways of classifying human thinking that closely, but not exactly, map onto the "implicit–explicit" distinction, such as System 1 and System 2 thinking: "System 1 operates automatically and quickly, with little or no effort and no sense of voluntary control. . . . System 2 allocates attention to the effortful mental activities that demand it, including complex computations. The operations of System 2 are often associated with the subjective experience of agency, choice, and concentration" (Kahneman, 2011, pp. 20–21). System 1 thinking involves implicit processes, but System 2 thinking involves both implicit and explicit processes. Another associated classification is two routes to persuasion, the central route, involving cognitive engagement, critical thinking, and deeper information processing, and the peripheral route, involving persuasion through emotions and feelings (Petty, Cacioppo, & Schumann, 1983).
45. Mullen and Hu (1989).
46. Osbeck, Perreault, and Moghaddam (1997).
47. Osbeck et al. (1997).
48. Moghaddam (2008b).
49. Moghaddam and Breckenridge (2011).

4

Attached Versus Detached Conceptions of Freedom

I was determined to come to Danzig only as a liberator. I now take Danzig into the great German community. . . . They . . . will remember with pride the time of the resurrection and rise of the German Reich, that Reich which welds all real Germans together.

—ADOLF HITLER[1]

On September 1, 1939, the German military steamrolled across Poland, crushed defending Polish forces, and took control of the invaded territories, triggering the start of World War II.[2] Hitler's victory speech to the people of Danzig, part of a territory he was forcibly "rejoining" to Germany, positioned himself[3] and the German forces as "liberators." In his speech, Hitler also positioned his moves as strengthening and bringing together all German people and launching a rebirth, a resurrection. This is the essence of the dictator's message, repeated across the ages: I am the person who will both free you and bring rebirth and glory to *our* sacred group; you will be liberated and strong through me!

FREEDOM THROUGH SACRED GROUPS

By supporting the dictator, people feel they have a path to freedom and glory through the greatness of their sacred group. The mass rallies, speeches, chants, and slogans, together with waving flags, banners, and other shared *cultural*

http://dx.doi.org/10.1037/0000142-005
Threat to Democracy: The Appeal of Authoritarianism in an Age of Uncertainty,
by F. M. Moghaddam

carriers,[4] the means by which culture is propagated and passed on from generation to generation, help to ferment a sense of community and to inspire supporters of the dictator to feel strong and positive about their sacred group, to give them a sense of resurgence and resurrection. Through the rise of the sacred group, the individual feels empowered, strong, and free. This is the essence of attached freedom, which I discuss in greater depth later in this chapter.

But attached freedom also involves a negative side because it is exclusionary. "We," "our group," "those who belong to our land," have the right to enjoy freedom, but "they," "those animals," "those who do not belong to our land," have no such right and must be excluded from our freedoms. This is how an organization such as the Austrian Freedom Party, which is populist political party with roots in Nazism and is antiminority, can "justify" including "freedom" in its name. In this case, *freedom* refers to the rights of the sacred ingroup, those who "truly belong" in Austria. Those who do not belong do not have the right to enjoy freedom.

The propaganda of dictatorship presents the sacred group as united and reflecting the free choice of the people. This "free choice" is (supposedly) reflected in the support and integration of all the people within the political party serving the dictator. The view that people support the dictator because he promises freedom through the sacred group is opposed by those who believe people want to escape from freedom because it (supposedly) brings them anxiety and even terror.

The Invalid Freedom as Terror Hypothesis

Whereas the traditional psychoanalytic interpretation is that alienation and isolation have resulted in modern people under some conditions escaping from freedom into the arms of dictators, my position is that people are attracted to dictators when the freedoms and greatness they associate with their sacred groups are threatened and strongmen persuasively promise to safeguard those freedoms and greatness. The psychoanalytic perspective is part of a widespread assumption that, deep down, people find freedom frightening—that they are threatened by freedom. This is what I call the *freedom as terror* hypothesis.

Those who view "freedom as terror" believe that human beings want to be dominated, that they want order and structure imposed on them, that they feel terrorized when restrictions are lifted and they are actually set free. Although they are not always explicit, the implication of this viewpoint is that it is best for humans to be regulated and governed, even in the details of their lives. Without such order, people become fearful and helpless; this is at the heart of the argument that modern humans rush to dictators as their saviors because freedom has terrorized them. I completely disagree with this perspective.

Rather than experiencing freedom as terror, most people find freedom liberating, exhilarating—it is through freedom that human creativity and genius come to fruition. It is when individuals are free to innovate that they can achieve greatness and, through their art, their businesses, and their ideas, bring wealth for everyone and benefits to society. Humans have a natural capacity and inclination to seek freedom as individuals, but the benefits of personal freedom also come to those around them.

However, being free to innovate and be creative is not the same as being free to exploit others. I am not advocating some kind of "trickle-down" economic model, according to which "great men" are given room to trample on the rights of others and concentrate as much wealth as possible in their own hands through the exploitation of others. Rather, I am arguing that freedom is essential for healthy entrepreneurial success, as well as artistic, scientific, and other types of creativity. Further, I believe that the urge to be free is rooted in the characteristics of all humans. By giving room and opportunity to all individuals to be creative and entrepreneurial, we enrich the larger society.

Anyone who doubts that there is among humans a universal urge to be free should consider the possibility of the opposite: a universal urge to be enslaved. Of course, humans want a functional level of order and structure in their lives, but this does not translate to a desire to live under tutelage. Dictatorial regimes can coerce and manipulate people to "give their ascent" to, and even vote in "elections" to support, an "unfree" form of life, as happens in Russia, Iran, and some other societies, but this does not demonstrate that people desire to "escape" from freedom.

The motivation driving people into the arms of strongmen is not escape from freedom but the safeguarding of freedoms. Unfortunately, charismatic strongmen are (mistakenly) seen by their supporters as saviors, and this is a fatal error because the strongmen invariably fail to deliver the glory and freedoms they promise. But the act of people mistakenly believing the promises of dictators is not proof of a rejection of freedom. The strongmen make false promises and mislead the people. The end result of manipulations by dictators is "escape to dictatorship" and the crushing of freedoms, but this is not what people want. We should not mistake what the dictator manipulates as the desires of the people with the actual wishes and motivations of the people.

The Genius of Dictators

The genius of the dictator is to persuade large parts of the population to believe that what people actually want is what the dictator personally wants. The dictator and his leadership group are able to create this confusion through sheer determination and the willingness to do whatever it takes to gain power. Even when in a numerical minority, as the Bolsheviks were in 1917 during the Russian Revolution and the fanatical followers of Khomeini were during and immediately following the Iranian Revolution in 1979, the dictator and his supporters manage to grab power because they are more focused and determined than their rivals to obtain power and willing to adopt an absolutist "our ends justify any means" approach to gaining monopoly control of society.

The dictator helps followers to cross borders in their minds, and particularly borders that limit their imagined future. These borders have developed through socialization and consist of strong norms, taboos, and other mechanisms that limit thought and the imagination—in this case, the imagined self in the future.

Internal borders can become ineffective through decay, or they can be discarded or rejected or leapt over or sidestepped in some other way. The dictator guides his followers to imagine and hope beyond internal borders regarding the life of the sacred group and the experience of followers as part of this group. He tells his followers that they must reject certain internal borders, so they—as individuals and sacred group members—will be liberated from the restrictions imposed on them by the "other" who does not want them to be free and great.

The "other" is depicted as the reason why the sacred group is unfulfilled, impaired, and prevented from achieving greatness. The "other" is different, foreign, sponging off the sacred group, a leach sucking the life out of "us." The "other" is animal, criminal, rapist, murderer, evil—the "other" must be discarded. The other is why we are not free.

Dictators are against some interpretations of freedom, but they are strongly supportive of some other types of freedom. To better understand this, we need to identify and distinguish among the different types of freedom.[5]

TYPES OF FREEDOM

Freedom and liberty, often used interchangeably,[6] have been discussed extensively over the centuries. For example, for Immanuel Kant (1724–1804), freedom is the only innate right; it is the basis of the principle of right.[7] Without freedom to choose and some measure of free will, there can be no morality. It is only when persons are free to choose that they can make a moral decision between right and wrong.[8] Isaiah Berlin (1909–1997) made a particularly influential distinction between *negative freedom*, the degree to which no other or others interfere with my activities, and *positive freedom*, the degree to which I am my own master and my life and decisions depend on myself.[9]

In the political domain, the treatment of freedom is central to the division between left-wing and right-wing political ideologies. Left-wing thinkers generally argue that freedom and justice are best served when the government intervenes in the economic marketplace and regulates, such as through taxation, to limit excesses. Right-wing thinkers argue that as a general rule, government interventions and regulations in the free market damage freedom and justice.[10]

In the contemporary world, there has been a proliferation of types of freedom, such as freedom of speech, freedom of the press, freedom of assembly, and freedom of movement.[11] Many of these types of freedom have been enshrined in the *United Nations Declaration of Human Rights* (1948). The influence of Western powers, and particularly the United States, has meant that freedom (and rights, as well as duties when they are mentioned) have been defined in terms of individuals and not collectives. Also, rights rather than duties have been emphasized. For example, in the *United Nations Declaration of Human Rights* (1948), collectives and duties are hardly mentioned, and the focus remains on individual rights.[12]

Another perspective, discussed subsequently, is the view that freedom involves the ability to exercise choice.

The "Capability Perspective"

The "capability set" . . . stands for the actual freedom of choice a person has over alternative lives that he or she can lead. In this view, individual claims are to be assessed not by the resources or primary goods the persons respectively hold, but by the freedoms they actually enjoy to choose between different ways of living that they can have reason to value. It is this actual freedom that is represented by the person's "capability" to achieve various alternative combinations of functionings, or doings and beings.

—AMARTYA SEN[13]

Sen is an economist who has developed a highly influential *capability approach* to freedom. This includes the basic human needs but adds the human ability to define and pursue one's own goals.[14] Since the late 20th century, the capability approach has been particularly influential in work on national development, with development conceived as a path for enlarging people's choices.[15] But there is a continuing tension and struggle between different views on "economic freedom"—how free should individuals be in their activities in the economic marketplace, and how much should governments intervene to limit economic freedom? There is a tension between economic freedom versus democratic freedom, as Michael Stroup discussed.[16] This relates to a distinction I have introduced between attached and detached forms of freedom, which I examine in greater detail later in this chapter.

Freedom and Group Identity

To appreciate the appeal and magnetism of the dictator, we need to examine closely the freedom and glory he promises and how exactly those promises match the needs and motivations of his core group of followers. We begin by noting that these potential followers are motivated to have a particular type of freedom and glory. By this, I do not mean freedom in the individualistic sense of being free from ties with others; rather, I mean freedom and the kind of glory that comes through positive collective identity and membership in sacred groups.

Social scientists have endlessly discussed how humans are social beings, echoing Aristotle,[17] but little attention has been given to what this implies for the exact nature of freedom we *in practice* aspire to achieve. Although freedom is often romanticized as independence and "going it alone" free from ties to anyone else, in practice freedom is realized through affiliation with collectives. To clarify this point, I begin by discussing in more depth the distinction between detached and attached types of freedom.

Detached Freedom and Individual Glory

The dominant conception of freedom in Western societies, and particularly in the United States, has been *detached freedom*, in which individuals are seen to be free if they can think and act independently and make choices as separate, unfettered, mobile units. Detached freedom is seen to be present when ties to groups either do not exist or are so weak that they do not restrain individuals. In the ideal of detached freedom, group memberships are like thin air: Individuals can pass through them unhindered.[18]

Detached individuals come to know themselves by looking inward and becoming absorbed in nature, not the society of other people. In his distinctly American style, Henry David Thoreau (1817–1862) explained his now famous retreat to the woods around Walden Pond in this way:

> I went to the woods because I wished to live deliberately, to front only the essential facts of life, and see if I could not learn what it had to teach, and not, when I came to die, discover that I had not lived. I did not wish to live what was not life.[19]

It is not that Thoreau neglected to think deeply about the larger, macro units of society and government; his thoughts on this subject are clear in his writings, particularly his essay "Civil Disobedience,"[20] which established a tradition of peaceful resistance, later followed by Dr. Martin Luther King (1929–1968) and others.[21] But the ideal he espoused was of the self-contained, self-reliant individual. The self is the source of greatness and goodness, and even provides company for itself, as Thoreau remarked: "To be in company, even with the best, is soon wearisome and dissipating. . . . I never found the companion that was so companionable as solitude.[22]

This ideal of detached freedom became central to mainstream culture in the United States, where ideas about the relationship between individuals and society, and democracy broadly, developed through and were profoundly influenced by Westward expansion. The influential work of Frederick Jackson Turner, first published in 1920, presented the classic image of the kind of democracy that evolved in the United States through Westward expansion:

> This democratic society was not a disciplined army, where all must keep step and where the collective interests destroyed individual will and work. Rather it was a mobile mass of freely circulating atoms, each seeking its own place and finding play for its own powers and for its own original initiative.[23]

We must keep in mind that Turner was presenting an ideal picture of glory through detached freedom, a picture that continues to be highly influential in the 21st century, despite being in major ways divorced from reality.

The Myth of Freely Circulating Atoms

Turner's imagery of Americans as *freely circulating atoms* matches the ideals espoused in the United States through the mass media and Hollywood films. In the classic cowboy movie, an art form with distinctly American origins, the hero lives according to his own, independent code of honor.[24] *Shane* represents the archetypical Western movie,[25] which begins with the lone cowboy riding into town, becoming embroiled in a local fight between good and bad people, helping the good side to win, and leaving town alone at the end of the movie.[26] Shane and other cowboy heroes do not become attached to communities. In those cases in which the lone cowboy does depend on the community, as in *High Noon*, where the sheriff (played by Gary Cooper) needs help to fight a gang of outlaws, the community abandons him (the only person who helps him is his wife, played by Grace Kelly). Ultimately, it is only by remaining independent from the community that the cowboy hero triumphs over evil.

In the economic and political spheres, Turner's freely circulating atoms translate to an ideology of self-help and individual mobility. In this scheme, the primary duty of individuals is to improve their personal situation through individual effort and personal responsibility. The job of the government is to create the conditions necessary for the "free circulation of atoms." Government intervention, either in the form of support for "weak people" or limitations on "strong people," can hinder such free circulation. We are reminded here of the first sentences in Thoreau's powerful and highly influential essay on *Civil Disobedience*:

> I heartily accept the motto,—"That government is best which governs least"; and I should like to see it acted up to more rapidly and systematically. Carried out, it finally amounts to this, which also I believe,—"That government is best which governs not at all."[27]

The ideal of detached freedom depicts society as being open, without any governmental and nongovernmental barriers, to the free circulation of atoms. It is assumed that irrespective of group membership—irrespective of whether a person is born Black or White, rich or poor, male or female, or whatever other group characteristics a person has—individuals enjoy the same opportunities and advantages. The achievements of individuals, the free circulation of atoms, depend completely on their individual characteristics.

The free circulation of atoms model is also the foundation for some of the most influential psychological research on human intelligence, leading to conclusion that the location of individuals on the socioeconomic hierarchy is dependent on individual intelligence, as indicated by IQ.[28] This body of psychological research serves as an assurance to the most affluent group in society that they are rich and powerful because of their personal talents and intelligence, not because of inheritance. But as Robert Putnam[29] and others[30] have demonstrated, inheritance is playing a greater part in determining the success of individuals. By inheritance, Putnam means more than just material wealth passed from generation to generation because another important part of what is passed on are social networks, connections, and informal knowledge about "how to get on in the world." In this sense, the American Dream is failing because inheritance works against the free circulation of atoms and the idea that anyone with talent and who works hard can make it in America.

GLORY THROUGH ATTACHED FREEDOM

Attached freedom involves individuals having opportunities to achieve freedom and glory through their membership and participation in a sacred group. Attached freedom has developed in various contexts, but in the present discussion I focus on this type of freedom as it developed in relation to two extremes on the political left and right, Marxism and fascism.[31] The common theme underlying attached freedom for both Marxist and fascist groups is the complete subservience of the individual to the collective and the destruction of civil liberties and personal rights, best captured by the policies of Hitler and Stalin.[32]

The terrible plight of individuals in a society characterized by attached freedom is reflected by the treatment of artists and thinkers who strive to develop their creativity in new ways and work toward new ideas and practices. Attached freedom only permits the development of individuals within the strict boundaries established by the dictator and within the limits set by the identity of the sacred ingroup. This explains the common plight of artists and "free thinkers" in regimes as apparently different as Nazi Germany, Stalin's and now Putin's Russia, the Islamic Republic of Iran, and North Korea. In all such contexts, the primacy of the sacred ingroup as determined by the dictator is absolute, ranging from "good Russians" in Putin's Russia to "good Muslims" in Khomeini's Iran.

In each case, we see that dictators seek to have control of the identity of the sacred group, as well as how individual citizens both desire the sacred group and become fulfilled through it. This is how the cruel and incredibly corrupt[33] Romanian dictator Nicolae Ceauşescu (1918–1989) positioned the communist party, through which he attained absolute power in Romania:

> Never has the Romanian people so fully merged its destiny with that of the communist party. The people's choice in favor of socialism is definitive and unanimous. . . . Whoever penetrates to the hearts of our people, whoever takes the pulse of this nation, understands fully the loyalty to communism and internationalism of these 20 million builders of the new order in Romania.[34]

The notorious Iraqi dictator Saddam Hussein (1937–2006) positioned the Baath Party, through which he ruled, in this way:

> We always say that the Arab Baath Socialist Party is . . . a party of the entire people. . . . We believe that any nationalist Iraqi . . . is prepared to defend his Party to the degree of martyrdom, since the Party represents his future and that of his children, his international reputation and record, both on local and Arab levels, of which he is proud.[35]

The key feature of Saddam Hussein's position is the emphasis on the "pride" that Iraqis must feel through group membership. But even though there is only one group to join in the dictatorship, the dictator positions the people as having choice and having freely chosen both the group and him as leader. This makes it necessary for the dictator to position his regime as "democratic," in the sense that the regime (supposedly) reflects the will of the people. The consequence is what, from the outside, seem like surprising statements, from dictators who obviously do not allow free choice and fair elections in their countries. For example, this is how the Chilean dictator

General Augusto Pinochet (1915–2006) positioned the "few" critics of the "Chilean democracy":

> I say to those bad Chileans who insult us . . . because they know we are in a democracy and we are not going to do anything to them: be careful, because patience has a limit and this limit can make itself known . . . we are going to show them, generously but proudly, we are going to wipe them off the map.[36]

Note how Pinochet first insists that he is leading a democracy but adds that the critics will be wiped off the map. The same contradiction appears in Russia where, despite the clear repression of opposition and clampdown on democratic movements in Russia, the dictator Vladimir Putin states: "Without liberty and democracy there can be no order, no stability and no sustainable economic policies."[37]

Even when a dictator rejects "Western ideas" about democracy, he still positions himself as having been selected by the people. In a famous interview with Ayatollah Khomeini in 1979, the Italian journalist Oriana Fallaci asked some pointed questions about freedom and democracy (and was abruptly told to leave). This is part of the exchange:

FALLACI: Imam Khomeini, the entire country is in your hands. Every decision you make is an order. So there are many in your country who say that in Iran there is no freedom, that the revolution did not bring freedom.

KHOMEINI: Iran is not in my hands. It is in the hands of the people, because it was the people who handed the country over to the person who is their servant, and who wants only what is good for them.[38]

In another part of the interview, Khomeini claims that "I act for [the people's] good" and "Islam means everything, all those things that, in your world, are called freedom, democracy. Yes, Islam contains everything."[39]

Khomeini's positioning is (a) the people chose me, (b) I am implementing Islam, and (c) Islam contains democracy, freedom, and everything else you say is good. Thus, it is through membership in the sacred group "Muslim" that people gain their freedom and glory.

No matter what the actual situation is, the dictator presents the group and the future of his people as involving freedom and democracy. President Xi Jinping is president for life but has always emphasized democracy in China:

> It is notable that shortly after installation as China's new leader, Xi Jinping, on December 29, 2012, gave his own "dream" speech, saying that by the one-hundredth anniversary of the CCP (2021) China would be a "well-off" (*xiaokang*) society and that by the one-hundredth anniversary of the PRC (e.g., 2049) China would be a strong, modernized, democratic, and socialist nation. "This is the greatest dream of the Chinese nation in modern history.[40]

Clearly, Xi Jinping is not bothered by the contradiction between being president for life, and the greatest dream of the Chinese nation being to become democratic.

CONCLUDING COMMENT

Populists desperately need enemies of the people to confirm the fiction that they speak and act in the name of the national community.

—FEDERICO FINCHELSTEIN[41]

The kind of freedom promised by the dictator, attached freedom, is exclusive and only for "our people," our sacred group; it takes shape through confrontation with enemies, those who are a threat to "our freedom." The strongman leader continuously places the spotlight on "those others" who are threats to "our freedoms." "Those others" do not belong to our sacred group and our land, they threaten our way of life, they are invaders. The exact nature of "those others" varies to some degree across time and place. For example, in Europe and the United States, Jews were a bigger target during the 1930s and Muslims are a larger target in the early 21st century. However, a constant feature of "those others" is that they are minorities, they are different, and they are seen as not fitting in with the majority group way of life.

Attached freedom is rooted in loyalty to and pride in the sacred group. The position taken up by the sacred group must be supported, and information must be interpreted to justify this support. Thus, "facts" are only useful if they are in line with the sacred group position. Of course, the position adopted by the sacred group is shaped by the bombastic, strongman leader. Bombastic leaders have in this way supported attached freedom, as they inspire the populous to battle against elites, particularly scientists and intellectuals.[42] Examples of this are the so-called cultural revolutions in China (late 1960s) and Iran (early 1980s) during which two ancient bombastic dictators, Mao and Khomeini, led the populace to attack the universities, scientists, and intellectuals in the service of attached freedom. Trump's attacks on scientists, science, and facts represent a more recent example of this same phenomenon.

ENDNOTES

1. Hitler (1939/1960).
2. Hitler's aggressive actions contrast with how he initially communicated with the people when he came to power, posing as a man of peace and claiming that his government would be very happy "if through a restriction of its armaments the world should make an increase of our own weapons never again necessary" (Kershaw, 1998, p. 265).
3. For a discussion of positioning theory, see Moghaddam, Harré, and Lee (2008).
4. Moghaddam (2002).
5. In this discussion I am not focused on the importance of group-based differences and freedom. As Polyani (1944) pointed out, "The comfortable classes enjoy the

freedom provided by leisure in security; they are naturally less anxious to extend freedom in society to those who for lack of income must rest content with a minimum of it." (p. 262).

6. For example, Berlin (1969) treats freedom and liberty interchangeably.
7. Bielefeldt (1997, p. 541).
8. Kant (1785/2016).
9. Berlin (1969).
10. For a contemporary empirical study reflecting these differences, see Ott (2018).
11. Bronislaw Malinowski (1947) provided an extensive discussion of types of freedom; his discussion looks back at the rise of totalitarianism in the 1930s and the Second World War.
12. Finkel and Moghaddam (2005).
13. Sen (1990b, p. 114); also see Sen (1990a).
14. Robeyns (2005).
15. United Nations Development Programme (1990).
16. Stroup (2007).
17. For example, see Aronson (2011).
18. Detached freedom is reflected in individualism, a behavioral style characterized by personal independence and self-reliance. Although individualism has been increasing across many countries, people in the United States and some other Western countries still record the highest scores on measures of individualism (see Santos, Varnum, & Grossman, 2017).
19. Thoreau (2003, p. 74).
20. Thoreau (2003).
21. See discussions in Cain (2000).
22. Thoreau (2003, p. 109).
23. F. J. Turner (1920, p. 306).
24. See Warshaw's (1962) seminal discussion.
25. See Lenihan (1980, p. 16); Wright (1975, p. 33).
26. Obviously Westerns have changed over their history (French, 2005). My discussion is about the classic form of the Western.
27. Thoreau (2003, p. 265).
28. For example, see Hernstein and Murray (1996).
29. Putnam (2016).
30. Chester (2016) showed that even in Australia, a relatively egalitarian society, wealthier parents tend to have children who are more likely to graduate from university, achieve higher occupational status, and be wealthier as young adults.
31. Included in the fascist groups is Islamic fascism, reflected by a variety of movements in Western and non-Western societies. Abdel-Samad (2014/2016) provides a compelling discussion of at least some forms of Islamic fascism.
32. See Bullock (1993).
33. For a glimpse of corruption in the regime of Nicolae and Elena Ceauşescu, see Pacepa (1987).
34. Quoted in Fischer (1989, p. 158).
35. Quoted in Balaghi (2006, p. 55).
36. Quoted in Spooner (1994, p. 223).
37. Quoted in Sakwa (2016, p. 33).
38. Johnstone (1986, p. 176).
39. Johnstone (1986, p. 177).
40. Lampton (2014).
41. Finchelstein (2017, p. 255).
42. See Moghaddam (2018a, 2018d).

5

Sacred Groups, Alienation, and Belonging

God is dead. God remains dead. And we have killed him. How shall we, the murderers of all murderers, comfort ourselves? What was holiest and most powerful of all that the world has yet owned has bled to death under our knives. Who will wipe his blood off us?

—FRIEDRICH NIETZSCHE[1]

Everything is indeed permitted if God does not exist, and man is in consequence forlorn, for he cannot find anything to depend upon either within or outside himself. He discovers forthwith, that he is without excuse . . . man is free, man is freedom. Nor, on the other hand, if God does not exist, are we provided with any values or commands that could legitimize our behavior. Thus we have neither behind us, nor before us in a luminous realm of values, any means of justification or excuse. We are left alone, without excuse. That is what I mean when I say that man is condemned to be free.

—JEAN-PAUL SARTRE[2]

The exaggerated position that "God is dead" has influenced existentialists, psychoanalysts, and various other intellectual movements since the 19th century. Connected with this position is another exaggerated argument: that the conditions of modern life have resulted in humans experiencing alienation, anomie, and loneliness. Various painters, poets, novelists, playwrights, film directors, and artists broadly have expanded and endorsed this thesis.[3] But religion continues to play a powerful and indeed in some ways resurgent role in the 21st century world, God is very much alive in this sense,

http://dx.doi.org/10.1037/0000142-006
Threat to Democracy: The Appeal of Authoritarianism in an Age of Uncertainty,
by F. M. Moghaddam

and many of the assumptions underlying the "God is dead, so humans feel alienated" thesis are shaky and need to be critically reexamined, particularly because this argument continues to be so widely influential (as reflected by the continuing international influence of Fromm's *Escape From Freedom* thesis, demonstrated by high and rising citations to this work).

THE GOD IS DEAD ALIENATION THESIS

Apparently, we humans have lost our way. Having "killed God," as Nietzsche put it, we no longer have the rules, rituals, and traditions of religion to guide us. We no longer have the holy books and the moral order derived from religion to tell us right from wrong, what to do and think, and what not to do and not to think. We only have as our guide the laws of society, constructed by ourselves and other fallible humans—and supposedly these do not provide certainty. After all, who is to say one set of laws is better than another? Who is to say I should obey your laws and not mine? We are lost, it seems, because normative systems and moral orders constructed by humans have no certainty; they are all fallible and relative.

The loss of religion as a guide to behavior has come at the same time that industrialization, mechanization, and urbanization have destroyed traditional social relationships. In traditional rural agrarian societies, people lived in communities where everyone knew everyone else and family members maintained close relationships with one another. Most people lived, worked, and died in the same village or town.

Industrialization and divisions of labor have also distanced humans from the products of their work. In preindustrial times, humans made things with their hands, and they produced crops and raised animals, all on a human scale. For example, a shoemaker would craft shoes from start to finish by himself, just as a farmer would grow his own food on his own farm. He and his family would know all or most of the members of their community. But with industrialization and the mechanization of farming came specialization of tasks and products, and higher productivity. Because fewer people were needed to work as farmers, there was large-scale movement of people from rural to vast new urban centers, where enormous numbers of people live in cities with masses of anonymous others. As Erich Fromm described it,

> Man has built his world; he has built factories and houses, he produces cars and clothes, he grows grain and fruit. But he has become estranged from the product of his own hands, he is not really the master any more of the world he has built; on the contrary, this man-made world has become his master. . . . He keeps up the illusion of being the center of the world, and yet he is pervaded by an intense sense of insignificance and powerlessness which his ancestors once consciously felt toward God. Modern man's feeling of isolation and powerlessness is increased still further by the character which all his human relationships have assumed. The concrete relationship of one individual to another has lost its direct and human character. . . . In all social and personal relations the laws of the market are the rule.[4]

The loss of traditional family and social ties, the loss of direct relationship with what they produce, the loss of religious systems and God—all these apparently have resulted in humans feeling lost, alone, and alienated. The freedoms humans gained proved illusory because they were accompanied with fear, anxiety, and alienation. This (supposedly) resulted in a desire to escape freedom and seek shelter in the arms of dictators.

RETHINKING "FEAR OF FREEDOM"

In my reexamination of this thesis, in this chapter, I focus particularly on two themes. First, psychological research suggests that human conceptions of right and wrong have evolutionary roots and despite being human constructions are, at least in some respects, universal rather than being in all respects relativistic. It is incorrect to assume that all human constructed systems of morality and justice are synonymous with relativism. Second, psychological research shows that humans universally create social categories, form groups, develop group memberships, and become strongly attached to what I have termed *sacred groups*. Importantly, through these sacred groups individuals gain a strong sense of identity and belonging. Later in this chapter, I discuss the nation as one of the most influential and powerful examples of sacred groups. The most important function of sacred groups is to enable individuals to achieve a sense of attached freedom.

Of course, religion continues to play a central role in the lives of many people; indeed, for many it is still the most important sacred group. The prediction that religion would disappear has not proven to be true,[5] and although there has been a decline in some traditional religious movements (e.g., the practice of Christianity in some European counties), new religious movements are developing.[6] Also, in some parts of the Islamic world, there has been a resurgence of fundamentalist Islam, as indicated by the surge of both Shia and Sunni radicalization. Thus, the very idea that "God is dead" is questionable, particularly among the masses, outside the experiences of highly educated elites. For many people, religion continues to serve as a buffer against the kinds of alienation and anomie discussed by existentialists and others.

Rather than being lost and alienated, the identities of most people evolve with strong connections to sacred groups. A major reason we value these groups is because through them we feel we can achieve and enjoy freedom. The moral order of each group is to some degree different and even unique, but in other respects, this moral order is universal and the same across all groups.

THE MORAL ORDER AS EVOLVED AND CONSTRUCTED

For long periods in human history, the dominant view was that our moral order has divine, natural origins, and we humans discover the laws set out for us; this is the *natural law* viewpoint. An alternative science-based viewpoint, referred to as *positive law*, is that we construct human moral orders. Moreover, the roots of our moral orders lie in our evolutionary past.[7]

I have argued that our sense of justice and morality derives from what I call *primitive social relations*, elementary behaviors that evolved as part of a repertoire of skills necessary for group survival.[8] Over millions of years, primitive social relations evolved out of functional needs; they are useful things that came out of our bad experiences and sometimes defeats.[9] For example, we are social beings and living in groups taught us that at times we need to take turns in an orderly manner, rather than perpetually fight one another to try to get in front and be the first in line. In this way, turn-taking became a primitive social relation—a behavior that we learn to engage in from a young age.

The simple behavior of turn-taking in grooming among apes and turn-taking in feeding among different animals[10] evolved to become the more complex behavior of turn-taking between newly born human infants and mothers during feeding and play,[11] turn-taking in gift giving and reciprocal behavior among adults, and more broadly turn-taking in human social, judicial, and political life. For example, consider how we turn-take to enable traffic to flow smoothly (most of the time!), turn-take in courts of law to present evidence and cross-examine witnesses, turn-take in political debates, and use term limits to enforce turn-taking in political leadership. Thus, turn-taking serves as a simple building block for far more complex sets of behavior, the foundation of which are ideas about right and wrong, correct and incorrect behavior.[12] From this perspective, then, our need to cooperate with one another in group life has led to the social construction of morality.[13]

FROM SOCIAL CATEGORIZATION TO BELONGING

To gain absolute power, dictators inspire, influence, and force citizens to develop the strongest possible sense of belonging to sacred groups. There is some variation in sacred groups from dictatorship to dictatorship, but irrespective of whether they are based on national, religious, ethnic, or some other categorization, they have in common their avowed superiority. It is through this superior sacred group that individual members feel they attain superior status (I experienced this in Iran with Khomeini pushing the superiority of "Islam and Muslims"). By being a "pure German" in Nazi Germany, for example, individuals were encouraged to feel they and their group had achieved greatness.

But membership in a sacred group also has consequences. Two processes immediately influence individuals who are categorized as sacred group members: *conformity*, changes in behavior arising from real or imagined group pressure;[14] and *obedience*, changes in behavior that arise when people follow the instructions of persons in authority.[15] Extensive psychological research demonstrates that ordinary people can be influenced in extraordinary ways, such as being pressured to take extremely harmful actions against others, through group pressure and orders from authority figures[16] (this topic is discussed in greater depth in Chapter 5, this volume).

But what is the psychological root of this trend of individuals "joining" sacred groups? Given that conformity and obedience to do harm to others begins with "belonging" to the sacred group, how can we better understand the process of group formation and belonging? This is the question I turn to next.

Social Categorization

Research in a variety of disciplines has led to the conclusion that *categorization*, the primary cognitive process of placing phenomena into categories, is integral to human intelligence and problem solving broadly.[17] As Stevan Harnan put it, "To cognize it to categorize."[18] *Social categorization*, the process of placing other people into groups, begins in infancy. The initial basis of social categorization is visible characteristics, such as faces and genders.[19] For example, within the first 12 months, infants learn to categorize both female and male faces, showing a preference for more attractive females and males.[20]

The neural capacity for categorization is common to all humans, as an essential means through which to process the infinite amount of social and nonsocial information bombarding us in our everyday lives.[21] Socialization processes build on this common human capacity within the first 2 years of life, by passing on through language and other means certain characteristics that different groups (e.g., based on gender and race) are believed to have.[22]

In the second half of the 20th century, Gordon Allport (1897–1967) discussed categories as the "basis for normal prejudgement,"[23] and Henri Tajfel (1919–1982) experimentally demonstrated that categorization can lead to within-group minimization of differences and between-group exaggeration of differences.[24] This results in feelings that "they are all the same, I can't tell them apart" and "they are very different from us." Recent research on *social vision*[25] has added to this picture in several important ways. First, social categorization enters very early in the process of perception; respondents differentiated between others on the basis of race only 100 ms after exposure to faces, and 50 ms later on the basis of sex.[26] Second, social categorization is heavily influenced by facial characteristics and is largely an implicit process,[27] meaning that it takes place without conscious awareness. That is, David will be categorized into a racial group a split second after being seen, but without onlookers being aware that they have made this categorization.

Implicit Processes and the Construction of Sacred Groups

When I was about 5 years old, an incident took place that I still remember vividly. I was living with my family in Tehran, Iran, at the time, and I had a group of friends I played with in the street outside our home. All of my friends were boys around the same age as me, but there was also a girl (I shall name her Zahra) who sometimes played with us. She was athletic and liked to play soccer; she was one of the best players in our group. The incident I want to relate took place one day when about 10 of us were playing soccer in the street, and Zahra was playing with us. Zahra's mother angrily interrupted our game to tell Zahra that she should be "ashamed of herself!" Her family had to go to a funeral ceremony, and Zahra was to clean up her face, change her clothes, and not play in the street "like a boy." Zahra went with her mother, and when she reappeared she was wearing a little chador, a form of Islamic hijab. According to Islamic custom, Zahra did not have to put on an Islamic hijab until age 9, but I could see she felt grown up dressed in her chador, copying her mother in her walk. I had seen girls as young as 3 or 4 years old trying on a chador, as a way of "looking grown up." This is akin to watching young Western girls trying on high-heeled shoes that belong to grown-up relatives.

By the time I left our neighborhood at age 8 (my family moved to England), Zahra had stopped playing soccer with the boys. I would see her from a distance, usually in the company of her mother and older sister, still an independent spirit but clearly modeling their behavior. The socialization of children in their religious identities begins early, probably as early as the first year when infants are able to use facial characteristics to distinguish between people. Infants do not yet know the meaning of emotions such as shame and guilt as interpreted by their particular cultures, but through gradual shaping by families, local communities, schools, and other agents of socialization, children learn precisely what kinds of behaviors should make them feel shame and guilt.[28] In the context of Iran, the most important sacred group is Islam (as interpreted by the fundamentalist mullahs ruling Iran), and stepping outside gender roles as prescribed by Islam will bring harsh pressures and punishments from authorities, intended to reinforce feelings of shame and guilt in the transgressor (in the next section, I discuss the nation, the most important sacred group in the United States and some other countries).

Sacred groups, such as religion and nation, come to acquire their enormous emotional, cognitive, and behavioral importance through stealth and implicit processes that few individuals become aware of. The little girl growing up in the mullahs' Iran, learning to feel shame and guilt when she is without the hijab, the little girl growing up in the United States, learning to feel shame and guilt when a person desecrates "Old Glory" in front of her—these are the outcomes of long-term socialization involving subtle implicit processes that we seldom become consciously aware of. So the young Muslim woman who vehemently defends the hijab and the young American woman who vehemently defends Old Glory are both standing up for a piece of cloth that has come to represent their sacred group. In both cases, this defense of the sacred group and its cultural carriers arises through long-term and mostly implicit socialization processes.

Freedom Through Sacred Group Membership

The main plank in the Nationalist Socialist program is to abolish the liberalistic concept of the individual and the Marxist concept of humanity and to substitute therefore the folk community, rooted in the soil and bound together by the bond of its common blood. . . . This is probably the first time and this is the first country in which people are being taught to realize that, of all the tasks that we have to face, the noblest and most sacred for mankind is that each racial species must preserve the purity of the blood which God has given it. . . . In the new German legal system which will be in force from now onwards the nation is placed above persons and property.

—ADOLF HITLER (1937)[29]

The most distinct and striking feature of potential and actual dictators is their positioning of the sacred group, whether it be based on national, racial, religious, or some other criteria, as being of supreme importance above individuals and above all other groups, social relationships, and values. For Hitler, the sacred group was racial, and all individuals who met the qualifications gained glory and freedom through the German race. In Khomeini's Iran, individuals gained glory and freedom through the sacred group Islam.

Individual members of the sacred group gain freedom through the power of the sacred group. Individuals become absorbed in the sacred group, and each of them adds to the strength and vibrancy of the collective. The sacred group enables individuals to achieve great feats, but only as a part of the collective. As Hitler puts it in the preceding quotation, the sacred group is placed above the individual, and the individual has to sacrifice for the collective.

But the sacred group can only succeed in carrying out its supremely important function through the leadership of the dictator. While ordinary members of the sacred group are subservient to the collective, the dictator shapes the direction of the collective and represents the values of the sacred group.[30] Of course, dictators often invoke "God" as the authority who justifies their supreme position. In Iran, Khomeini established the principle of rule by a supreme religiously qualified leader (*velayat-e-faghih*) who has authority from God to lead the nation.[31] Of course, he meant himself: He ruled the country with an iron fist until his last breath.

THE NATION AS A SACRED GROUP

Nationalism has assumed many forms since its birth in the eighteenth century. . . . But it seems to me, in all its guises, to retain . . . four characteristics . . . : the belief in the overriding need to belong to a nation; in the organic relationships of all the elements that constitute a nation; in the value of our own simply because it is ours; and, finally, faced by the rival contenders for authority or loyalty, in the supremacy of its claims.

—ISIAH BERLIN[32]

The supremely strong surge of nationalism sweeping the modern world has come as a surprise, in that before the 20th century, most thinkers believed nationalism to be a passing phase.[33] But in the 21st century, we see continued and even rising strength in nationalism, which Joshua Searle-White, in his book *The Psychology of Nationalism*, defined as a "sense of identification with a group of people who share a common history, language, territory, culture, or some combination of these."[34] Researchers have distinguished between *nationalism*, a belief in the superiority of one's nation over other nations, and *patriotism*, a noncompetitive concern for the welfare of one's nation.[35]

Psychologists have been particularly concerned with nationalism because it is often associated with war, and violence more broadly—modern wars are between nations, and an urgent research question is why nations go to war.[36] By appealing to a sense of nationalism, political leaders can motivate and mobilize people to fight and sacrifice themselves, and even their loved ones, in aggression against others. Nationalism is associated with "hot" emotions (such as strong anger, pride, and shame); people are emotionally moved by their strong sense of belonging to a nation.[37] I was in the capital city Tehran in 1980 when Saddam Hussein's military invaded Iran. Khomeini and other mullahs ruling Iran first attempted to mobilize Iranians to defend their country by appeals to religion but found this was not effective enough. The "antinationalistic" mullahs were forced to use nationalistic propaganda to mobilize Iran's defenses to push back Saddam Hussein's forces. Even fanatical Muslims with dictatorial power in Iran had to fall back on the power of modern nationalism.

In addition to questions about nationalism and violence, we must ask: What makes nationalism so powerful? In answering this question, we are led to the role of the nation as a sacred group, a "cause" that strongly moves people emotionally to sacrifice and die for. The nation gives meaning to people's lives; it provides them with deep, lifelong, and extraordinarily strong identity, a "frame of devotion"[38] so that they are ready to do anything and give up everything for "our country," which many experience as the most practical and concrete sacred group.

Freedom and Glory Through "My Country"

Most importantly, the nation provides the strongest avenue for people to achieve freedom. I do not mean freedom in the detached sense—in the isolated sense that Eric Fromm[39] discussed the problem of freedom experienced by people in capitalism:

> freedom from the traditional bonds of medieval society, though giving the individual a new feeling of independence, at the same time made him feel alone and isolated, filled him with doubt and anxiety, and drove him into new submission and into compulsive and irrational activity.[40]

The experience of alienation and isolation that Fromm postulated is associated with detached freedom, but nationhood provides attached freedom, giving individuals a sense of power, a feeling of invincibility, greatness, and pride. In the extreme, nationalism is associated with ethnocentrism and intolerance toward dissimilar others.[41] However, nationalism is also a path to individual empowerment and freedom, in the sense of feeling strong to achieve more and fulfill their individual potential—to become actualized.

To appreciate the ability of nationhood to liberate individuals, to empower them to feel free and capable of achieving far more than is possible as isolated individuals, we need to reverse traditional thinking and see the group as sovereign, as Michael Hogg has argued.[42] The group is the root of individual consciousness and identity.[43] It is the sovereignty of the group, and particularly sacred groups such as the nation, that enables nationalism to exert great influence on individual behavior, particularly through cultural carriers (discussed in Chapter 4). Some cultural carriers become sacred, in the sense that they become things for which people are ready to sacrifice and die.

The National Flag as a Sacred Carrier

The nation as a sacred group sustains and builds on its power through cultural carriers, which have evolutionary roots[44] and arise out of ancient symbols, emblems, and signs used to signify affiliation with and loyalty to bands and tribes well before ways to document sacred carriers evolved. The function of cultural carriers is to achieve cultural continuity, to carry forward the normative system and culture broadly from one generation to the next, teaching the young how to think, act, and feel correctly. For example, in the United States, the Pledge of Allegiance to the flag is recited by most elementary school children as part of everyday school activities. In many modern societies, legislation is used to enforce the "correct" socialization of the young with respect to sacred carriers such as the national flag.[45]

The result of socialization is that from an early age, people develop strong emotional ties with cultural carriers such as the national flag.[46] In essence, the national flag becomes integrated within the self and elicits a particularly strong reaction from us, as suggested by research on brain activity when individuals are presented with their own and other national flags.[47] Behavior that in any way disrespects the flag is felt to be not just wrong but also morally reprehensible and associated with emotions such as disgust.[48] For example, in the Winter Olympic Games of 2018, an American gold medal winner was severely criticized when he let the American flag he was carrying drag "disrespectfully" on the floor; some people expressed anger and outrage and felt he had to offer a public apology.[49]

The strong emotional ties people develop to the national flag have behavioral consequences. There is experimental evidence that exposure to the American flag can result in a shift in both thought and actions (e.g., voting) in favor of the Republican Party, a shift that persisted 8 months later.[50] Exposure to the American flag was also shown to result in a sense of superiority over other groups, reflecting a jingoistic sense of nationalism.[51] However, we must be cautious in interpreting such findings because exposure to the national flag has also been found to result in more moderate behaviors. For example, in a set of three studies carried out in the post–9/11 era, exposure to the American flag led to more egalitarian attitudes and more acceptance of Arabs and Muslims.[52] In another set of studies, presentation of the Israeli flag influenced Israelis to hold more moderate "middle" political positions, both in attitudes and actions.[53]

The research literature clearly shows that the national flag and other cultural carriers have a powerful influence on behavior. The flag is just a piece of cloth, but it is a piece of cloth strongly connected to emotions and identities.

Sport as a Vehicle for Nationalism

Sport has played a central role in the construction of nationhood and the shaping of the nation as an imagined community.[54] For example, consider the role of the Tour de France in shaping French national identity, ice hockey in shaping Canadian national identity, and football (soccer) in shaping Brazilian national identity.[55] Sport also plays an important role in the organization of collective identities within nations, where different sports teams are associated with different emblems and symbols (e.g., the football teams Manchester United and Tottenham Hotspur wear red shirts and white shirts, respectively). These kinds of "tribal" differences are enhanced through business marketing and identity construction.[56]

The nation as an imagined community comes to life more vividly as a sports team of players with individual names and identities, to paraphrase Eric J. Hobsbawm.[57] National sports teams play an important role in the "production of collective belonging,"[58] arriving at a single collective identity. This process can help to bridge cultural and political gaps. For example, after the fall of the Berlin Wall and the reunification of Germany in 1990, Germany has been represented by united national sports teams.[59] The united German national football team has played a particularly important role in the reunification process, embodying a single Germany.[60] By shouting in unison in support of their single unified German team, Germans from the East and West are feeling and acting as members of one united nation.

Sports also structure and regulate activities in everyday life. This is achieved through rituals shared by team supporters, involving chants, emblems, social behaviors, and special terminology that are learned through socialization among groups of supporters. Importantly, the sporting calendar regulates the activities of supporters all year round, increasingly all around the world.[61]

Sport and Banal Nationalism

Nation-states have emerged relatively recently in human history,[62] yet many people feel that their nation has always existed, and it is only natural that they are nationalistic and have a strong sense of belonging to their nations. Michael Billig[63] argued that to understand the nature and continuation of nationalism, we need to pay attention to the numerous ways in which national identity is integrated into the routine practices of our everyday lives. Although nationalism in non-Western countries and radical movements is often depicted as problematic, our Western nationalism is seamlessly and mindlessly remembered and practiced: "The national flag hanging outside a public building in the United States attracts no attention. It belongs to no special, sociological genus. Having no name, it cannot be identified as a problem."[64]

The role of sport in nationalism fits well with Billig's thesis that nationalism is a form of life that "is daily lived in a world of nation states."[65] From this perspective, the nation is not some abstract idea, but part and parcel of the daily activities of ordinary people—for example, as they watch, with great emotion and agitation, "their" national football team play the rival team of another nation. This does not mean that people uncritically support their national team; they criticize and debate what went wrong in the game, how the team should have played better, and engage in conflicting debates and dilemmas about what should be done.[66] Their thinking is through debate and argument.

The supporting of national sports teams has become part of a routine, an everyday practice for the populations of nations. Nobody questions the strong emotional ties between the citizens of a country and their national sports teams. Nor do we question the association between sporting events and national holidays, so that engagement with sport (as a spectator or player) becomes integral to a national event. This is part of what Billig sees as the "mundane" everyday practice of nationalism, mindlessly played out in a routine way in different nations, but capable of shaping our identities and giving meaning and structure to our everyday lives.

Thus, in the 21st century, sport has become a powerful vehicle for shaping and strengthening nationalist sentiments, emotionally binding the individual to the nation. Sport is treated as a politically neutral arena. However, the emotional ties created through sport become influential in politically charmed arenas, such as international war. National leaders are able to call on citizens to make sacrifices in war, tapping into the emotional ties created by sport between citizens and the nation as a sacred group.

CONCLUDING COMMENT

Industrialization, urbanization, and modernization have been associated with widespread changes in human societies. Fromm and others have claimed that the decline of traditional church, traditional communities, and traditional family relations and values, have resulted in greater individual freedoms but at the same time created feelings of alienation and anomie. There has been broad discussion of how humans have (apparently) "lost their place" and now feel "alienated," particularly because of a loss of religiosity and the abandonment of God.

Yet in many parts of the world, including in societies where religious fundamentalism is on the rise,[67] humans are far from abandoning God. Besides, humans continually construct and reconstruct their moral orders, conceptions of how they arrived in the universe, and their ideas of justice. Importantly, humans construct their social worlds and identities using groups, and some such groups, particularly those based on national, ethnic, and religious boundaries, become sacred. When sacred groups are threatened, individual group members feel they must sacrifice and mobilize in collective defense.

It is in defense of sacred groups that the potential dictator rises in popularity and gains the opportunity to use the springboard to dictatorship. By positioning himself as the greatest defender of sacred groups, the (potential or actual) dictator champions attached freedom. He positions himself as the savior, the only person who can lead the sacred group to greatness again. The promise is that through his strong leadership, the sacred group and its members will achieve freedom and glory. The cost is that group members must show unswerving loyalty and obedience to the strongman, even as rule of law is trampled upon, inequalities increase, and their group (in objective terms) experiences one chaotic disaster after another.

ENDNOTES

1. Nietzsche (1956, p. 105).
2. Sartre (1956, p. 295).
3. For example, see broad discussions by McMullen (1968) and Read (1967), was well as the essay by Pavlikova (2015) that explores aspects of Kierkegaard's concept of despair in relation to Walker Percy's 1961 novel *The Moviegoer*.
4. Fromm (1941, pp. 117–118).
5. For a broad discussion of the continued role of religion in 21st-century societies, see Christiano, Swatos, and Kivisto (2015).
6. P. Oliver (2012).
7. See Moghaddam and Riley (2005).
8. Moghaddam (2002).
9. As Dershowitz (2004) put it, they are "Rights from Wrongs."
10. For a broad set of discussions about moral behaviors in animals, see the readings in Crane (2016).
11. See the discussion in Moghaddam and Riley (2005).
12. Franz de Waal (2016) suggested animal empathy as another such building block.
13. See Curry (2016).
14. For an overview of conformity research, see Moghaddam (2005a, Chapter 15).
15. For an overview of research on obedience, see Moghaddam (2005a, Chapter 16).
16. Zimbardo (2008); also, Chapters 15 and 16 in Moghaddam (2005a).
17. See discussions in Cohen and Lefebvre (2017).
18. Hernad (2017, p. 21).
19. See particularly the chapters in Part V of Cohen and Lefebvre (2017).
20. Rennels, Kayl, Langlois, Davis, and Orlewicz (2016).
21. Gazzaniga and Ivry (2013) discussed the neural circuitry underlying categorization processes in memory, perception, and other important psychological fields is discussed.
22. Rhodes, Leslie, Bianchi, and Chalik (2018).
23. Allport (1954, p. 20).
24. Tajfel and Wilkes (1963).
25. A useful overview is provided by K. L. Johnson, Lick, and Carpinella (2015).
26. Ito and Urland (2003).
27. Macrae, Quinn, Mason, and Quadflieg (2005).
28. For a broad discussion of emotions in very young kids, see Lieberman (2018).
29. Adolf Hitler, speech before the Reichstag, January 30, 1937. Retrieved from http://www.worldfuturefund.org/wffmaster/Reading/Hitler%20Speeches/Hitler%20Speech%201937.01.30.html.
30. Freud (1921/1955) gave particular importance to the role of the strong leader in group processes; see also Chapter 3 in Moghaddam (2008b).

31. The basic idea of *velayat-e-faghih* was explained in Khomeini (1979).
32. Berlin (1980, p. 345).
33. Berlin (1980, p. 337).
34. Searle-White (2001, p. 3).
35. See Kemmelmeier and Winter (2008) and readings in Bar-Tal and Staub (1997).
36. This is the title of Stroessinger's book, which came out in its 10th edition in 2007.
37. Pope, Rolf, and Siklodi (2017) discussed the hot emotions associated with nationalism. For a more expansive review of theories of nationalism, see Özkirimli (2017).
38. This phrase is Erich Fromm (1970, p. 97).
39. Fromm's analysis has found many defenders over the years; see McLaughlin (1996).
40. Fromm (1941, p. 103).
41. Li and Brewer (2004).
42. Hogg (2001).
43. Moghaddam (2006b).
44. G. R. Johnson (1997).
45. See the examples of such legislation given by Butz (2009).
46. Helwig and Prencipe (1999).
47. Fan et al. (2011).
48. See Haidt, Koller, and Dias (1993).
49. See Bieler (2018).
50. Carter, Ferguson, and Hassin (2011); Hassin, Ferguson, Shidlovski, and Gross (2007).
51. Kemmelmeier and Winter, 2008.
52. Butz, Plant, and Doerr (2007).
53. Hassin, Ferguson, Shidlovski, and Gross, 2007.
54. The source is Anderson's (2016) and Carretero (2011).
55. For more extensive examples, see Campos (2003), Cardoza (2010), Dóczi (2012), and Cronin (1999).
56. Meir and Scott (2007).
57. Hobsbawm (1992).
58. Fox (2006, p. 217).
59. Kersting (2007).
60. See Ismer (2011).
61. T. Miller, Lawrence, McKay, and Rowe (2001).
62. Hobsbawm (1992).
63. Billig (1995).
64. Billig (1995, p. 6).
65. Billig (1995, p. 68).
66. Billig's (1992) study of people talking about the British royal family highlights this point.
67. Emerson and Hartman (2006).

6

Political Plasticity and Dictatorship

The most important question a psychologist might attempt to answer is why so few programs of revolutionary action succeed.

—ROM HARRÉ[1]

For elites and a small minority of well-placed individuals, social change implies new opportunities and positive experience which facilitate the process of adaptation. However, social change represents a devastating experience for the vast majority of individuals who are less advantaged and unable to reap its direct benefits.

—ROXANE DE LA SABLONNIÈRE, DONALD TAYLOR, CHRISTINA PEROZZO, AND NAZGUL SADYKOVA[2]

One of the great puzzles in human history is why revolutions against dictatorships so often result in the overthrow of one dictatorship, only to be replaced by another.[3] Revolutions do bring about some change, but they also involve strong continuities; one of these continuities is that elites tend to benefit from change more than nonelites. In this chapter, I delve deeper into the puzzle of change and continuity by examining political plasticity, the ability to change (or not) social relations when structures change, and vice versa. The concept of political plasticity enables us to better understand why there are continuities in behavior. I examine two sources of influence on continuity: hardwiring inside and outside individuals. I also discuss examples that show interactions between hardwiring inside and outside individuals.

http://dx.doi.org/10.1037/0000142-007
Threat to Democracy: The Appeal of Authoritarianism in an Age of Uncertainty,
by F. M. Moghaddam

PLASTICITY AND TWO TYPES OF HARDWIRING

> For a long time, it was thought that the adult mammalian brain was hard-wired and that once circuits were laid down and their functions assigned, little change was possible. This notion is no longer tenable. The brain has a lifelong inherent ability to change and adapt.[4]

As Andres Lozano explained in *The New England Journal of Medicine*, 21st-century research has revealed the malleability of the brain. The term *hardwiring* in the brain is now taken to mean characteristics that have lower malleability, rather than being fixed and unchanging. It is also in this sense that I am using the term *hardwiring* to refer to characteristics that are less flexible, more rigid, in the brain. I am also using the term in a new way, however, by extending it to the larger social world outside the individual.

The concept of political plasticity leads to a focus on two sources of hardwiring or rigidities: the first inside individuals, such as hardwiring in the brain, and the second outside individuals, in the larger culture. As discussed here, in practice these different sources of influence become effective through interactions with one another.

Plasticity Inside Individuals

Since the 19th century, research attention has been given to how brain characteristics relate to behavior, and since the latter part of the 20th century, researchers have also explored the relationship between brain processes and collective behavior.[5] The relationship between the brain and collective life in humankind has several aspects. The first is the *social brain hypothesis*, which proposes that the evolution of large brains in humans and other primates was in response to the cognitive demands of their complex social lives.[6] Life in groups, which became particularly elaborate and complicated for humans, imposed the need to develop a sophisticated *theory of mind*, to attribute motivations, beliefs, and mental states broadly to oneself and others.[7]

The second aspect of the relationship between the brain and collective life is the influence of brain characteristics on how we perceive, experience, and behave in the social world. Probably the most important of these influences is through the process of categorization, grouping the social world and seeing (and treating) the groups as different (a topic discussed at some length in Chapter 5, this volume). Although a great deal of attention has been given to hardwiring in the brain[8] and its implications for behavior, far less attention has been given to another form of hardwiring, these being rigidities in the world outside individuals.

Plasticity Outside Individuals

Before we arrive in this world, there is a strongly structured normative system "out there" waiting to guide our cognitions and actions; after we leave, the normative system continues to regulate the thoughts and actions of subsequent generations. This normative system consists of norms, rules, values, attitudes, beliefs, motives, and broadly "correct ways of making sense of the world and behaving in it." The normative system acts like "hardwiring" in society, influencing our behavior just as neural networks inside the brain influence behavior. We learn what is polite and impolite behavior, in what situations it is correct to express emotions such as shame and anger, how to interpret signals that another person wants or does not want to socialize with us, and endless other skills that are essential for effective functioning in society.

Highly resilient mechanisms have evolved to ensure the continuity of normative systems across generations. Perhaps the most important of these mechanisms is the family, which can vary in shape, size, and structure within and even more across societies. However, the school, the neighborhood, religious organizations, and other groups and institutions also help to teach the young how to think and act correctly according to the local normative system.

An extremely powerful but underestimated mechanism that ensures the continuity of normative systems is the built environment, including the landscaping and buildings around us.[9] Our behavior is shaped in important ways by the built environment, from the external shape of buildings to the interior arrangement of space and the design and organization of furniture. For example, through architectural design and town planning, the physical activity level of residents can be increased.[10]

Revolutionaries who topple a government and come to power can immediately change the names of cities, airports, hospitals, public squares and spaces, schools and universities, roads, and buildings, but changing the physical landscape and the actual shape of buildings takes a lot longer. Continuity in the built environment is one of the most important factors leading to continuity in styles of thinking and acting before and after revolutions. This includes the parts of the built environment that are symbolically important, such as statues, cathedrals and different places of worship, as well as other major landmarks (this influence is widely acknowledged, as reflected in the continuing conflicts over Confederate monuments in the United States).

The influence of the built environment is on such a vast scale that it is extremely difficult to change, even through major political revolutions. For example, imagine if after a revolution, there was a decision to radically change the shape and size of the family. Instead of two spouses and their children, the postrevolution family would comprise 20 men and 20 women and their children all living together. Such a postrevolution family would number around 100 people. But such a plan would face a major obstacle: The vast majority of homes have been built for what we now regard as a traditional family numbering around three to five people. There would not be enough homes to house families numbering 100 or so members. Of course, such homes could be built, but it would take many decades or even centuries to transform all the homes from a standard of housing three to five people to housing 100 people.

Continuity Through Traditions

After the 1979 revolution in Iran, Khomeini and his radical supporters attempted to eradicate everything "non-Islamic" in Iran and to strengthen and enforce everything they interpreted to be Islamic. For example, the traditional Persian New Year celebration Nowrooz has Zoroastrian roots and involves activities related to pre-Islamic Iran. On the 13th day of the New Year, for instance, Iranians participate in a ceremony involving jumping over fire and chanting special verses rooted in Zoroastrianism, a type of activity the Islamic fanatics condemn as "fire worshipping."

I witnessed how in the years immediately following the 1979 revolution, Islamic fundamentalists attempted to prevent Iranians from celebrating the Iranian Nowrooz in the traditional way. The fundamentalists would literally march through neighborhoods, going from street to street, preventing people from holding celebrations and carrying out traditions such as jumping over fires. They punished, threatened, beat people up, hauled youngsters away to jail, humiliated parents in front of their own children—they did just about everything they could to kill the traditional Nowrooz, but they failed. The traditional pre-Islamic Persian New Year continues to be celebrated in Iran.

Traditions such as the Iranian Nowrooz celebration and important ceremonies in the Christian calendar (e.g., Easter) have evolved over long time periods and are part of the continuity of styles of thinking and acting. Such traditions rely on normative systems that are "out there" in the wider culture, embedded in relationships between people—relationships that are resilient to change.

However, while the internal and external sources of hardwiring can be differentiated in the abstract, it is their combined, interactional impact on the world that should be our focus. Internal and external sources do not influence individual and collective behavior independently; rather, the influence of one is always achieved through the influence of the other. Consequently, in practice we must consider these two sources of influence together. Under certain conditions, the two sources of hardwiring combine to help create the springboard to dictatorship that potential dictators then use to spring to power and move their societies back toward dictatorship.[11] In the next section, I use the illustrative case of China to highlight the way some features of society, such as leadership style, remain fairly stable in a context in which many other features are changing.

LOW PLASTICITY OUTSIDE INDIVIDUALS: THE EXAMPLE OF LEADERSHIP

To recognize the role of both internal and external sources of low plasticity or hardwiring, and how they interact, consider the role of leadership in human societies. There have been explorations of follower-centered styles of group and organizational management,[12] as well as collective leadership.[13] However, there is general agreement that traditional individual leadership is one of the important human universals[14]: All major societies and organizations function with individual leaders. The universality of leadership probably has evolutionary roots, as Mark Van Vugt, Robert Hogan, and Robert Kaiser have argued:

> groups with an effective leader–follower structure would have higher aggregate fitness. Under the right conditions . . . leadership might create enough variation between groups for natural selection to operate. It is possible that well-led groups are so much better at group hunting, food sharing, and warfare that the relatively lower within-group payoffs for followers are compensated for by between-group fitness benefits. That is, followers may not be as well off as their leaders, but they are better off than individuals in poorly led groups.[15]

There is no doubt that the universality of leadership is influenced by the interaction of dispositional (within-person) and contextual (environmental) factors. Variation in styles of leadership, such as dictatorial (top-down) versus "servant–leadership" (bottom-up),[16] reflect the power of context to shape the solutions humans develop to problem solve.

Change, Continuity, and Leadership: The Example of China

In March 2018, the delegates of the National People's Congress of China voted on the momentous issue of whether to end the two-term limit for presidency of the country. Out of 2,964 delegates, only two voted against and three abstained, thus almost unanimously making Xi Jinping president for life.[17] Through this endorsement, Xi Jinping continues an autocratic tradition that goes back thousands of years in China; as Zhengyuan Fu noted,

> The most enduring and significant characteristic of Chinese political tradition is autocracy. This autocratic tradition is embodied in the social order in which society is almost totally subordinated to the state. Such a social order was installed when China was unified under one centralized political authority in 221 B.C. with the establishment of the Qin dynasty.[18]

Since the death of Mao Zedong (1893–1976), the last "president for life" in China, almost half a century has passed, and enormous economic, cultural, and social changes have taken place in Chinese society, as well as the relationship of China with the rest of the world. As summed up by three leading economists,

> China's economic growth has lifted hundreds of millions of individuals out of poverty. The resulting positive impacts on the material well-being of Chinese citizens are abundantly evident. Beijing's seven ring roads, Shanghai's sparkling skyline, and Guangzhou's multitude of export factories—none of which existed in 1980—are testimony to China's success.[19]

We can clearly see the economic success of China by looking at all the "made in China" goods we use in our everyday lives—Chinese goods have flooded just about all the countries of the world. This export success has brought enormous wealth for China and created an elite "super-rich" Chinese group (there are now more billionaires in China than in the United States[20]). The standard of living of ordinary Chinese people has also been lifted: Between 1992 and 2007, average real wage in China increases by 202%.[21] A study of a rural community in China showed that as economic changes have taken place, bringing increased interaction with tourists and other outsiders, there have also been changes in the identities of rural Chinese.[22] For example, more pride and less shame is now associated with the rural identity. Gender roles are also changing, as more women advance in education and become middle-class professions.[23] Political changes also seemed possible: The growth of a large Chinese middle class with degrees from world-class research universities[24] led to rising democratic aspirations, culminating in the momentous 1989 Tiananmen Square protests.[25] Despite all this, the political system of China continues its long tradition of autocracy, in the midst of rapid and large-scale economic and social changes.

Thus, on the one hand, there have been enormous transformations in China, particularly in terms of higher income, advances in technology and infrastructure, and also gender roles. On the other hand, the "emperor for life" autocratic political tradition continues. China is not the only country experiencing this contradiction between economic and social changes on the one hand, and political stagnation on the other. For example, consider how, in terms of technological advances, Russia has sped ahead, as reflected in its space program and computing capabilities, but in the political sphere, the leader–follower relationship has not changed; autocracy continues with Putin enjoying unrivaled control of Russian society. Clearly, change in Russia has not extended to important parts of the political domain.

Low Plasticity in Social Relations: The Example of Perceived Threat, Instability, and Escape

The psychoanalytic perspective postulates that "the despair of human automation is fertile soil for the political purposes of fascism."[26] According to this line of thinking, industrialization and urbanization have resulted in individuals feeling isolated and alienated. This argument seems to fit with a rise in individualism and a decline in social capital in modern societies, meaning that there is more "bowling alone," acting as independent individuals, and less community life.[27] Participation in Boy Scouts, Girl Guides, and numerous other traditional groups and communities has declined. These trends, one might argue, are resulting in greater alienation and isolation of individuals and are creating fertile ground for the greater influence of "charismatic strongman leaders"[28] and possible slide to dictatorships.

A more viable alternative explanation for these recent developments is to see community ties as changing rather than evaporating. For example, numerous new communities have emerged through the Internet; the new paths for social interaction, such as Facebook, are different, but they can lead to strong bonds and a sense of belonging to certain groups.[29] Indeed, research on the *minimal group paradigm*,[30] a procedure that arbitrarily places individuals into groups on the basis of trivial criteria, demonstrates that what objectively seem to be trivial criteria for group formation can lead individuals to bond with the group. There are numerous examples of this in real life. For example, football (soccer) involves teams in different-colored shirts kicking a ball up and down a field, but the next soccer World Cup will involve billions of football (soccer) fans strongly identifying with their national teams and experiencing emotional turbulence with each goal.[31] People have been known to kill and be killed for this "game."[32] Thus, communities can come alive through the Internet, based on criteria that seem from the outside to be "trivial," but result in group identities that are powerful and important for behavior.

In the 21st century, it is more accurate to view patterns of identification with groups as changed, rather than as in decline or in the process of extinction. The "alienation" or "anomie" that psychoanalysts, existentialists,[33] and others have postulated, if it has taken place, has not prevented us from bonding strongly with sacred groups, such as our national, ethnic, or religious group. The sacred groups with which we identify have changed, but this does not mean that the intensities of group identifications have diminished. For example, in 21st-century Western societies, individuals tend not to identify as strongly with a village, neighborhood, or extended family, but identification with nations tends to be particularly strong. Immigrants seen as identifying with the nation are more readily accepted by host societies.[34] Even in a "traditional" collectivist society with strong ethnic ties, such as India, the nation-state can serve as a strong enough superordinate group to result in positive behavior toward the "ethnic other."[35] That is, in some conditions, nationhood can overpower ethnic and regional differences.

In the context of modernization theory, even more surprising than the rise of nationalism is the resilience and resurgence of religion. As discussed in Chapter 5, rather than decline in some regions, the power of religion has increased in the 21st century—with religion and capitalism surging in the same regions of the world.[36] The resurgence of Islam in the context of 21st-century globalization has received a great deal of attention because it has been associated with radicalization and terrorism.[37] However, Christianity and other major religions also continue to be robust and to defy the predictions of modernization theory about the impending decline of religion.[38] In addition, strong identification with sports teams has become a norm internationally, influenced by marketing efforts to sell products through sports teams such as Real Madrid, the world-famous football club.[39]

Thus, rather than 21st-century individuals suffering from alienation and isolation, they are identifying strongly with nation, religion, and various other groups, including ethnic and language groups, and also sports teams. Group identifications satisfy a basic psychological need for people to belong to collectives, particularly those that enable individuals to enjoy a positive and distinct identity.[40] But strong identification with nation, sports team, or any other group leaves the individual vulnerable in an important way: Such groups could be threatened and could suffer a decline. Next, I examine what happens when 21st-century conditions create threats for collective identities based on sacred groups.

Consequences of Perceived Threat to Sacred Groups

An important implication of the concept of political plasticity for the resilience of dictatorship concerns the consequences of perceived threat to sacred groups. Specifically, the implications are that human response to such perceived threat is, first, a result of long-term evolutionary processes; second, stable across most human cultures; and third, resilient and can only be changed through focused programs.

Most important, the implication is that perceived threat results in humans seeking a way to safeguard the freedoms and security provided through membership of sacred groups, such as nations and religions. When these freedoms are threatened, people gravitate toward and become magnetized by strong leaders who promise to protect their sacred groups and associated freedoms. Thus, the pull of strongmen who become dictators is not an "escape from freedom" as Fromm argued, but an attempt to safeguard freedom through the misguided path of dictatorship.

Human response to threat is integral to our general adaptive strategies for survival. As Steven Neuberg and colleagues described,

> Rather than being designed by engineers to process information in a dispassionate manner, the human brain has been designed by natural selection to be something of a motivational device to promote adaptive behavioral responses to critical challenges directly related to survival and reproductive fitness.[41]

The self-preservation instinct has resulted in humans developing a number of psychological responses to perceived threats.[42] Groups that responded to threats more effectively were more likely to survive and socialize their young to adopt and adapt similar responses. Over time, these responses have become fairly stable and do not change easily.

A fascinating body of psychological research sheds light on the kinds of reactions people show to perceived threat. A large number of these studies were triggered by the terrorist attacks of 9/11; researchers were interested to learn how the terrorist threat would impact support for civil liberties and democracy more broadly. The results were disheartening in that the greater people's sense of threat, the lower their support for civil liberties.[43] However, threat does not influence everyone in the same way; for example, African Americans and individuals less trusting of government were less willing to drop support for civil liberties when under threat. Those who feel more threatened by terrorism[44] and are higher on authoritarianism[45] were more likely to drop support for civil liberties as a result of feeling threatened.

There is strong evidence that when group members feel threatened, they adopt more conservative positions,[46] support strong leaders who can provide aggressive responses to threats,[47] and become more prejudiced against outgroups.[48] Tolerance for dissimilar others decreases in particular when people feel threatened in situations of uncertainty.[49] In other words, in situations in which there is uncertainty and threat, such as terrorist threat coupled with large-scale immigration and economic change, people become more closed-minded and ethnocentric.

CONCLUDING COMMENT

Change is at the heart of the puzzle of dictatorship—both why dictatorships persist and why, under certain conditions, some societies that become relatively open move back again toward dictatorship. The concept of political plasticity is useful because it helps us to focus on the tendency for behavioral resilience that maintains dictatorships and slows down change toward democracy. The concept of political plasticity leads to two main questions: First, why has it proven to be so difficult for societies to move from lower to higher stages of political development toward democracy? This question is particularly puzzling in the 21st century because international surveys[50] show that there is a general sentiment among the majority of people that democracy is an improvement on dictatorship in terms of adherence to human rights and basic freedoms. Perhaps because of this, even primitive dictatorships add the word "democratic" to their official name (e.g., the official name of North Korea is the Democratic People's Republic of Korea) or go through the formalities of holding "elections" (e.g., as occurs in Iran), even though clearly such elections are not free or fair. Obviously, attempts to present regimes such as Iran and North Korea as "democratic" reflect the popularity of democracy among the majority of populations in these countries.

The second question raised by the concept of political plasticity is: Why is there sometimes "backward movement" from democracy toward dictatorship? This is a highly timely question for the United States and the European Union because populist antidemocracy leaders such as Donald Trump and Silvio Berlusconi highlight the danger of return to dictatorship.[51] The two chapters in Part III of this book explore the global context of, first, the springboard to dictatorship and, second, the relationship between dictators and their followers.

ENDNOTES

1. Harré (2018, p. xii).
2. de la Sablonnière, Taylor, Perozzo, and Sadykova (2009, p. 341).
3. See Moghaddam (2013) for a more detailed discussion.
4. Lozano (2011, p. 1367).
5. For example, see the discussions in Mikulincer and Shaver (2014).
6. Dunbar (2009).
7. Dunbar (1998); Premack and Woodruff (1978).
8. For example, the journals *Neural Plasticity* (https://www.hindawi.com/journals/np) and *Brain Plasticity* (https://www.iospress.nl/journal/brain-plasticity) publish research that illuminates the nature of hardwiring in the brain.
9. For discussions of how the built environment influences behavior, see Steg, Van den Berg, and De Groot (2013).
10. Handy, Boarnet, Ewing, and Killingworth (2002).
11. Moghaddam (2013).
12. See readings in Shamir, Pillai, and Bligh (2007).
13. For example, Sveiby (2011).
14. Brown (1991).
15. Van Vugt, Hogan, and Kaiser (2008).
16. Greenleaf (1977/2002).
17. BBC News (2018, March 11).
18. Fu (1993, p. 1).
19. Autor, Dorn, and Hanson (2016, pp. 36–37).
20. PwC Press Room (2017).
21. Ge and Yang (2012).

22. Xue, Kerstetter, and Hunt (2017).
23. An example is women in accountancy and consultancy firms in China; see Cooke and Xiao (2014).
24. There has been rapid growth of excellent universities in China; see Huang (2015).
25. Among the books on China in the turbulent late 1980s, Lim's (2015) is particularly moving.
26. Fromm (1941, p. 256).
27. Putnam (2000).
28. World Economic Forum (2018, see p. 10 and p. 37).
29. See the studies on Facebook and social capital by Ellison, Steinfield, and Lampe (2007) and Ellison, Vitak, Gray, and Lampe (2014).
30. For an example of the original research studies, see Tajfel, Billig, Bundy, and Flament (1971); for a broad discussion of the literature, see Moghaddam (2008b).
31. Allison (2000).
32. An example of a football game embroiled in violent disputes is the "never-ending" game between Dinamo Zagreb and Red Star Belgrade in May 1990 (see Dordevic, 2012). This football game, which was abandoned because of violent clashes between rival groups of supporters, is seen by some to be the start of Croatian–Serbian conflicts and the end of Yugoslavia as a country.
33. I am thinking here particularly of the popular works of Jean-Paul Sartre and Albert Camus, but also of Fyodor Dostoevsky, Søren Kierkegaard, Friedrich Nietzsche, Karl Jaspers, and Martin Heidegger.
34. Roblain, Azzi, and Licata (2016).
35. Charnysh, Lucas, and Singh (2014).
36. Heslam (2016).
37. Moghaddam (2008a).
38. B. S. Turner (2010).
39. Baena (2016).
40. I am referring here to the extensive research on social identity theory, which began in the late 1960s and is continuing to expand (see Moghaddam, 2008b).
41. Neuberg, Kenrick, and Schaller (2011).
42. Terror management theory is one of the psychological theories that highlights this point; Pyszczynski, Greenberg, and Solomon (1997).
43. Davis and Silver (2004); Huddy, Feldman, and Weber (2007).
44. Huddy et al. (2007).
45. Duckitt and Fisher (2003).
46. Nail, McGregor, Drinkwater, Steele, and Thompson (2009).
47. Laustsen and Petersen (2017).
48. Das, Bushman, Bezemer, Kerkhof, and Vermeulen (2009).
49. Haas and Cunningham (2014).
50. Wike, Simmons, and Fetterolf (2017).
51. Albright (2018) and others have pointed out the dangers of fascism, as well as the institutional safeguards that have (so far) helped the United States avoid becoming a dictatorship.

III

GLOBALIZATION AND DICTATORSHIP

Alas, the storm is come again.

—WILLIAM SHAKESPEARE,
THE TEMPEST (2. ii. 38)

The chapters in Part III explain changes societies undergo along the dictatorship–democracy continuum by exploring the perfect storm that is being created for the rise of dictatorships in the 21st century. Integral to the perfect storm is the match between the characteristics of what I have called *fractured globalization,* when the pull of the global economic forces is opposite to the pull of local identity needs, and the mind of the dictator. Fractured globalization involves macroeconomic and technological forces pushing for greater integration of different societies, but the identity needs of people pulling toward nationalism, localism, and antiglobalism broadly. Fractured globalization is associated with collective identity threats, particularly against national identity, being experienced by ordinary people. This creates opportunities for strongmen leaders—potential dictators—to grab power.

During certain historical periods, such as Europe in the 1930s, the combination of contextual characteristics and the availability of leaders who are potential dictators results in a storm surge toward the dictatorship end of the dictatorship–democracy continuum. The signs indicate that in the early 21st century, another such storm surge is sweeping across the globe. The election of Donald Trump has accelerated this trend.

Extremist right-wing groups and individuals are now shaping political changes and events around much of the world. Commenting on this unexpected situation, Francis Fukuyama argued,

> Something strange is going on in the world today. The global financial crisis that began in 2008 and the ongoing crisis of the euro are both products of the model of lightly regulated financial capitalism that emerged over the last three decades. Yet, despite widespread anger at Wall Street bailouts, there has been no great upsurge of left-wing American populism in response . . . the most dynamic recent populist movement to date has been the right-wing Tea-Party. . . . Something similar is true in Europe as well, where the left is anemic and right-wing populist parties are on the move.[1]

The surge of global right-wing populism that brought Trump to the White House in the United States has brought authoritarian rulers back to power in Eastern Europe and shaken up the European Union. As a 2018 *Washington Post* headline put it, "E.U. faces a rebellion tougher than Brexit. In Eastern Europe, members openly deride the bloc's values, principles and rules."[2]

The two chapters in Part III explore the psychological foundations of what seem at times to be repeated patterns in history, of societies moving toward democracy and then back again toward dictatorship. The difference now is that accelerating globalization has resulted in a far more integrated and interdependent world, so that political changes in one part of the world have a greater impact on other parts. Consequently, the right-wing political surge is not isolated in particular countries but spreading across borders. For example, in the European Union the rightward shift in Poland, Hungary, and Italy is impacting all other E.U. countries, as well as spilling outside the Union.

ENDNOTES

1. Fukuyama (2012, p. 53).
2. Witte and Birnbaum (2018).

7

Globalization and the Springboard to Dictatorship

Context is everything in understanding popular support for dictatorship. The most common mistake is to focus attention disproportionately on the personality of the potential or actual dictator and to see personality features such as "narcissism," "Machiavellianism," and "charisma" as the key to explaining why in certain historical periods so many people flock to support authoritarian strongmen. Of course, the personality of the leader is important, but even more important is the context; it is the context that determines the type of leader that can emerge to lead a nation.

For example, the "pro-fascist" context of the 1930s in Japan led to a more important role for absolute dictatorship, the alliance with Hitler, and the terrible acts committed by Japan before and during World War II, such as the forced prostitution of several hundred thousand "comfort women" abducted mostly from China and Korea.[1] After the defeat and surrender of Japan in 1945, and the occupation of Japan by U.S.-led forces, leadership in Japan was compelled to change direction.[2] Even though the Japanese emperor was permitted to stay in place after the war, occupying forces diminished his role to enable the development of a Japanese form of democracy, one that turned away from militarism. Thus, a change of context forced changes in leadership style, from dictatorial to relatively more democratic.

The most important force changing the context for political leadership in the 21st century is globalization. My goal here is not to attack globalization as evil[3] but to point out some consequences of globalization that require attention from

http://dx.doi.org/10.1037/0000142-008
Threat to Democracy: The Appeal of Authoritarianism in an Age of Uncertainty,
by F. M. Moghaddam

prodemocracy forces because these particular consequences tend to result in movement toward dictatorship rather than democracy.

GLOBALIZATION AND DICTATORSHIP

The illusion that globalization will inevitably bring more openness and democracy continues to be widespread. It has mistakenly been assumed that as the world becomes smaller, everyone will become better informed and more open-minded because information, cultural products, and people will flow more smoothly across borders. Other parts of this optimistic illusion are that the sharing of cultures will lead to greater similarities between people, and as the members of different countries become more similar to one another, there will also be more liking and attraction between them. Also, it is assumed that globalization will result in governments around the world becoming more tolerant, national borders and national biases melting away, and people becoming less ethnocentric in general.

But in reality, these optimistic possibilities associated with globalization have been thwarted by opposing forces, one of them being terrorism, which poses an enormous threat, although not for the reasons usually given. In the next section, I examine the deeper threat terrorism poses, which concerns the danger to democracy and civil liberties as a result of subjective threat. Next, I examine the subjective threat host populations experience in the European Union and the United States, in response to perceived "invasions" by non-Western populations. In the final section of this chapter, I discuss traditional accounts of conflict and introduce an alternative cultural evolution account centered on the role of subjective threat.

THE DEEPER THREAT OF TERRORISM

I visited Israel several times during a period in which suicide bombings in buses were relatively common—though of course quite rare in absolute terms. . . . For any traveler, the risks were tiny, but that was not how the public felt about it. People avoided buses as much as they could. . . . I was chagrined to discover that my behavior was also affected. . . . I was ashamed of myself, because of course I knew better. I knew that the risk was truly negligible, and that any effect at all on my actions would assign an inordinately high "decision weight" to a miniscule probability. . . . My experience illustrates how terrorism works and why it is so effective: It induces an availability cascade.

—DANIEL KAHNEMAN[4]

Terrorism brings to mind bloody and mutilated bodies, destroyed buildings, scenes of confusion and carnage, people in bomb explosions and gun attacks, victims being assaulted by vehicles crashing through pedestrian areas; terrorism triggers such horrifying scenes of destruction and death. But despite the hysteria of the global mass media, deaths and injuries are not the most serious danger posed by terrorism—far from it. As Kahneman points out in the preceding quote, terrorism is not effective because of the number of deaths and injuries it inflicts but because terrorist events work through the *availability heuristic* (a mental rule of thumb leading to estimates of the likelihood of an event on the basis of how readily instances come to mind) to result in a huge overestimation of terrorist events. This individual-level heuristic process can multiply and become part of a collective process, described by Timur Kuran and Cass Sunstein as *availability cascades*, "social cascades, or simply cascades, through which expressed perceptions trigger chains of individuals responses that make these perceptions appear increasingly plausible through their rising availability in public discourse."[5] As a consequence of the availability heuristic and availability cascades, we greatly overestimate the probability of getting killed or injured in terrorist attacks.

Our magnifying the "threat of terrorism" becomes clear when we evaluate the impact of terrorism in its larger context. According to the World Health Organization, around 800,000 people die in the world due to suicide each year.[6] Within the United States, there was an increase in suicides in 1999–2014,[7] and about 30,000 to 35,000 people die from firearm-related incidents annually.[8] In comparison, a small number of people die each year in the world and in the United States from terrorist attacks: between 1970 and 2012, the annual number of deaths from terrorist attacks was around 2,526 in the world[9] and a few dozen in most years in the United States (obviously 2001 was an exception, when almost 3,000 people were killed in attacks on one day on U.S. soil). In her analysis of terrorist attacks on U.S. soil, Carolyn Gallaher concluded: "Between 1970 and 2012, just over ninety percent of attacks involved no fatalities (1,986). Of the attacks that did involve fatalities (197), ninety-six percent involved ten or fewer people. Only four attacks involved more than 100 fatalities."[10] She continued:

> Incidents of terrorism in the United States are also on the decline. In 1970, for example, there were more than 450 recorded cases of terrorist attacks. After the early 1970s, the number of incidences decreases sharply; after 1977, the number of recorded cases never exceeds 100. In 2012, there were thirteen recorded cases.[11]

Of course, even one death from terrorism is too many, but in terms of sheer numbers, suicide and firearm-related deaths are far, far more serious than terrorism. Why do we not have a war on suicide or a war on firearms? The widespread fear and anxiety created by terrorism has prevented this question from being seriously considered.

But there is an additional important factor that results in terrorism creating such enormous fear and alarm, when the number of people killed and injured through terrorism is relatively tiny: Terrorism has become associated with "the other," "the alien," "the enemy force"—Islam. The Norwegian ultranationalist Anders Brevik, who became infamous for his 2011 terrorist attacks, warned of the "Islamic invasion," and his hysterical proclamation finds echoes in the wider debate about terrorism in Europe and North America. The global mass media have noted that extremist nationalists, antigovernment groups, and many other non-Muslim attackers are also responsible for terrorist acts, such as the 1995 Oklahoma City bombing that killed 168 and injured almost 700 people in the United States and the 2011 Brevik attack that killed 77 people in Norway. Despite terrorism carried out by non-Muslims, Americans who lean to the political right tend to see an association between terrorism and Islam, and about half of all U.S. adults believe that Islam is not part of mainstream American society.[12]

Even in places where people have had extensive experience with terrorist attacks perpetrated by non-Muslims, such as in the United Kingdom where there is a history of Irish Republican Army (IRA) attacks, Islamic terrorism inspires new levels of fear and general anxiety. I lived in the United Kingdom during the 1970s, when the IRA waged a bombing campaign against targets in England. The British faced these attacks with the "Dunkirk spirit" and a "stiff upper lip." After all, the IRA is something the Brits know well. But terrorist attacks in the United Kingdom (and in other parts of Europe and North America) by Muslims have raised an altogether different and higher level of stress and fear.[13] These attacks are from an alien source.

THE SO-CALLED NEW INVASIONS

The movement of millions of people each year across national borders and entire continents, mostly from non-Western to Western countries, has created new perceived threats among host populations in Western societies. Some locals welcome the incoming "hordes," but many spurn them as dangerous and unwelcome "invaders." In this section, I discuss so-called invasions of the European Union and the United States.

The "Invasion" of Europe?

In the summer of 2017, I taught at the University of Oslo and had the opportunity to travel to a number of European countries. In cities large and small, I found that many local people showed a high level of anxiety and obvious discomfort in reaction to the arrival of what seems to them to be unstoppable waves of mostly Muslim refugees and immigrants, particularly from Syria, Iraq, Iran, Afghanistan, Yemen, Libya, and other parts of the Middle East and North Africa. Mixed in with these people, who are escaping their homelands because of violence and political repression, there are also Pakistanis, Bangladeshis, and people from many other parts of Asia and Africa who are moving to Europe and North America as economic refugees; they seek to escape the poverty and dire material hardships of their homelands. Whether the main motive for moving is to escape political repression, economic hardship, war, or all of these problems, the result is the same from the perspective of global migration patterns: Each year millions of people, many of them Muslim, have flooded from non-Western into Western societies. Research by the Pew Research Center shows that between 2010 and 2016, the Muslim population in Europe increased by one million a year to reach 27 million.[14]

According to the *distance-traveled hypothesis*,[15] the Muslims moving to Western societies can be divided into two groups: those who are eager to escape the restrictions of traditional Islam, turn their backs on traditional mosques and see a "reformation" in Islam and those who continue to embrace traditional Islam, are eager to build mosques, and attempt to spread traditional Islamic values in their adopted Western lands. Most of the higher educated immigrants from Muslim lands fall into the first category, whereas most of those with low education fall into the second category.

The distance-traveled hypothesis postulates that the material and non-material resources available to immigrants and refugees will determine the distance they are able to move away from their lands of origin. The greater the distance between the land of origin and the host country, the greater the resources needed to successfully make the move. For example, those who originate from the Middle East will need greater resources to reach the United States than to reach the European Union. In practice, this means that Muslims moving to the European Union require fewer resources; they are less likely to be among the Western-educated, multilingual, secular Third World elite who could fit into Western societies relatively easily. Rather, many of the new arrivals in the European Union are low in education, unilingual, traditional in values, and clinging to the Muslim religion as traditionally interpreted.

The arrival of millions of Muslims in Europe comes at a time when both Europe and Muslim societies are grappling with enormous challenges. On the one hand, European societies are experiencing high tensions that arise from European integration. Countries as varied as the United Kingdom, Lithuania, Poland, Romania, France, Croatia, Austria, Greece, Bulgaria, and Germany, with their different cultures, languages, and religions, have to integrate and try to become one, united, cohesive, economic and cultural unit: the European Union. One of the challenges facing the European Union is demographic; Europeans are not having enough babies. A 2.1% total fertility rate (TFR) will allow a society to maintain a steady population level, but the TFR in European countries has been around 1.4, well below replacement level (it has been as low as 1.2 in Italy and Spain, two traditionally Catholic countries).[16]

Low fertility rates have arisen at the same time as longer life expectancy and the rise in the number of seniors among Europeans. Since 2008, the proportion of people 15 years and younger has been smaller than those 65 years and older.[17] The proportion of people 80 years and older, the "very old," is expected to triple between 2008 and 2060. Europe is not producing enough young workers to fill vacancies and pay the pensions of the fast-expanding retired community of Europeans; whereas there was at least four persons aged 15 to 64 for every person aged 65 years or older, there were only two by 2060.

The decrease in the size of the young population in Europe relative to the older population might suggest that unemployment among the young would be very low, but in Spain, Italy, and a number of other European countries, this is far from the case. A major problem has been a lack of flexibility in the labor market, which has made it difficult to take advantage of new technologies:

> the EU countries suffering from the highest youth unemployment rates are not the ones experiencing faster rates of technological development and adoption. Moreover, youth unemployment rates in these countries have remained at extremely high levels for the last forty years.[18]

A major problem has been the lack of fit between work opportunities and the skills and motivations of local workers. Robotics and mechanization are helping to compensate for the shortage of young workers with the needed motivations and skills in Europe (as well as in some other parts of the world, particularly Japan), but the change has not taken place fast enough. Tens of millions of additional workers are needed, particularly to fill unskilled jobs. Go to Germany, France, Italy, the United Kingdom, and any other major European country and look to see who is doing the cleaning and maintenance work in airports, hospitals, hotels, universities, business offices: It is workers from non-Western societies. In most cases, the workers will be from non-Western countries with historic colonial ties to the European country they work in, such as South Asians in the United Kingdom and North Africans in France.

The arrival of tens of millions of workers from non-Western countries has benefitted affluent Europeans because it has provided them with a large pool of highly motivated cheap labor. Go to the businesses and homes of affluent Europeans and you will see that it is mostly non-Westerners working for them as nannies, gardeners, mechanics, cleaners, garbage collectors, cooks, and so on. In senior homes in European countries, old people are being looked after almost exclusively by non-Western caretakers. Similarly, it is the non-Western workers who look after the babies and toddlers of affluent Europeans; Europeans are now cared for almost exclusively by non-Westerners at the beginning and end of their lives.

Yet White working-class Europeans often find themselves (actually) in direct competition with the refugees and immigrants from non-Western societies. Whereas affluent Europeans find it convenient to have the imported laborers available as nannies, gardeners, cleaners, and so on, it is the White working-class Europeans who feel they are being displaced from neighborhoods and jobs by the newcomers. It is the White working-class Europeans whose children share schools with immigrant children; schools that are typically underresourced and underperforming academically.[19]

Baluchestan in Midland England

I lived in England for 18 years and especially enjoyed visiting cities in the Midlands. Birmingham, Bradford, Coventry, Leicester, Wolverhampton—these cities grew rapidly during the Industrial Revolution and developed cultures and languages that were to some extent distinct. Some of the greatest English authors originated from the Midlands, including William Shakespeare, Charles Dickens, and George Eliot.

From the late 18th century, the mechanization and modernization of farming pushed millions of people from rural to urban areas, where they found employment in newly expanded industries in the Midlands. The lack of regulations meant that factories and factory workers developed in a rough environment, and for most people, life in urban slums was harsh.[20] The working-class culture that evolved in the industrial cities of the Midlands was authentic and unpretentious, but it was also infused with some pride in nationhood. After all, in the 19th century, the sun never set on the British Empire.

The two World Wars in the 20th century were associated with the decline of British global power and British manufacturing industries, even though Britain was on the "winning" side in both wars. From the end of World War II, the importation of cheap labor from former British colonies sped up: By 2011, 20% of people in England and Wales described their ethnic groups as other than White British.[21] The mostly South Asians who moved to towns such as Birmingham and Blackburn faced major challenges in the assimilation process, however.[22] Although evidence suggests there has been steady integration of minorities in England and Wales,[23] the emergence of ethnic economic enclaves in Midland England has created pockets of cultural separatism, "Baluchestans in England," where not only the White English but also other groups feel alienated from Muslim immigrants in particular.[24] The backlash to the perceived "invasion" by Muslims[25] is part of the explanation for Brexit (the vote for Brexit was higher in the Midlands than in the south of England[26]), as well as what Jacques Rupnik has referred to as the specter of "surging illiberalism" across most of Europe.[27]

The "Invasion" of the United States?

Growth of the foreign-born population is projected to exceed that of natives, resulting in an increasing share of the future U.S. population that is foreign born.

—SANDRA COLBY AND JENNIFER ORTMAN[28]

When Mexico sends its people, they're not sending their best. They're not sending you. . . . They're sending people that have lots of problems, and they're bringing those problems with us. They're bringing drugs. They're rapists.

—DONALD TRUMP[29]

The United States has historically been a nation of immigrants, and the preceding quotations represent two contrasting ways of discussing immigration. On the one hand, Colby and Ortman provided an objective summary statement in their 2015 report concerning projections of the size and composition of the U.S. population; on the other hand, Donald Trump provided an emotion-laden and controversial statement, referring to Mexicans as "rapists" and "bringing in drugs." However, despite their very different tones, the statements both refer to America reaching the majority–minority point, when the White population will make up less than 50% of the nation's total population—a trend that a substantial group of White Americans find troubling (66% of registered voters who support Trump in the general election see immigration as a "very big problem"[30]). As things stand, this point is expected to be reached in 2044.[31]

The chant "Build the Wall! Build the Wall!" continues to be highly popular among Trump supporters, reflecting a strong desire to keep out immigrants and refugees from Central and South America and some other parts of the world, particularly Muslim countries. Trump supporters believe minorities are working against the meritocratic American system.[32] This "antiminority" and "anti-newcomer" attitude has to be considered in light of recent trends and future projections in immigration to the United States. From the perspective of some Americans, these trends and projections indicate an "invasion."

The U.S. population is projected to increase from 319 million in 2014 to 417 million in 2060.[33] This increase comprises mostly foreign-born individuals. Between 2014 and 2060, the native population is expected to increase by 22% but the foreign-born population to increase by 85%. The Hispanic population in the United States is expected to rise from 17.4% of the total population in 2014 to 28.6% of the total in 2060 (more than 50% of the Hispanic population are born in the United States).[34] The Black population will remain more stable, increasing from 13% of the total U.S. population in 2014 to 14% of the total in 2060. By 2060, Black Americans and Hispanic Americans alone will make up 42.6% of the U.S. population. The share of the non-Hispanic White group is 50% of the total U.S. population in 2014 but will decline to 44% by 2060.

These enormous population changes are seen by some Americans of European descent as an "invasion" because they represent huge increases in the number of "dissimilar others." The majority of early immigrants to the United States were from Europe; in the 30-year period 1820–1850, 90% were from Europe.[35] As more and more non-Europeans attempted to move to the United States, various laws were enacted to limit non-European immigration, including the 1924 national origins quota system that attempted to "freeze" the proportion of Americans with different heritages and was only repealed in 1965. The percentage of Americans who claim European heritage has dropped from 80% in 1990 to 75% in 2000 and 72% in 2010.[36]

Thus, in both the European Union and the United States, actual competition between White working-class "locals" and non-Western "newcomers" over jobs, housing, educational resources, and other areas has led to certain changes in group and intergroup dynamics—changes that are predicted on the basis of psychological research.

EXPLANATIONS FOR GLOBALIZATION AND CONFLICTS

A wide range of psychological theories are available to explain conflict in the context of fractured globalization. I first briefly outline the conventional psychological theories then put forward a complementary theory that fills a vital gap in the existing literature. What I propose does not replace the existing explanations but adds to them.

The Conventional Explanations

The conventional psychological theories of conflict can be conceived as lying on a continuum,[37] with theories that give primacy to "material factors" as the drivers of conflict at one extreme and those that give primacy to "psychological factors" at the other extreme (see Figure 7.1).

The *materialist* theories, such as realistic conflict theory, propose that conflict is driven by competition for material resources, and this intergroup competition will shape the psychological experiences of group members. For example, according to materialist theories, competition over land, water, and other material resources is leading Israelis and Palestinians to develop negative attitudes and stereotypes of each other and to engage in violent conflict. On the other hand, theories that give more importance to psychological factors as the drivers of conflict, such as psychodynamic theory and social identity theory, argue that the deeper reasons for conflict are related to collective identity, unconscious emotions (e.g., irrational hatred of the outgroup), and other such nonmaterial factors. In short, land, water, oil, and other such resources are used as excuses for fighting, but the deeper reasons for conflict are psychological and often outside the conscious awareness of those engaged in the fighting.

The conventional *psychological* theories cover a wide range of factors and have important strengths. An important dimension has been added to the traditional theories, through sociobiology, social dominance theory, and other theories that have strengthened the evolutionary theme in explaining human conflict.[38] In the next section, I build further on the evolutionary theme by outlining an account of conflict that more firmly places human intergroup conflicts in the larger context of the natural world and in relation to the functioning of all plants and animals. The evolutionary perspective adds an important dimension to the available psychological explanations but it does not replace them.

A Complementary Explanation: Threatened Identities and "Catastrophic Evolution"

Globalization in the 21st century is creating certain conditions that lead to people experiencing collective threat, particularly in relation to sacred groups such as nation-state, religion, and ethnicity. This threat arises in part because of large-scale movements of people and cultural phenomena across national borders and entire regions. It is useful to consider these changes from an evolutionary perspective and particularly in relation to the concept of *invasive species*—an animal, plant, or other living organism that is not native to a territory but is introduced there, reproduces, and spreads in a way that damages the local

FIGURE 7.1. The Materialist-Psychological Continuum of Psychological Explanations of Conflict

Primacy given to material factors	————————————————	Primacy given to psychological factors

species and ecology. Invasive species are often introduced to a local ecology by accident. For example, pythons have been introduced to Florida, probably by pet owners who found that their pet snakes grew too large to keep in their homes and abandoned them in the Everglades. However, pythons have flourished in their new habitat and are wiping out some local species in South Florida.

Among animals and plants, there are many examples of how the introduction of invasive species has resulted in *catastrophic evolution*, "a swift, sharp and often fatal decline in the numbers of a particular life form."[39] Catastrophic evolution is more likely to come about after *sudden contact*, the swift coming together of life forms with no previous history of contact and with *low postcontact adaptation* speed. That is, a life form is likely to go into decline or even extinction when it suddenly comes into contact with invasive species without having had time to develop the defenses necessary for surviving interactions with the invaders. For example, the flightless birds known as moa were soon wiped out after the arrival of Maori settlers in New Zealand in the 13th century.[40]

Catastrophic evolution also takes place among human groups. This trend is probably as old as human evolution; in recent history, we can see the trend clearly in the "discovery" and colonization of Africa, Asia, and the Americas by Western powers. Indigenous populations often suffered sharp decline or even extinction as a result of sudden contact with European colonizers. For example, Tasmania was discovered by Europeans in 1642, but by 1876, the last indigenous Tasmanian perished.[41] The majority of the tens of millions of people indigenous to what is now the United States were also killed within a few centuries after their "discovery," mostly because sudden contact brought them within the range of diseases against which they had little immunity.[42]

Sudden contact and catastrophic evolution can be clearly seen in the trend of "language death."[43] About two thirds of the languages that were thriving when Columbus arrived in North America have already disappeared; there are hundreds of languages with only a few speakers left alive; most of the languages spoken today will be wiped out by the end of the 21st century. This is in large part because of the global dominance of a few languages, particularly English.[44] For the first time in human history, a dominant world empire, Great Britain, has immediately been followed by another, the United States, using the same language, English. The global dominance of English and a few other major languages has meant that many local languages are struggling to survive. The example of language death shows how sudden contact and catastrophic evolution can result in the decline and even extinction of entire groups. Not surprisingly, the members of threatened groups often attempt to take "defensive" actions to protect themselves.

Thus, in the face of collective threat to their sacred group, members evolve a variety of defensive behaviors, ranging from prejudice and discrimination to collective violence and genocide. Radicalization and terrorism can be part of these defensive behaviors, as in the case of Islamic extremists and white nationalist extremists, who see each other as a serious threat and engage in mutual radicalization, each pushing the other to take more extreme positions.[45] The concept of catastrophic evolution, then, complements existing explanations by pointing to longer term evolutionary processes, and the vitally important role of perceived collective threats in intergroup conflicts.

CONCLUDING COMMENT

In the context of the wider critical attention given to globalization over the last half century,[46] I have complemented existing explanations of intergroup conflict by interpreting the process of globalization in an evolutionary context in which humans, animals, and plants sometimes experience collective identity threat and catastrophic evolution. The vast movements of people and cultural artifacts across national boundaries and regions have created enormous feelings of collective threat experienced among sacred group members. In some instances, the perceived threat is well grounded because entire languages and ways of life are disappearing in the face of large-scale "invasions," such as the flood of "Hollywood culture" and the English language into non-Western societies. Even Islamic fundamentalist societies have found it difficult to resist this flood,[47] despite draconian measures taken by "morality police" in various countries (particularly Iran and Saudi Arabia).

Collective threats to sacred groups have also been intensely experienced in Western societies, however. This perceived collective threat is at the heart of support for populist strongmen who (falsely) promise freedom and glory for the sacred group members. In the next chapter, I further explore the nature of the relationship between the dictator and his followers.

ENDNOTES

1. S. J. Friedman (2015).
2. See Rikki Kersten's (1996) analysis of how democracy developed in postwar Japan.
3. There are already numerous pessimistic accounts of globalization, such as Bremmer (2018).
4. Kahneman (2011, p. 322).
5. Kuran and Sunstein (1999, p. 685).
6. See World Health Organization (2018).
7. Curtin, Warner, and Hedegaard (2016).
8. Grinshteyn and Hemenway (2016).
9. See LaFree, Dugan, and Miller (2015), particularly Figure 7.1.
10. Gallaher (2015, p. 325).
11. Gallaher (2015, p. 325).
12. Pew Research Center (2017, July 26).
13. Pew Research Center (2017, May 24).
14. Pew Research Center (2017, November 29).
15. Moghaddam (2008a, p. 11).
16. Chesnais (1998).
17. Rechel et al. (2013).
18. Annunziata and Bourgois (2018, p. 12).
19. Several good publications have examined the plight of White working-class children in schools, for example, Evans (2016).

20. Rose (1992).
21. For discussions of ethnic groups in the United Kingdom, see papers in Jivraj and Simpson (2015).
22. Marketing is now taking place on the basis of ethnic enclaves in the United Kingdom, see Ojo, Nwankwo, and Ghadamosi (2015, pp. 97–116).
23. Catney (2016).
24. Storm, Sobolewska, and Ford (2017).
25. For a study of the daily hassles experienced by Muslims in Europe, see Göle (2017).
26. Zoega (2016).
27. Rupnik (2016).
28. Colby and Ortman (2015).
29. Part of a speech made by Donald Trump June 16, 2015, announcing his run for the Republican nomination for president. Retrieved from https://www.newsday.com/news/nation/donald-trump-speech-debates-and-campaign-quotes-1.11206532
30. Doherty (2016).
31. Colby and Ortman (2015).
32. Cech's (2017) research shows Trump supporters to be "rugged meritocratists" (p. 1).
33. The statistics in this paragraph are mostly from Colby and Ortman (2015).
34. Ngai (2014) provided a nuanced discussion of the role of Hispanics in modern America.
35. Hing (2004).
36. Census Briefs (2010).
37. See Moghaddam (2008b) for a critical review of these theories.
38. See Chapter 4 in Moghaddam (2008b).
39. Moghaddam (2006a, p. 421).
40. Baskin (2002).
41. Ryan (1981).
42. Mann (2006).
43. *Language Death* is the title of an excellent book by Crystal (2000), but it is also now the term used for an entire domain of research.
44. Crystal (2003).
45. Moghaddam (2018a).
46. For example, consider the debate about "McDonaldization" (Ritzer, 1998).
47. See Fulu and Miedema (2016) for a discussion of how globalization is influencing gender roles and family relations in some Muslim societies.

8

The Dictator–Follower Nexus

He jeered at prodemocracy protesters in Istanbul for their liberal lifestyle, calling them "Marauders" and mocking their drinking habits: "They drink until they puke." And he made a notoriously coarse remark about a socialist feminist protester who climbed onto an armored vehicle in Ankara, wondering if she were a girl or a woman, essentially questioning her virginity.

—CARLOTTA GALL,[1]
DESCRIBING THE ACTIONS
OF THE TURKISH LEADER TAYYIP ERDOGAN

In 1980, I was in Tehran listening to "Supreme Leader" Khomeini making a fiery speech. He spoke in simple, direct, threatening language. He threatened America ("The Great Satan") and Israel ("The Little Satan"), he condemned his opponents, and in particular, he targeted the Western-educated elite in Iran. The crowd was mesmerized as Khomeini lambasted those who (he said) had abandoned their Islamic roots, and again and again he told his followers that they were great, they were superior because they had Islam. Khomeini's speech was full of exaggerated claims about the power of Islamic Iran and about the weakness of the "evil enemy." His frenzied followers shouted slogans, chanting in unison to show their support, vying to sacrifice themselves for him. In that scene, I could sense an extraordinarily strong bond between Khomeini and his core followers. They would do anything for him, and he knew how to reach out and touch each of them, even though the

http://dx.doi.org/10.1037/0000142-009
Threat to Democracy: The Appeal of Authoritarianism in an Age of Uncertainty,
by F. M. Moghaddam

educated elite in Iran mocked his speeches as simplistic and unsophisticated, just as the educated elite in Turkey ferociously mock Erdogan and find him crude and frightening.

Leaders such as Khomeini, Erdogan, Putin, and Trump have an instinctive understanding of their core supporters and how much these supporters are willing to sacrifice and remain loyal to them. Donald Trump famously boasted during the 2016 presidential campaign that "I could stand in the middle of Fifth Avenue and shoot somebody and I wouldn't lose voters."[2] Trump was not exaggerating because, as events showed, no matter how many women came forward to explain in detail how he accosted them, no matter how much proof was put forward to reveal Trump's devious past, no matter how many business scandals swirled around him, and no matter how many critics pointed out that Trump refused to disclose his tax records and to separate his private business interests from his government role, his core supporters kept on shouting, "We don't care! We don't care! We don't care!" and remained loyal to him.

The political scientist Jan-Werner Müller[3] argued that populist leaders get away with what looks like corruption and nepotism from the outside by convincing core supporters to see the world in terms of tribal categories of "us" and "them." Whatever is done to strengthen the sacred group, "our tribe," is not only forgiven but also justified and celebrated. So while outsiders are horrified when the populist leader violates the rule of law and attacks the free press, his loyal followers cheer him on. In this sense, Trump was absolutely correct to claim that he could shoot someone in a crowded street and still not lose a vote. So far, his supporters have not faulted him for his use of his government position to further the private business interests of himself and his family.

The communication strategies and messages Trump and other populist leaders use tend to alienate some groups, particularly those who are better educated,[4] but to energize their fanatically loyal base. Loyal supporters who stand by the potential or actual dictator tend to have very similar psychological characteristics across different nations. This includes the core supporters of populist strongmen as apparently varied as Khomeini, Erdogan, Chavez, Putin, and Trump, despite their different expressed ideologies and physical appearances.

Dictatorial leaders have important commonalities, across different societies. In this chapter, I first examine the psychological characteristics of dictatorial leaders and their followers; second, I explore the dictator–follower nexus. The relationship between dictatorial leaders and followers is symbiotic; they thrive together and die together. They both emerge under certain environmental conditions, involving increased perceived threat to sacred groups, particularly nation-state, ethnicity, and religion. In parts of this chapter, I select particular dictatorships, such as Cuba, as illustrative examples of the dictator–follower nexus. My focus is on commonalities across actual or potential dictators, not unique features of particular dictatorships.

CHARACTERISTICS OF THE DICTATORIAL LEADER AND HIS FOLLOWERS

The potential or actual dictator takes shape in relation to his core followers and is in this way shaped by his environment. Because of the "strongman" image we have of dictators, an image dictators publicize themselves, we make the mistake of assuming that how they think and act is purely shaped by themselves—independent, self-reliant, separate from everyone else. The "great dictators"—Stalin, Hitler, Mao, and the "little dictators"—Castro, Khomeini, Saddam Hussein, Assad, all publicize themselves as standing apart from everyone else, but at the same time "representing the interests of the common people." However, in practice dictators' surroundings and particularly their core supporters highly shape their actions.

A number of traits are central to the personality of the dictator (these were discussed in Chapter 3, this volume): charisma, craving for centralized power, illusions of control, Machiavellianism, narcissism, paranoia, self-glorification. Not all dictators have all of these traits to the same degree. For example, Stalin had little charisma,[5] but he had all the other preceding traits to a high degree. Hitler could be described as a "complete dictator" in terms of personality traits because he possessed all of the preceding listed traits to a very high degree. Culture also influences how dictators manifest personality traits. For example, in both Cuba and Iran, being "one of the people" is part of the myth of the great leader, manipulated by Castro and Khomeini. Fidel Castro and his brother discouraged having their pictures displayed in public spaces, and Khomeini tried hard to present himself as "humble." But behind these facades, the Castro brothers, Khomeini, and other dictators share the characteristic of being utterly intolerant of disobedience: Anyone who crosses them is immediately shut down.

In addition to the basic traits of the dictator personality, we can identify certain features of the *cognitive style*, a distinct way of thinking and problem-solving, as well as the *emotional and motivational style*, a distinct way of feeling and being moved to take action, associated with each feature of cognitive style. These cognitive style features are interconnected, and we can envisage them as loosely linked in a circle (see Figure 8.1). They are not in any order or hierarchy, but they do form a cluster together.

Cognitive Styles

Cognitive Style 1: Sacred Groups Are Separate and Different

The world is divided into sacred groups that are very different from one another; cross-cutting categories (i.e., people with multiple races, nationalities, and so on) are not a consideration for the dictator, and there are no ambiguities about which sacred group each person belongs to or the characteristics of the different sacred groups.

Emotion–Motivation Style: We must trust and accept those who are in our sacred group and distrust, fear, and reject those who are in other sacred groups.

FIGURE 8.1. Features of Cognitive Style Characteristic of Dictators

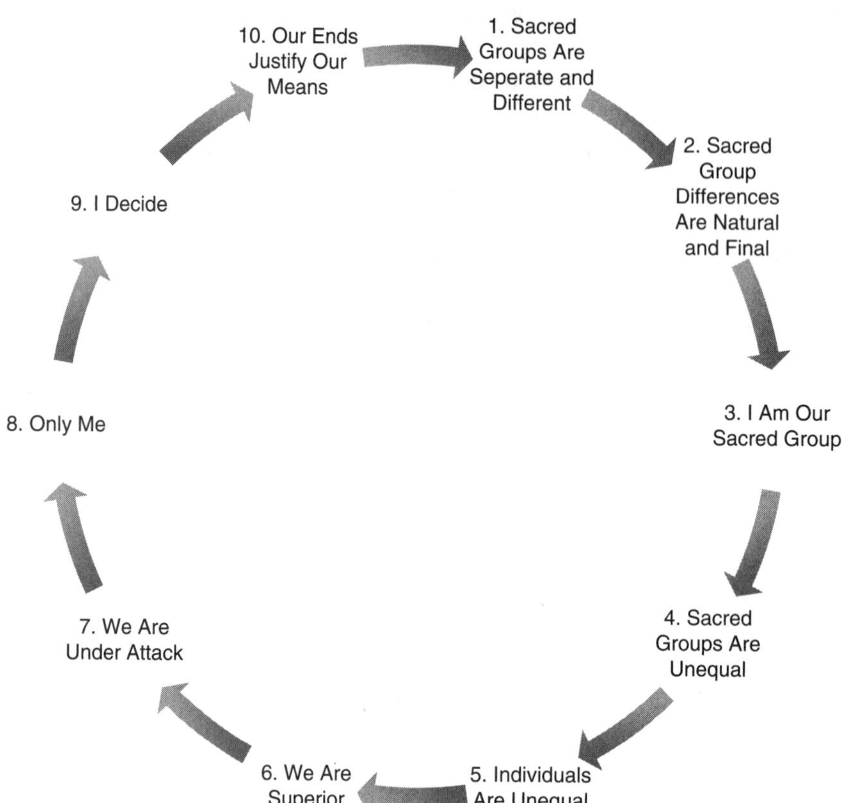

Cognitive Style 2: Sacred Group Differences Are Natural and Final

The differences between sacred groups, between us and them, are natural and unchanging, final. Our sacred group and those other sacred groups will always remain far away from one another, separated by unbridgeable differences.

Emotion–motivation style: We must not attempt to go against the natural order, by trying to bridge the distance between sacred groups. The world is a threatening and dangerous place, where the "others" are bad, disgusting, never to be trusted, and harmful to us.

Cognitive Style 3: I Am Our Sacred Group

Our sacred group depends on me; without me, our sacred group falls apart and fails, but with me it achieves greatness.

Emotion–motivation style: I feel pride in my leadership and those who remain loyal to me, so that we can reach our greatness. Loyalty to me is the highest priority.

Cognitive Style 4: Sacred Groups Are Unequal

There is a hierarchy of sacred groups, with winners and losers.

Emotion–motivation style: I feel pride in the natural order of the world. I feel anger and hatred toward those who refuse to accept their position; some of these traitors are born as members of our sacred group but are disloyal to me.

Cognitive Style 5: Individuals Are Unequal

The world is hierarchical, divided into individuals who are winners (like me) and losers (those many others), leaders and followers.

Emotion–motivation style: I feel pride in my power to defend the natural order and anger toward those individuals who refuse to accept their inferior position, below me.

Cognitive Style 6: We Are Superior

Our sacred group is naturally great, victorious, and superior.

Emotion–motivation style: We must maintain pride and joy in our natural collective superiority. Loyalty to me is part of the natural order.

Cognitive Style 7: We Are Under Attack

We are constantly being attacked by dangerous, devious, and cowardly internal and external enemies. They deny our superior collective qualities and work in secret to try to destroy us. We are also under attack from disloyal members of our own sacred group; they are cowards and traitors.

Emotion–motivation style: We have to destroy our internal and external enemies first, before they have a chance to attack us. They are deviants and can't be trusted.

Cognitive Style 8: Only Me

I alone can lead and save our sacred group, and the entire world. Everyone must put their faith entirely in me.

Emotion–motivation style: I loathe and destroy those who are disloyal and disobedient to me.

Cognitive Style 9: I Decide

I must be the center, the decision point, for everything; all roads that matter must lead to me. When people accept this truth, our sacred group fulfills its destiny to be great, and the world is saved.

Emotion–motivation style: I feel safe and assured when I am in control and in command, but I know there are cowards who are disloyal to me.

Cognitive Style 10: Our Ends Justify Our Means

Our goals are pure and virtuous and justify whatever means we need to adopt. Those who are loyal to me can do no wrong.

Emotion–motivation style: I feel pride in our goals, which are pure and virtuous. We are justified to use all necessary means to reach our goals, and to shame and shun those who show disloyalty and opposition to me by criticizing our methods.

The Underlying Characteristic of Narcissism

Although a number of personality traits characterize the dictatorial leader, the core binding mechanism of these traits is extreme narcissism. The personality of the dictator leader is centered on self-love, self-adoration, self-loyalty, and self-infatuation. Next, I discuss narcissism as the hallmark of the dictator personality.

During the final days of his life in Berlin, when German and Axis military forces had been completely defeated and American, Russian, British, and other Allied forces were closing in on the crumbling German capital, Hitler inspected the thin line of German defenders made up of very young boys and very old men. Rather than face justice, Hitler and Eva Braun, who were married in their last days, took their own lives in a bunker in Berlin on April 30, 1945. Among all the horrific images from the Second World War, none is more haunting than that of Hitler inspecting the ragged old men and patting the cheeks of young boys defending his bunker, urging them to fight to the death.[6] Hitler is a supreme example of a narcissist, characterized by self-centeredness and self-love, exaggerated sense of one's own importance and talents, and neglect of the needs and feelings of others. Rather than try to save Germans from further pain and suffering, in the final days of the war, Hitler was consumed with urging more Germans to die for him.

The same narcissistic characteristic is clearly evident in all of the major dictators. It leads to a terrifying disregard for the lives of others and a willingness to sacrifice their nation for the sake of their own ideas, plans, and egos. The grandiose sense of importance often leads dictators to produce books that they believe must serve as a blueprint for the lives of everyone else, such as Mao's Little Red Book[7] and Muammar Gaddafi's *Green Book*.[8]

Among the secondary personality characteristics related to narcissism is *antisocial* (also known as *psychopathy*), involving a disregard for right and wrong and for the rights and feelings of others. The antisocial personality is motivated to do what he (or she) feels like doing, irrespective of morality and how others will be affected. In the case of the all-powerful dictator, this can lead to enormous pain for others, as when the Khmer Rouge leader Pol Pot (1925–1998) attempted to create an ideal communist society through radical economic and social programs in Cambodia, resulting in about 20% of the entire population being killed. The self-love and self-centeredness of dictators is commonly associated with a strong *craving for power* to be concentrated in their own hands. With decision-making concentrated completely in their hands, dictators often make enormously costly mistakes, as when Saddam Hussein (1937–2006) invaded Iran in 1980 and Kuwait in 1990, plunging his country into devastating wars with huge human and material costs. Dictators tend to also have *illusions of control*,[9] exaggerated views of how much they actually do influence events and people. An example of this is the Libyan dictator Muammar Gaddafi (1942–2011), who was making grand speeches about his importance and power even in his last days when the revolution against him had succeeded and he was being hunted down. Soon after his grand speeches, he was caught hiding in a drainage pipe and was killed in 2011, shot with his own golden gun.

Narcissism in Dictatorial Relationships

> His majesty would take his place on the throne, and when he had seated himself I would slide a pillow under his feet. . . . I was His Most Virtuous Highness's pillow bearer for twenty-six years. I accompanied his majesty on travels all over the world. . . . His Majesty could not go anywhere without me, since his dignity

> required that he always take his place on a throne, and he could not sit on a throne without a pillow, and I was the pillow bearer. I had mastered the special protocol of this specialty, and even possessed an extremely useful, expert knowledge: the height of various thrones. This allowed me quickly to choose a pillow of just the right size, so that a shocking ill fit, allowing a gap to appear between the pillow and the Emperor's shoes, would not occur. In my storeroom I had fifty-two pillows of various sizes, thicknesses, materials and colors.[10]

Haile Selassie (1892–1975) ruled Ethiopia for 47 years, first as regent, and then as emperor. In his account of Haile Selassie's reign, Ryszard Kapuściński (the preceding quote is from his *The Emperor: Downfall of an Autocrat*) provided a stark picture of what happens when a ruler has absolute power over a population. On the one hand, the emperor led the defense of his country at the League of Nations in 1936 when it was attacked by the fascist regime of Benito Mussolini, and he attempted some modest reforms in Ethiopia, such as curbing the power of feudal landowners. However, the absolute power that Haile Selassie enjoyed for almost half a century meant that corruption and nepotism inevitably grew and enveloped all aspects of life in his country. Total power resulted in total corruption.

When the military officers who deposed Haile Selassie in 1974 arrived at his palace and ask him to return the money he has stolen from the nation, he claimed there was no money. The officers

> get up from the armchairs, lift the great Persian carpet from the floor, and there under the carpet are rolls of dollar bills stuck together, one next to the other, so the floor [looks] green. In the presence of his August Majesty they order the sergeants to count the money, write down the amount, and carry it off to be nationalized.[11]

However, the wealth that the emperor and his clan put away in bank vaults abroad would never be returned.

The condition of absolute power to a large degree shaped the personality of Haile Selassie. Similar to the shah of Iran, the king of Saudi Arabia, Bashar al-Assad of Syria, and a number of other absolute rulers, Haile Selassie was born into his position, and it was this inherited position that largely shaped his personality. In many other cases, the dictator is not born into his position but springs to power, using the springboard to dictatorship. Vladimir Putin of Russia, Saddam Hussein of Iraq, Muammar Gaddafi of Libya, Idi Amin of Uganda—these are among the notorious dictators who were not born into their positions but sprang to power. Irrespective of whether a dictator inherits his position or springs to power using the springboard to dictatorship, absolute power leads him and his regime to become absolutely corrupt.

Dictatorial Followers and Authoritarianism

With the rise of extreme right-wing authoritarian movements in Europe and elsewhere in the 1930s, some psychologists turned their research attention to the characteristics of individuals who supported dictatorships and potential dictators.[12] After the Second World War, researchers developed far larger and more systematic programs to study the personality of prodictatorship individuals, one result of which was the 1950 publication of the seminal work *The Authoritarian Personality*.[13] Researchers identified a set of features or *subsyndromes* that they believed characterize the authoritarian personality: submissiveness to authority, being punitive toward minorities and people who are different (seen as "deviants"), and rigid adherence to traditions and conventions (such as the idea that the family can only consist of a male husband, female wife, and their children). Stanley Milgram's research, conducted from the late 1960s, demonstrated that high authoritarians are more obedient to leadership, including when they are ordered to do harm to others.[14]

The cognitive style of those high on authoritarianism is particularly relevant to the antiscience approach they, and their leaders, tend to adopt: They are categorical thinkers who have a high need to avoid ambiguity and achieve certainty in a simplistic manner.[15] They have low tolerance for nuanced thinking and fuzzy categories; their world consists of "us versus them," "good versus evil," "black versus white." This is how the original researchers discussed the antiscience aspect of the authoritarian personality:

> The inability to "question" matters and the need for definite and dogmatic answers, as frequently found in high scorers (on authoritarianism), leads either to an easy acceptance of stereotyped, *pseudoscientific* answers . . . or else to an explicitly *antiscientific* attitude.[16]

This antiscientific attitude manifests itself in dismissal of scientists and their findings if the "facts" do not correspond to what the potential or actual dictator presents as the truth. Historically, this has resulted in great catastrophes in the Soviet Union under Stalin and China under Mao, costing tens of millions of lives.[17] For example, Stalin's interference in Soviet farming programs on the basis of a false knowledge of genetics helped to create food shortages and famine (e.g., in 1946). Mao's ill-conceived and antiscience "Great Leap Forward" of the late 1950s and "Cultural Revolution" of the 1960s brought equally disastrous outcomes, costing millions of lives and wasting enormous human talent. Looking to the future, Trump's dismissal of scientific findings regarding the role of human activities in climate change could prove to be even more costly for humankind.[18]

THE AUTHORITARIAN LEADER–FOLLOWER NEXUS

"Comparing his regime with Jesus Christ and his opponents to Barabbas may have disgusted many observers who read about Pinochet's remarks . . . yet the speech was typical of his improvised presentations and illustrated well Pinochet's own mindset."[19] General Augusto Pinochet led a U.S.-backed coup against the democratically elected Marxist government of President Salvador Allende and established a military dictatorship in Chile that lasted from 1973 to 1990 (Pinochet was finally pushed out from the head of the military in the mid-1990s). The military dictatorship faced widespread opposition both inside and outside Chile, but lasted so long because of the eagerness of the United States to support "anticommunist" governments and also the strong support of prodictatorship groups inside Chile. But who were the pro-Pinochet groups? During the Pinochet dictatorship, agents of the regime murdered thousands of people; who supported these attacks? When Pinochet made speeches comparing his regime with Jesus Christ and his opponents to Barabbas, depicting "our side as pure good and their side as pure evil," who applauded and agreed with him?

The key psychological characteristic of Pinochet's supporters was high authoritarianism. His supporters sharply demarcated their sacred group as different and superior. As with all dictatorships, the nexus of leader–follower relations in the Chilean dictatorship involved a moral justification of actions. Pinochet's supporters convinced themselves that they were doing the right thing not only for the economy of Chile but also for the higher morality and culture of their homeland, "The junta commanders portrayed their mission as morally, even divinely, inspired. Most soldiers became convinced that they had saved Chile from catastrophe and that they alone stood as guardians of the nation's values against the forces of subversion."[20]

The potential or actual dictator helps the sacred group members achieve glory through their (supposed) collective moral and cultural superiority. The message is clear: "Those other leaders, my rivals, have failed us, they have failed our sacred group, because they weakened us! I am the only one who will make us great again!" This is the essence of the "Make America Great Again" slogan. In the context of Russia, Putin has a "Make Russia Great Again" slogan, criticizing those who lost Russia world superpower status. Putin has argued that

> Russia must not only preserve its geopolitical relevance, it must multiply it, it must generate demand among our neighbors and partners. I emphasize that this is in our own interest. This applies to our economy, culture, science and education, as well as our diplomacy, particularly the ability to mobilize collective actions at the international level. Last but not least it applied to our military might that guarantees Russia's security and independence.[21]

According to Putin, Russia is not just another country, but a nation with "special responsibility for maintaining peace, stability, and prosperity" in the world. Putin's goal is to position Russia as a nation with enormous global responsibilities, with the implication that Russia must be great because only a great nation can have such responsibilities.

THE PROBLEM OF "TRICKLE-DOWN CORRUPTION" IN DICTATORSHIPS

The aroma of cigars and dark rum fills the small restaurant where I sit. I am writing these lines in Cuba, a dictatorship ruled by the Castro brothers for nearly 60 years. After Fidel Castro, his brother Raul Castro came to power. However, Raul set a 10-year term limit for the Cuban presidency, and as planned he stepped aside from power in 2018. For the first time in the post-revolution period, the Cuban president is not a Castro but President Miguel Diaz-Canel, another member of the Castro inner circle. This is a small step toward "opening up" Cuba. China is increasingly influential in Cuba, so perhaps Cuba's way of "opening up" will be to follow the Chinese model, freeing up the economy to grow faster but at the same time maintaining one-party rule and severely limiting political freedoms. But the "Chinese way" does not mean change in dictatorial leadership; after all, China now has a leader for life.

Cuba is very slowly opening up economically, and many Cubans are grateful for this small sign of improvement. The number of "51/49 businesses" is growing; these are business where 51% is owned by the Cuban government and 49% by private (often foreign) investors. The restaurant I sit in used to be a private home, but the owner obtained permission from the government to open this business. The clients are international visitors like me who bring in much-needed foreign currencies, as well as Cubans who somehow manage to gain access to higher income, mostly through the vibrant black-market economy. Associated with the thriving Cuban black market is *trickle-down corruption*, pervasive petty corruption in the everyday lives of ordinary people, which parallels corruption involving far larger "favors" at the top of the political power structure.[22] Of course, I could have chosen any other dictatorship to discuss trickle-down corruption; Cuba happens to be a convenient illustrative example.

The main source of trickle-down corruption in dictatorships is the total intolerance of any kind of criticism or questioning of authority, from top to bottom. Trickle-down corruption means that at every step, in all the details of daily life, ordinary people living in dictatorships find themselves enmeshed in corruption. The individuals who conscientiously try to do their jobs correctly and efficiently and not become involved in corruption are treated as simpletons. However, there are differences across individuals. In an innovative study, Vineeta Yadav and Bumba Mukherjee showed that there is variation in the level of corruption in dictatorships and lower corruption in regimes with "directly elected multiparty legislature that contains de facto opposition parties, and the presence of a national business association organized by and representing private-sector small- and medium-scale firms."[23] But Cuba meets neither of these conditions and is closed in terms of feedback on regime performance.

Because ordinary Cubans cannot criticize or even seriously question Castro and the Cuban political elite, there is a trickle-down effect so that even minor government officials become impervious to criticism. Nobody dares point out inefficiency among officials, for fear of being labeled "antirevolutionary." This buffer from criticism creates all kinds of opportunities for trickle-down corruption in everyday life and the growth of "mini-dictators" on every street corner. Under every dictator with an iron fist hammering the nation, there are thousands of mini-dictators with iron fists hammering factories, schools, shops, offices, and homes.

Trickle-down corruption leads to warped job preferences in dictatorships such as Cuba. The main criterion for choosing a career becomes the opportunities a person can find to steal from the workplace and participate in the black-market economy.

What job would you choose in Cuba, being a highly qualified factory engineer or being a low-status clerk with access to the factory warehouse inventory? You might imagine that the highly qualified engineer would be the more lucrative and highly sought job, but actually the clerk who has greater opportunities than the engineer to gain access to the goods in the warehouse will have a much better income for the simple reason that the clerk has opportunities to steal supplies and sell them on the black market, thus benefiting from a second income. A few dozen cans of paint this month, some metal sheets next month, office supplies the month after that—a fluctuating but ongoing string of "missing" supplies means that the clerk has an alternative revenue stream. The school cook steals three cans of oil from the school kitchen and sells them to neighbors; the woman in charge of washing hospital sheets steals five bottles of detergent and sells them to a local shop, which sells them to customers under the counter; the mechanic at the main taxi repair station in town occasionally gets away with stealing (supposedly) "faulty" or "worn-out" car tires—the possibilities are varied, and Cubans dedicate a lot of creative energy to continue to discover new avenues for participating in the underground economy.

A major reason dictatorships are economically inefficient is that so much of the creative energies of the population is poured into finding new ways to steal, cheat, and "shake down" other people, mostly within the government system. The underground economy in dictatorships is extensive and often efficient in its own way, at least for people who have the money to pay for black-market goods at black-market prices. As a rule of thumb, everything can be bought for a price in dictatorships, including all the banned goods and services. Of course, the black market is controlled by those who have strong ties with the regime, as in the case of the Republican Guards who control so much of both the official economy and the black market in Iran. The banking system in Iran has been particularly hard hit because of trickle-down corruption. A banking crisis arose from around 2016 when the Ponzi schemes ran by a number of banks, with regime cronies as beneficiaries, came crashing down.[24]

I also had opportunities to experience corruption in East European dictatorships before the collapse of the Soviet Union in 1990. When I was a university student in England in the 1970s, I drove overland from England to Iran several times. This journey took me through the communist Eastern Bloc countries, which at that time were petty dictatorships controlled by the U.S.S.R. The only exception was Yugoslavia, which under President Tito enjoyed more independence from Moscow relative to other Soviet satellite states. In countries such as Hungary, Romania, and Bulgaria, the police would routinely target cars with foreign number plates and impose fines for various incomprehensible reasons. The solution was to pay the police in cash with U.S. dollars. Of course, I never received a receipt for such payments.

Corruption is certainly also present to some degree in Western capitalist societies, and more so during Donald Trump's tenure in the White House. As *The Economist* put it,

> Mr. Trump . . . promised to run the country as he ran his family business, which would logically mean nepotistically, autocratically, with great regard for his personal interests and little for the rules. And so he has. . . . He has retained his business interests and cloaked his finances in secrecy.[25]

Despite Trump's corrosive influence on democracy, the level of corruption is still far higher and more pervasive in Russia, Iran, Cuba, and other such dictatorships. Since 1995, *Transparency International* has published the "Corruption Perception Index," which lists countries on how corrupt their public sectors are seen to be.[26] As a general rule, the more open and democratic a country, the lower the level of corruption. As Wayne Sandholtz and William Koetzle showed, there is a two-way relationship between corruption and democracy: On the one hand, corruption is higher when democratic norms and institutions are weaker; on the other hand, corruption corrodes core democratic values.[27] A study of 100 countries over a 16-year period suggests that the impact of corruption is much higher in dictatorships than in democracies, one reason being that in democracies, voters have opportunities to defeat politicians in elections, thus getting rid of politicians seen to be corrupt.[28] Another important reason is freedom of expression and the free press: In democracies, people are able to speak out against corrupt individuals and groups. Such freedom is not available to people in dictatorships. Unfortunately, just as globalization does not necessarily lead to more openness and democracy, globalization does not necessarily lead to a decline in corruption, at least not for lower income countries.[29]

The pressure on Cuban society is to become more economically diverse, to allow the private sector to grow and to become more open to foreign investment. Of course, the Castro regime is terrified that if it allows more economic freedom, then it will lose political control. However, the example of China has shown that a diversified economy does not necessarily lead to, or require, political diversification. Indeed, one of the paradoxes of globalization is that in some respects, it is placing enormous pressure on most societies to become more closed rather than more open.

One of the reasons globalization is leading to more closed societies is that from the perspective of traditionalists, conservatives, and those concerned with preserving the status quo, globalization is a threat that involves so-called invasions of foreign people, ideologies, religions, and cultures. This foreign invasion means that our sacred group could be swamped and even taken over, wiped out, by outside groups. Also, globalization opens the possibility of "our young people" being seduced and lured away to join other groups. In response to these threats to sacred groups, there is a tendency to retreat and close up, to engage in varieties of Brexit.

Would-be dictators and actual dictators are instinctively aware of the power they acquire through collective threats. It is by focusing on the threat of "the other" and exaggerating dangers of "the other" for the ingroup that potential and actual dictators mobilize their core base and achieve a "rally around the flag" outcome, having already wrapped the flag around themselves so in the minds of their supporters they embody the nation.

TRIBAL MORALITY: OUR SACRED GROUP IS GOOD, AND OUR ACTIONS ARE JUSTIFIED

"Only He Can Save Us"

The dictator's mind produces lethal tactics for grabbing and keeping power. The most potent of these create feelings of threat and helplessness in both supporters and opponents. Supporters react to feelings of threat and helplessness by becoming more and more dependent on the dictator. He presents himself as the only one who can save the sacred group from the crisis they are facing. "Only he can save us!" is a message supporters take to heart, passionately and sometimes violently attacking those who oppose this message. Their attacks arise out of the pride and strength they feel in being associated with the powerful and dominating figure of the dictator.

Fear and helplessness are also what the dictator wants opponents to feel, so they literally can do nothing and become helpless against him. The gut instinct of the dictator is to exaggerate threats against the sacred group, highlight the ruthlessness of "enemies," point to the evil nature of the "other"—whether it be Islamic terrorists, Jews, Mexican gangs, or any outsiders deemed different and frightening. As I discuss next, research shows that this tactic can have exactly the outcome the dictator is looking for: less public support for civil liberties and human rights and further movement toward authoritarianism and dictatorship.

The terrorist attacks of 9/11 served as a natural experiment, giving researchers the opportunity to test the impact of highly serious threat. Terrifying scenes of the Twin Towers burning and collapsing with thousands of people trapped inside, and the possibility that there could be new and perhaps even more devastating terrorist attacks, resulted in widespread feelings of threat among many Americans. A national survey carried out soon after 9/11 by University of Michigan researchers[30] demonstrated that people who experienced more threat were less supportive of civil liberties and agreed more with statements such as "to curb terrorism in this country, it will be necessary to curb some civil liberties" and "Everyone should be required to carry a national identity card at all times to show a police officer upon request."[31]

Additional research has shown that those Americans who feel threatened by future terrorist attacks are more supportive of aggressive antiterrorism government policies.[32] When people feel threatened and uncertain, they are less tolerant of those who disagree with them politically.[33] A study of trends across 32 countries demonstrates that when there is civil conflict in society, people show lower tolerance for those who are different.[34] The general impact of feeling threatened is for people to show less support for civil liberties and more support for aggressive measures against others—at home and abroad.[35] Although liberals are less willing to sacrifice civil liberties than are the politically moderate and conservative, liberals also move to the conservative position when they feel threatened.[36] However, trust also plays an important role in support for civil liberties: Those who have less trust in the U.S. government are less willing to sacrifice civil liberties for security.[37]

Research is showing that emotions play a huge role in how we understand and participate in politics.[38] We are "hot" and "emotional" political animals, not "cold" and "rational" ones. Although there are some disagreements among researchers about how exactly emotions influence us,[39] there is agreement that we often make irrational decisions and interpretations in politics as a result of acting out of emotions such as anxiety and anger.[40]

The bottom line is that by making people feel frightened and under attack, the strongman gets them to support his policies for clamping down on civil liberties and persecuting minorities and those who think and act differently. But some people are more easily persuaded by the strongman and are stronger supporters of his policies from the start. These "strongman supporters" are highly authoritarian and believe there is a natural hierarchy in society; they are more obedient to those above them in the hierarchy, and punitive and discriminatory toward those below them.[41] As discussed earlier, these high authoritarians are the core supporters of strongmen who will use the springboard to dictatorship when given the opportunity.

Mobilizing Core Supporters Through Fear Tactics

> Donald Trump has faced bipartisan criticism after failing to explicitly condemn the role of white supremacists in clashes with counter-protesters in Charlottesville, Virginia, that culminated in a car running into a crowd, killing at least one person. The president said he condemned "hatred, bigotry and violence on many sides" on Saturday. He then repeated the phrase "on many sides" for emphasis. . . . Senator Orrin Hatch of Utah [Republican] who lost a brother in the second world war [tweeted]: "My brother didn't give his life fighting Hitler for Nazi ideas to go unchallenged here at home."[42]

On August 12, 2017, a group of neo-Nazi White supremacists held a rally in Charlottesville, Virginia. These "Alt-Right" groups had been emboldened by the election triumph and presidential style of Donald Trump and saw new possibilities for mobilizing and increasing their national influence. Violence erupted and one person was killed during the rally when a White supremacist drove a vehicle into the counterdemonstration, as clashes flared up between the two sides (charges were announced against some far-right rioters[43]). The background to this clash was the fight over confederate statues and attempts to remove them as symbols of racism and slavery.

In reaction to the neo-Nazi rally and the violence, President Trump tweeted and talked in a way that depicted the two sides as morally equivalent. He repeatedly placed blame on both sides and refused to condemn the White supremacists, even for driving a car into protesters. But he had no hesitation in (correctly) placing blame on Islamic terrorists who drove a vehicle into pedestrians and killed three people in Barcelona, Spain.[44] In this case, he did not treat the "two sides" as morally equivalent. Trump's refusal to condemn neo-Nazi White supremacists may appear to be a puzzling reaction from a purely political point of view because Trump lost the support of key figures in the private sector and had to disband two groups of business leaders he had brought together under the Strategic and Policy Forum and the Manufacturing Jobs Initiative.[45] But the approach Trump adopted is not puzzling when we consider his instinctive link with his core group of authoritarian supporters and his "natural" tactic of depicting his sacred group, "our tribe,"[46] as morally superior and always justified in whatever actions "we take," because our goals are virtuous and pure, any means we use are justified.

CONCLUDING COMMENT

In analyzing the rise to power of potential and actual dictators, there is a tendency to exaggerate the role and personal characteristics of the individual strongman. Strongmen themselves encourage this tendency because their narcissism leads to self-glorification and the presentation of their stories as the personal successes of self-contained individualists. But there are present in all societies individuals with the personality characteristics necessary for functioning as dictators; it is only when the conditions are conducive, when the springboard to dictatorship becomes ready, that the potential dictator can spring to power. An essential part of this springboard is the availability and readiness of a large enough core authoritarian group that supports the rise of dictatorship.

The characteristics of those who are more likely to support dictatorship are well known: They are high on authoritarianism, low on tolerance for ambiguity, categorical thinkers, ethnocentric, intolerant toward minorities and "uppity" women, and obedient to "strongmen." This group has always been present to some degree in all societies, and the springboard to dictatorship makes clear the conditions in which this group will mobilize as a populist antidemocratic, pro-strongman force. Fractured globalization in the 21st century is helping to create the springboard to dictatorship in countries around the world.

The global shifts taking place are enormous, and their consequences could be highly detrimental for open societies everywhere. It is important to attend to future trends and develop and implement solutions so that we return to movement toward democracy rather than dictatorship. The final two chapters of the book, in Part III, address future developments and solutions toward strengthening democracy.

ENDNOTES

1. Gall (2018).
2. Diamond (2016).
3. Müller (2016).

4. The findings of Choma and Hanoch (2017) pointed to the expected association between authoritarianism and support for Trump, but also (less directly) lower cognitive ability and support for Trump.
5. Bullock (1993) described how Stalin developed "a plain style of speaking" (p. 174) and had to develop characteristics other than charisma to become the dominant power in the Soviet Union.
6. See such photographs online (https://www.pinterest.com/pin/322922235759659089).
7. See Cook (2014).
8. Gaddafi (2005).
9. For a more in-depth discussion of illusions of control in individuals and groups, see Moghaddam and Studer (1998).
10. Kapuściński (1978/1989, pp. 27–28).
11. Kapuściński (1978/1989, p. 157).
12. For example, see Stagner (1936).
13. Adorno, Frenkel-Brunswik, Levinson, and Sanford (1950).
14. As in the obedience to authority experiments of Milgram (1974).
15. Intolerance for ambiguity was identified by Adorno et al. (1950) as an important theme in the highly authoritarian personality, and more recent research has expanded on this theme through concepts such as need for closure and need for certainty (Kruglanski & Orehek, 2012).
16. Adorno et al. (1950, p. 464).
17. Moghaddam (2013).
18. Appenzeller (2017).
19. Spooner (1994, p. 248).
20. Constable and Valenzuela (1991, p. 62).
21. Quoted in Tsygankov (2016, p. 243).
22. There have been some interesting discussions of trickle-down corruption in the electronic media, such as Wilcox (2017).
23. Yadav and Mukherjee (2016, p. 246).
24. Erdbrink, Kirkpatrick, and Tabrizy (2018).
25. "Lexington: The coming collision" (2018).
26. See the list online (http://www.nationsonline.org/oneworld/corruption.htm).
27. Sandholtz and Koetzle (2000).
28. Drury, Krieckhaus, and Lusztig (2006).
29. Asongu (2012).
30. Davis and Silver (2004).
31. Davis and Silver (2004, p. 44).
32. Huddy, Feldman, Taber, and Lahav (2005).
33. Haas and Cunningham (2014).
34. Hutchison (2014).
35. Huddy, Feldman, and Weber (2007).
36. Davis and Silver (2004).
37. Davis and Silver (2004).
38. Demertzis (2013).
39. For example, see the discussions in Ladd and Lenz (2008) and Marcus, MacKuen, and Neuman (2011).
40. Weeks (2015).
41. Cohrs, Kielmann, Maes, and Moschner (2005).
42. B. Jacobs and Murray (2017).
43. Benner and Spencer (2018).
44. Nakamura (2017).
45. Gelles, Thomas, Sorkin, and Kelly (2017).
46. See Frances (2017) for further discussions of use of "tribal" tactics by Trump.

IV

FUTURE TRENDS AND SOLUTIONS

. . . we have only to look below the surface of any historical event, to inquire, that is, into the activity of the whole mass of people who took part in the event, to become convinced that the will of our historical hero, so far from ruling the actions of the multitude, is itself continuously controlled.

—LEO TOLSTOY, *WAR AND PEACE*[1]

In examining future trends and solutions to dictatorship, the most direct and simple explanation would be to see dictatorships as arising from the characteristics of individuals such as Hitler and Stalin, and in recent times Putin, Xi Jinping, Castro, Khomeini, Saddam Hussein, and so on. But as Tolstoy points out in the preceding quote, this would be an enormous mistake because the behaviors of the leaders themselves are also arising out of, and shaped by, particular contexts. I have already given detailed attention and importance to the nexus between dictatorial leaders and followers (Chapters 7 and 8), and the symbiotic leader–follower relationship. The two chapters in this final part of the book explore the dangers that continue to confront democracies and create conditions that are conducive to dictatorship (Chapter 9), as well as the solutions to preventing movement toward dictatorship (Chapter 10).

In both chapters, priority is given to contextual conditions. The proposition is that by creating conditions that stimulate and encourage prodemocracy changes at micro, meso, and societal levels, the general direction of societal change will lead to the creation of more democratic citizens.[2] There will be individual differences in how much and how fast people change toward democratic citizenship, but the broad direction of change will be toward openness. In this way, there will be a decrease in the size of the authoritarian core support that typically is associated with dictatorial leadership. Through the appropriate civic education, directed toward the goals I set out for socializing psychological citizens, it will be possible to achieve greater openness even in the context of threats associated with globalization.

I discuss the contextual changes that will diminish the likelihood of a springboard to dictatorship, which potential dictators use to spring to power. I have argued that in terms of personality characteristics, in every population there are always potential dictators available and ready to use the springboard to dictatorship if and when it should come into being. The challenge for supporters of democracy and the open society is to minimize the possibility of the springboard to dictatorship coming to life, keeping in mind that such a possibility is *never* completely eliminated. Even the most open and democratic society could experience events that lead to a regression toward dictatorship, bringing to life once again the conditions for the springboard to dictatorship and the springing to power of a dictator to end democracy. The fight to prevent dictatorship is never-ending.

ENDNOTES

1. Tolstoy (1869/1957, vol. 2., p. 1168).
2. See chapter 2 in Moghaddam (2013).

9

Continuing Dangers

Social Media, Illiberal Education, Politics as Show Business, Unbounded Bureaucracies

The 21st century brings with it enormous and complex challenges for democracy and those who desire to live in open societies. These challenges are driven in part by life-changing technological innovations, such as the Internet and numerous new social media services that have come with it (e.g., Facebook, Twitter). Another factor behind these challenges are large-scale transformations associated with globalization, such as vast movements of people across nations and regions and the backlash against immigrants, refugees, and so-called invaders in general. Common to all these factors leading to new challenges is that at least some of them also bring benefits. For example, Twitter can facilitate communications, but it can also be used as a tool to drum up populist, antidemocratic sentiments and actions.

In this chapter, I explore four main interlinked areas, starting with social media, where changes that bring some benefits also lead to serious challenges for democracy and the open society. For example, Twitter can be used to disseminate useful and accurate information, but it can also be used to spread false information. Social media "educates" the larger public, but the second and related topic I discuss in this chapter is formal mass education in the United States, which has failed to provide a robust and widespread program of civic education, leading to a public both politically engaged and capable of critical thinking about politics. Mass civic education remains weak in the United States, and this weakness opens the door to politics as show business, the topic of the third section of this chapter. In the current climate when, for many people,

http://dx.doi.org/10.1037/0000142-010
Threat to Democracy: The Appeal of Authoritarianism in an Age of Uncertainty,
by F. M. Moghaddam

politics and show business have merged, the door is open to political persuasion through emotions and surface-level arguments. This represents an insidious shift in mass American culture. In the final section, I focus on another overlooked feature of contemporary culture that is acting against the open society and democracy: the overlooked role of bureaucracy.

Received wisdom tells us that bureaucracy is politically neutral; it may be bad, but it does not favor the political left or right. This assumption is false because bureaucracy is determinedly against democracy. Wherever bureaucracy grows, openness diminishes and the spirit of democracy languishes. Academics might imagine that they are exempt from this tendency, but an examination of bureaucracy in universities demonstrates they are not exempt. Moreover, by looking at universities in other countries, we can recognize how political changes can lead Western and particularly American universities backward, toward being closed and dictatorial. I discuss my experiences in Iran as an illustrative example of the universal detrimental influence of bureaucracy at universities.

SOCIAL MEDIA

Not long ago social media held out the promise of a more enlightened politics, as accurate information and effortless communication helped good people drive out corruption, bigotry and lies. Yet Facebook acknowledged that before and after last year's American election, between January 2015 and August this year, 146m users may have seen Russian misinformation on its platform. Google's YouTube admitted to 1,108 Russian-linked videos and Twitter to 36,747 accounts. Far from bringing enlightenment, social media has been spreading poison.

—*THE ECONOMIST*[1]

Rising dictatorships are even more dangerous in the 21st century because the world is now far more integrated and democracies are more vulnerable to influence from dictators such as President Vladimir Putin of Russia. We have entered a new era in which, rather than democracies spreading the values of the open society and influencing dictatorships to become more open, dictatorships are increasingly influencing events in democracies and maneuvering them to become more closed. The influence of the Russian dictatorship in Western elections, such as in the United States and France, reflects this dangerous trend.[2]

Moreover, as pointed out in the same *Economist* article just quoted, the assumption that social media will necessarily enlighten people and strengthen democracy has proved to be too simplistic. Social media can serve as a force for democratic values, but only if safeguards are in place and great care is taken to limit the influence of dictatorial and reactionary forces. As things stand, dictatorial powers are manipulating social media to fight democracy and weaken those societies that are relatively more open.

Part of the challenge for defenders of democracy is that certain "automatic" psychological tendencies seem to favor movement toward closed rather than open societies, dictatorships rather than democracies. For example, in an important study on the spread of true and false news online, Soroush Vosoughi, Deb Roy, and Sinan Aral[3] examined a large data set of "rumor cascades" on Twitter over the years 2006 and 2017. They explored how about three million people were involved in the spreading of about 126,000 true and false rumors. They demonstrated that false rumors spread to more people than did the truth; the truth rarely reached more than 1,000 people, whereas false rumors sometimes reached 100,000 people. The truth took about six times as long as falsehood to reach 1,500 people, and falsehoods were about 70% more likely to be retweeted than the truth. Importantly, the authors found that the retweeting of false news more than the truth was characteristic of people, not robots. An earlier study by Sarita Yardi and Danah Boyd[4] showed that Twitter exposes people to a more varied viewpoints, but they need better skills to constructively engage these different others. By implication, better education is needed for people to reap the benefits of diversity in viewpoints.

Why does false news spread faster, farther, deeper, and more broadly than the truth? This is probably because false news tends to be seen as more novel and to evoke stronger emotional reactions, particularly fear, disgust, and surprise. In contrast, true stories evoked less "exciting" reactions, such as trust, joy, and sadness. The tendency for false news to spread faster helps dictators, "strongmen," and, in general, those who want to spread false news to distract from and distort the truth. Of course, the tendency for false news to travel faster than the truth is not unique to the 21st century; this trend was probably present in the 19th and earlier centuries. However, the availability of Twitter and other social media platforms magnifies the effect of false news traveling faster than the truth. This is an example of how new technologies are changing the factors associated with democracy and dictatorship.

A related challenge is to minimize the tendency for the Internet and new social media tools to magnify resource inequalities, with the poor as particular targets. Virginia Eubanks argued that whereas these new electronic systems are seen as bringing huge benefits and profits by affluent groups, the poor see them as oppressive:

> The cheerleaders of the new data regime rarely acknowledge the impacts of digital decision-making on poor and working-class people. This myopia is not shared by those lower on the economic hierarchy, who often see themselves as targets rather than beneficiaries of these systems.[5]

Similarly, Safiya Umoja Noble[6] argued that, far from being neutral, the Internet embodies and magnifies the racism and group-based inequalities of the larger society. This becomes clear when we conduct searches using key phrases such as *Black men* rather than *White men*, or *Black women* rather than *White women*, and reach very different results in terms of larger implications, reflecting various stereotypes and biases in the larger society. The monopoly of certain search engines and the tendency of powerful interest groups to promote certain websites exaggerates biases, ensuring that "web neutrality" is nonexistent—at least for the poor.

ILLIBERAL EDUCATION

I am using the term *illiberal education* here to mean education that fails to teach students *democratic citizenship*, or the ability to think and act critically in the political domain, including in political decision-making and participation. What I do not mean by this term is for students to be taught to become liberals in their political persuasion. Critical, independent thought and action is the goal, rather than any particular political orientation.

The modern education system, and particularly the U.S. system, has been the target of severe criticism and controversy, at least since the 1960s. Initially, left-wing critics of schooling, such as Ivan Illich and his call for "deschooling society,"[7] attracted the most attention. Illich and other left-wing critics depicted American schools as institutions (prisons) where young people are socialized to become conformist and obedient consumers in the capitalist marketplace. This line of criticism arose out of the broader 1960s left-wing counterculture.

But from around the 1980s, American education—and by extension, schools in Western societies—came under attack from right-wing critics who saw the demise of American and Western schools as reflecting a broader decline in Western societies. This avowed decline was reflected in test scores: Students from "disciplined" Asian societies were outperforming the "undisciplined" American and Western students. This has continued to be a theme in criticisms; as Ludger Woessmann pointed out in 2016,

> On the most recent international achievement tests in math and science, the average 15 year old student from Singapore, Hong Kong, Korea, Japan, and Taiwan is more than half a standard deviation ahead of the average student of the same age in the United States.[8]

Discussions about the "American education deficit" have varied considerably and have been influenced by politics. For example, Joel Klein, a chancellor of New York City's school system, decried the "failure of American schools."[9] John Gatto,[10] a prize-winning schoolteacher, turned against what he called the "prison" of modern schooling (in some ways echoing criticisms raised by Ivan Illich). But David Berliner and Bruce Biddle argued that the so-called crisis in America's public schools was a "myth" and a "fraud" concocted by the same financial interests who sell schools tests, textbooks, and educational technology broadly.[11] Also, behind attacks on American public schools are financial interests motivated to channel government money from public to private schools. In line with this, Steven Singer argued that "U.S. public schools are not failing. They're among the best in the world."[12]

But rather than become mired in the controversy of test scores and what they mean, my concern is with the outcomes of the kind of civic education students are (or are not) receiving. There is general agreement that schools play an important role in shaping citizenship and political engagement,[13] and there are strong arguments and solid evidence showing that people who lack information and critical-thinking abilities are less able and interested to participate in democratic politics.[14] Even in U.S. presidential elections, there has been a decline in voter participation, and only about 50% of eligible citizens now vote.[15] Participation rate is particularly low among the young; as William Galston noted,

> In the early 1970s, about half of the 18–29-year-olds in the United States voted in presidential elections. By 1996, fewer than one third did. The same pattern holds for congressional elections. . . . Only 26% of freshmen think that keeping up with politics is important, down from 58% in 1966. Only 14% say they frequently discuss politics, down from 30%.[16]

In a 2018 update on the state of civic engagement, Sarah Shapiro and Catherine Brown wrote,

> Civic knowledge and public engagement is at an all-time low. A 2016 survey by the Annenberg Public Policy Center found that only 26 percent of Americans can name all three branches of government, which was a significant decline from previous years . . . public trust in government is at only 18 percent and voter participation has reached its lowest point since 1996.[17]

The long-term trends, then, are clearly toward a less informed and less engaged citizenry.[18] My contention is that weaknesses in civic education is an important factor in this decline in political knowledge and participation. At present, civic education lacks specific goals and ideals in terms of the democratic citizen we are aspiring to socialize. In the final chapter, I propose such ideals. Next, I discuss one of the consequences of feeble civic education in the United States: politics being transformed into show business.

POLITICS AS SHOW BUSINESS

One of the greatest dangers to democracy and the open society is the merging of politics and show business, as symbolized by the presidency of Donald Trump. The role of the media and "entertainment" in politics is not new, just as merchants and owners of media always had influence in shaping political propaganda and political outcomes.[19] However, in the 21st century, we have reached a more complete merging, so that with a reality show host in the White House, everyday politics has become entertainment. We have entered what Kathryn Brownell called "showbiz politics."[20]

To better understand the deeper implications of the merging of politics and show business, we need to consider the relationship between different kinds of persuasion and the level of Machiavellianism of the leader. A very useful distinction is between *central routes to persuasion*, which involve deeper cognitive engagement, information processing, and rational problem-solving, and *peripheral routes to persuasion*, which involve persuasion more through emotions and feelings than through deep thinking.[21] For example, if I want to persuade you through the central route to buy a car from me, I would provide you with detailed written information about the car so that you could think about the technical details, costs, performance, energy savings, environmental impact, and so on. If I want to use the peripheral route, I might show you a video of glamorous people riding in the car on an open road or beside a sunny beach and get you to feel great about what you are watching. Yes, you could be driving that car with those beautiful people on the open highway.

The second factor we must consider is the level of Machiavellianism of the leader. The measure of Machiavellianism was developed by psychologists[22] using Niccolò Machiavelli's masterpiece *The Prince*[23] as a source. Those who score high on Machiavellianism see the world as a dangerous place, where nice people finish last, you have to cut corners, and you had better get the other guy before he has a chance to get you.

The interactions of high and low Machiavellianism, with central and peripheral routes to persuasion, provide various alternatives that can be conceived of as lying at some point in a space delimited by two vectors (see Figure 9.1). The polar opposites of the first vector are high Machiavellianism and low Machiavellianism, and those of the second vector are the central route and the peripheral route to persuasion. The resulting four possibilities are as follows:

1. *High Machiavellian/central route:* There is some danger to democracy because the leader is highly Machiavellian and inclined to try to manipulate events to create a closed society. However, citizens are engaged through the

FIGURE 9.1. Diagrammatic Representation of Routes to Persuasion and Level of Leader Machiavellianism

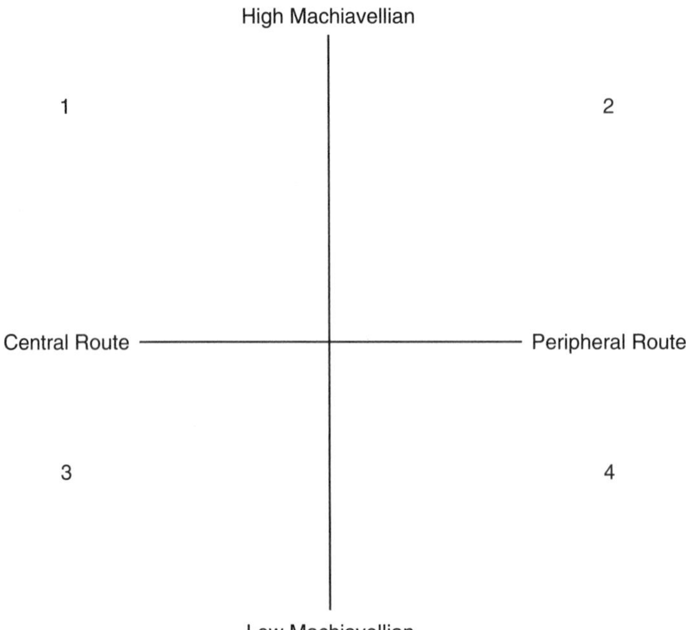

central route; therefore, they are alert to the dangers and there are safeguards (e.g., a free press, an independent judiciary) against the establishment of dictatorship.

2. *High Machiavellian/peripheral route:* There is serious danger to democracy because the leader is intent on manipulating events to try to create a closed society, and the citizens are persuaded primarily through emotions and feeling, rather than serious critical thinking.
3. *Low Machiavellian/central route:* This situation poses the least danger to democracy. This is because the leader does not tend to manipulate events to create a closed society, and at the same time, citizens are cognitively engaged in critically assessing political issues.
4. *Low Machiavellian/peripheral route:* There is not a danger to democracy directly from the leader, but there is still some danger because individuals close to the leader might try to manipulate his decisions to damage democracy. Also, because the citizens are persuaded though the peripheral route, antidemocratic manipulations perpetrated through the leadership have a chance to succeed.

Thus, when the peripheral route to persuasion is more available and the leader is highly Machiavellian, there is a greater probability that "fake news" and "we make reality up as we go along" will become the norm. Related to this, Trump made 3,001 false or misleading claims in his first 466 days in office; the nonpartisan fact-checking organization PolitiFact rated 69% of Trump's statements as "mostly false," "false," or "pants on fire," compared with 26% of statements made by Obama.[24]

Perhaps even more insidious than deception in politics is the influence of factors that work against democracy but are seldom recognized. In the next section, I examine the illustrative example of bureaucracy, which tends to work against democracy and openness.[25] I turn specifically to bureaucracy in universities because there is a tendency for academics to imagine that they are immune from this problem.

UNBOUNDED BUREAUCRACIES

"Rule by Nobody"

—HANNAH ARENDT[26]

Bureaucracies are the unseen and insidious enemies of democracy. As Arendt pointed out, in bureaucracies "nobody" rules, and so nobody can be held accountable. Bureaucracies have enormous subterranean power, in the sense that it is covert, often invisible power, and thus extremely difficult to fight against. Brazilian dictator Getúlio Vargas (1882–1954) hinted at this as he promised, "For my friends everything, for my enemies the law."[27]

Bureaucracies can entangle critics and nonconformists in legal quagmires. Of course, bureaucracies are not unique to dictatorships. Armies of bureaucrats also thrive in North America, the European Union, and other relatively open parts of the world. Some characteristics of bureaucracies are universal and not confined to any particular society.

The universal aspects of bureaucracies become more apparent when we compare the same institutions functioning in different societies. I have had an opportunity to visit many different universities around the world over the past 40 years. A startling feature of universities since the 1960s is the rapid expansion of bureaucracy in the shape of "university administration." As in so many other areas, the United States has set the pace, with the growth of "top-down" administrations in American universities being nothing less than startling.[28] Between 1993 and 2007, inflation-adjusted spending on university administration increased by 61%, while instructional spending increased by 39%.[29] It is one thing to review the statistics on how full-time administrators are being hired at a much faster rate than full-time faculty, but it is very different to actually experience this dramatic change (and the accompanying increases in tuition) in my everyday life at work.

In a detailed critical assessment, Todd Zywicki and Christopher Koopman identified the expansion of administrations in universities as probably the main reason for the rapid rise in tuition in American universities.[30] On the one hand, pay for the senior administrators has risen sharply, with the highest paid university president receiving more than $7 million in 2012 and 36 university presidents receiving more than $1 million that year.[31] On the other hand, there has been a rise of the number of administrators in universities: "In 1990, at both private institutions and public research universities, full-time faculty outnumbered administrators (executive and professional staff), but by 2012, administrators outnumbered full-time faculty."[32]

The universal features of university administration became clearer to me during my work in universities in Iran following the 1979 revolution. The universities in Iran became a thorn in the side of Khomeini and his fanatical followers, as they pushed hard to transform Iranian society according to their particular extremist interpretation of Islam. Khomeini decided that he could not control opposition forces centered in universities, so he copied Chairman Mao's so-called Cultural Revolution and forcibly closed down the universities (as discussed in the Introduction to this volume). Whereas Mao unleashed his Red Guards against universities and intellectuals in China, Khomeini's attack on universities and intellectuals was spearheaded by "Students in the line of the Imam," who in terms of personality and mission were very similar to Mao's Red Guards. They were dogmatic and dedicated to shutting down intellectual inquiry and showed complete obedience to their ancient leader (Mao in China and Khomeini in Iran).

I was active on the campus of both the National University and Tehran University during the last days of freedom, before those two institutions were forcibly shut down and successive destructive purges were carried out to enforce obedience and conformity with Khomeini's wishes. These purges were highly detrimental with respect to Iran's national interests because they eliminated a generation of highly trained Iranian professionals and intellectuals, just as Mao's purges during his Cultural Revolution of the 1960s eliminated a generation of the most highly educated Chinese. However, the university closings and academic purges in Iran helped Khomeini suffocate opposition to his dictatorship.

At the start of the "cultural revolution" in Iran in 1980, I resigned from university work. I was not willing to be "reeducated" to fit with Khomeini's reactionary and utterly backward ideas about what a university should be. It was relatively easy for me to take this step because I was single and did not have a wife or children to worry about—or them to worry about me. Some other faculty members were married with children and had heavy financial responsibilities. It was far more difficult for them to resign from their university positions, although many of them were forcibly removed in the course of Khomeini's "revolutionary" purges over the next few years.

Having resigned, I still needed to visit the National University to resolve my final salary payment. I assumed that I would be able to collect my back pay quickly because nothing was going on at the National University—or any other university in Iran. All the students and faculty had been kicked off campus, all classes and research had come to a standstill, and only administrators were on campus. I imagined that in this situation, the administrators would be sitting around with nothing to do, and I would quickly finish my business and leave the university. How wrong I was!

When I went to the main administration building at the National University, I found it was difficult to get an appointment—the administrators were busy! Yet there were no students or faculty on campus, no classes and no research; the main activities of the university had come to a complete stop. What were the administrators doing? After asking around and trying in different ways to make appointments to get my back pay, I realized that the university administrators did not need students or faculty, classes or research, to keep them busy: They created work for themselves and set up meetings and committees to keep up a fast pace of activity. It was as if the main job of the university was administration; the students and faculty were an addition, or even a nuisance.

I eventually did receive my back pay, but more important, I learned that the university administration behaves as a self-regulating independent system, with a strong tendency to survive and even expand irrespective of events outside itself. The fate of universities in countries such as Iran and China might seem remote and far-removed from Western universities, but it would be a grave mistake to imagine so. Universities in Western countries, and particularly in the United States, have become overwhelmed by bloated administrations and enormous bureaucracies. This is one of the factors resulting in faculty having less and less real influence on how universities are governed and of the universities failing to serve as strong enough safeguards for democracy in the larger society.

CONCLUDING COMMENT

The road to actualized democracy is long and winding. At times, this road bends back toward dictatorship, as is now taking place in a number of countries around the world. The examples of countries taking this route are varied. In some cases, such as Russia, Iran, and Egypt, there was a collapse of dictatorship, and a brief "opportunity bubble" presented a real possibility of societal movement toward democracy. However, limits on political plasticity mean that the collapse of one dictatorship often leads to the rise of another, with a different front. In some other cases, countries that seemed to have taken a slower, longer road toward democracy, such as Turkey and Venezuela, have now once again turned back toward dictatorship. A third group of countries are the more developed democracies, such as the United States, Italy, and Hungary, which have now voted to empower populist antidemocratic leaders and face a more uncertain future. In this chapter, I have examined four of the main factors behind these developments, associated with a turn away from the open society. In the next chapter, I explore solutions and the question of how we can better safeguard democracy.

ENDNOTES

1. "Do Social Media Threaten Democracy?" (2017, p. 11).
2. See Calabresi (2017).
3. Vosoughi, Roy, and Aral (2018).
4. Yardi and Boyd (2010).
5. Eubanks (2017, p. 9).
6. Noble (2018).
7. Illich (1970).
8. Woessmann (2016, p. 3).
9. Klein (2011).
10. Gatto (2017).
11. Berliner and Biddle (1996).
12. Singer (2017).
13. For international debates on "teaching for democracy," see discussions in Laker, Naval, and Mrnjaus (2014).
14. Elkin and Soltan (1999).
15. See Teixeira (1992).
16. Galston (2001).
17. S. Shapiro and Brown (2018).
18. See also the extensive review of 50 years of survey data on what Americans know about politics by Delli Carpini and Keeter (1996).
19. The readings in Schulman and Zelizer (2017) suggest that the United States has always been a "media nation," with entertainment part of politics.
20. Brownell (2014).
21. See Petty and Cacioppo (1986).
22. Christie and Geise (1970).
23. Machiavelli (1532/1950).
24. Morris (2018).

25. Gormley and Balla (2013) have examined ways in which the detrimental impact of bureaucracy on democracy might be mitigated.
26. Arendt (1970).
27. See O'Donnell (2004, p. 40).
28. As far back as the 1980s and 1990s, critics were pointing out the sharp rise in administrative costs in U.S. universities; see Leslie and Rhoades (1995).
29. Greene (2015).
30. Zywicki and Koopman (2017).
31. P. Jacobs (2014).
32. See American Institute for Research (2014), which actually attempts to avoid the conclusion that administrative costs are to blame for rising university costs.

10

Solutions

How to Defeat Dictatorship

Every function in the child's cultural development appears twice: first, on the social level, and later, on the individual level, first between people (interpsychological) and then inside the child (intrapsychological). . . . All the higher functions originate as actual relationships between individuals.[1]

—LEV VYGOTSKY (1896–1934)

Solutions are only as good as the theories they are based on. In this chapter, I put forward practical solutions to defeating dictatorship based on what I call the *foundational position*: that social processes and relations between people shape cognitive processes and how people think at the individual level, an idea that goes back in modern times[2] to Lev Vygotsky. The foundational position has vitally important implications for our understanding of human behavior.[3]

Intraindividual processes and dispositional characteristics, such as personality traits, are also important in influencing thinking and action, but only at a secondary level. One of the advantages of this approach is to avoid *reductionism*, the tendency to explain phenomena through reference to the smallest units (e.g., to processes within individuals rather than to group or societies processes), and the *mereological fallacy*,[4] the tendency to attribute the qualities of wholes (e.g., collectives) to parts (e.g., individuals), a topic discussed in more detail later in this chapter.

http://dx.doi.org/10.1037/0000142-011
Threat to Democracy: The Appeal of Authoritarianism in an Age of Uncertainty,
by F. M. Moghaddam

THE FOUNDATIONAL POSITION

The foundational position proposes that dictatorship arises primarily out of the political, economic, and cultural conditions of the larger society. It is these macro-level conditions that give rise to the emergence of a springboard to dictatorship.[5] The springboard to dictatorship establishes the larger context and creates possibilities for a power-grab by potential dictators. Thus, the concept of springboard to dictatorship is in line with the foundational position, conceptualizing individual-level thinking and action as emerging from collective processes and relations between people.

When individuals enter this world, there is already a normative system in place, guiding people and indicating what are correct and incorrect ways of thinking and acting. The normative system, which consists of norms, rules, values, attitudes, and all other facets of a culture, socializes people and guides behavior. The power of this normative system arises from its shared and collective nature: It functions above and beyond individuals and is to be found in the collectively upheld processes that are passed on from group to group, generation to generation.

Individual-level factors, such as personality traits, do play a role in behavior. However, there is a tendency in the context of the United States, and to some degree all Western societies, to engage in reductionism and to exaggerate the role of individual level characteristics. In essence, the tendency is to engage in the mereological fallacy, attributing the properties of wholes to parts, mistaking what are societal sources of influence to individual sources. This strong tendency toward reductionism stems in large part from the deeply engrained "self-help" and "individual responsibility" ideology pervading the United States and to some degree all capitalist societies.[6]

The individualistic ideology of the United States and other capitalist societies holds individuals responsible for their successes and failures. This ideology proposes that if Manon is a billionaire and Mary is unemployed and penniless, this is because of the individual characteristics of Manon and Mary, such as Manon being more hardworking, intelligent, and highly motivated and Mary being lazy, low in intelligence, and lacking talent and motivation. In other words, the poor are poor because each of them individually lacks what is needed to be rich, and the rich are rich because each of them individually has the characteristics needed to be rich. Research such as the *marshmallow test*, which showed an association between a child's ability to delay gratification and adult achievement and behaviors,[7] seemed to support this individualistic view. But on closer inspection, it turns out that family background, particularly social class, strongly influences behavior on the marshmallow test.[8] Increasingly, researchers are recognizing the behavior of individuals as highly context dependent.[9]

The foundational position leads us to a number of specific policy solutions, which I will discuss in turn. The first policy solution for movement toward fuller democracy is to adopt specific ideal goals in programs for socializing democratic citizens. These ideal goals should become integral to civic education.

A great deal of attention has been given to the link between education and democracy,[10] but civic education for democracy continues to languish in the vast majority of countries. In the previous chapter, I discussed the weakness of civic education in the United States, as reflected in decreasing political engagement and participation, particularly among younger citizens. In this chapter, I propose specific ideal goals for this education.

Second, I propose civil society action groups that will be effective from the ground up to fight against dictatorship and move societies toward greater openness.

Third, I put forward a model for managing diversity, which maximizes inclusiveness and prevents displacement of aggression, a favorite tactic used by authoritarian strongmen.

EDUCATION AND SOCIALIZATION

In recent history, the ideas of John Dewey[11] have been particularly influential in arguing that education promotes democracy. Economists such as Seymour Martin Lipset[12] have worked with the same assumption, adding that along with education, economic growth also contributes to the growth of democracy. A series of empirical studies have put forward strong evidence in support of the link between education and democracy,[13] a link that is generally assumed to be true, at least in Western intellectual circles. It seems to make intuitive sense that education should promote democracy. However, Daren Acemoglu and colleagues[14] are among a number of researchers who empirically test this relationship and find it to be invalid. They document that "the lack of a relationship between education and democracy is highly robust." So, what are we to make of these contradictory arguments and findings?

The main reason for the differences in findings is that education has been treated as something uniformly good: More education has been assumed to be better, irrespective of the content of education. But this is an incorrect assumption: More years of schooling will not lead to a democratic citizen if the schooling is socializing children to be antidemocratic. To take two extreme examples, more years of schooling in an extremist Christian/White supremacist school in the United States or a fundamentalist Islamic seminary (*madrassa*) in Pakistan will not lead to a democratic citizen. Education has the power to shape young people, and more education can create democrats, but it can also create anti-science, antidemocratic citizens who support authoritarian strongman rule.

We now have available the objective criteria necessary to distinguish between prodemocracy and antidemocracy education.[15] We can also identify the psychological characteristics we need to nurture to socialize democratic citizens. In what follows, I summarize the main psychological characteristics of the democratic citizen; these are the characteristics we must nurture in the young so that they grow up to support democracy rather than dictatorship.

We can identify a cluster of 10 psychological characteristics essential for democratic citizenship. These characteristics were developed as part of a larger research project on the psychology of democracy,[16] and in 2018, an international research conference was held at Aarhus University, Denmark, to critically evaluate and explore the psychology of democracy project. A book was published[17] based on this international conference, resulting in further development of the basic ideas in democratic citizenship. These developments underscored the importance of considering the characteristics of democratic citizens as an integral whole. Democratic citizenship develops through individuals acquiring all of these characteristics to a large degree, not just one or a few of them.

We can conceptualize the 10 characteristics of democratic citizenship as forming a circle, with each of 10 "slices" in the circle representing a key characteristic. The first characteristic is the ability to begin any action or thought with the acceptance that "I could be wrong." This acceptance is easier in some domains than others. For example, most people find it easier to accept that they could be wrong about their beliefs in the area of cooking than about their beliefs in the area of politics or religion. However, the ability to leave open the possibility that one might be wrong forms a doorway for future healthy growth and development. Second, the individual must adopt the view that "I must critically question everything, including the sacred beliefs of my society." Thus, it is not only personal but also societal beliefs that must be continuously and critically evaluated, with the acceptance that sacred societal beliefs could be wrong. Extensive psychological research[18] demonstrates that the questioning of sacred societal beliefs is difficult because it can lead to a clash with others in the ingroup, resulting in extreme pressures on the individual to conform, obey, and "fall in line" with the normative system of the ingroup.

Related to the first two characteristics, the third characteristic is the belief that "I must revise my opinion as the evidence requires." The reference to "evidence" is important and connects to science and evidence-based reasoning. Democratic citizens are able to identify and absorb objective evidence and revise their own worldviews based on new evidence. In contrast to this, authoritarian citizens dismiss objective evidence that contradicts their worldviews and in essence reject science.

The next two characteristics concern the relationship between citizens and others who are different from the sacred group in important ways, such as being from a different ethnic, language, or religious group: fourth, "I must seek to understand those who are different from me" and fifth, "I can learn from those who are different from me." The first step involves understanding others who are different. After understanding, the possibility opens up of learning from others who are different. Again, this is easier to achieve in some areas than others. For example, it is easier for most people first to understand how the Chinese cook rice and, second, to learn from how Chinese cook rice, than it is to understand and learn from religious beliefs and practices among Chinese people.

The next three characteristics of democratic citizenship involve information-seeking and the gaining and sharing of experiences: sixth, "I must seek information and opinions from different sources"; seventh, "I should be actively open to new experiences"; eighth, "I should be open to creating new experiences for others." The underlying theme of these three characteristics is openness: being open to new information and experiences, on the understanding that the acquisition of new information and experiences is essential to both collective and individual human growth and actualization. To achieve such openness, citizens need to have high *tolerance for ambiguity*, a tendency to view ambiguous situations positively, and also high *open-mindedness*, a tendency to revise one's own position in light of evidence.[19]

The first eight requirements for democratic citizenship tend to move the individual toward a relativistic orientation. These requirements involve individuals questioning the beliefs they and their societies hold, being ready to revise beliefs based on evidence, being open to learn from others, and provide learning experiences for others. The result might be a citizen who adopts an "anything goes" attitude and lacks principles. However, the final two requirements are designed to rectify this situation and move citizens away from relativism. The ninth requirement is "There are principles of right and wrong," and the tenth "I should actively seek experiences of higher value." These two requirements are clearly based on the belief that everything is not relative, and we can identify certain criteria and values that are universally acceptable as better, as reflected, for example, by the *Universal Declaration of Human* Rights[20] (discussed in Chapter 4, this volume) put forward by the United Nations.[21] Of course, there continue to be violations of human rights, but the Declaration stands as an ideal, reflecting universal principles. Similarly, the 10 requirements for democratic citizenship outlined here present an ideal toward which we should aspire—a set of goals we should adopt in schools, families, and other units engaged in the socialization of children with the end result of "making democratic citizens."

CIVIL SOCIETY ACTION GROUPS

The successful path to defeating dictatorship will always be bottom-up, mobilizing the masses to be directly involved. This is not only to topple the existing dictatorship but also to increase the probability that the existing dictatorship will be succeeded by a more democratic society rather than by yet another dictatorship—the pattern of one dictatorship being followed by another, even after major revolutions, has become very familiar in history.[22]

The solution of bottom-up civil disobedience and activism is suggested by in-depth explorations of resistance to dictatorship. For example, Adrian Karatnycky and Peter Ackerman[23] used Freedom House data to explore changes from dictatorship to democracy over a 33-year period and concluded that

> dictatorships collapse and new states and new democracies arise by a variety of means . . . **far more often than is generally understood, the change agent is broad-based, nonviolent civic resistance—which employs tactics such as boycotts, mass protests, blockades, strikes, and civil disobedience to de-legitimate authoritarian rulers and erode their sources of support, including** the loyalty of their armed defenders [bold in the original].[24]

In another extensive study focused on 323 violent and nonviolent movements that took place between 1900 and 2006, Erica Chenoweth and Maria

Stephan[25] showed that 53% of the nonviolent movements succeeded compared with 27% of violent movements. Experimental research also suggests that nonviolent movements are perceived as more legitimate and more likely to influence public opinion.[26]

This bottom-up approach to resisting dictatorship is influenced by Henry Thoreau's famous essay *Civil Disobedience*,[27] in which he argued for the importance of action on the basis of personal conscience ("The only obligation which I have a right to assume is to do at any time what I think right"[28]) and the power of the minority when people act collectively ("A minority is powerless while it conforms to the majority . . . but it is irresistible when it clogs by its whole weight"[29]). Since the 20th century, Thoreau's ideas have been associated with the Gandhian model[30] of nonviolence, and civil disobedience movements in India and South Africa are taken to be prime examples of how this approach can be successful. In the United States, the nonviolent movement is associated with the historic advances made by civil rights movement and the leadership style of Martin Luther King (1929–1968).

But the discussion of nonviolent movements needs to be strengthened in several ways. First, it is a mistake to see bottom-up movements as synonymous with nonviolent movements. There are various movements that resist dictatorship using bottom-up support but are not nonviolent. This includes resistance shown by smaller nations against larger nations. For example, President Josip Broz Tito (1892–1980) led Yugoslavia to resist Soviet domination during the very difficult post–World War II era.[31] Even though the Soviets considered Yugoslavia on "their side" of the Iron Curtain, Tito was able to push back against Stalin and attain some independence for Yugoslavia because he used his World War II experiences of building up the resistance to the Nazis invaders. The Soviets were aware that if they invaded Yugoslavia, they would face the same kind of bottom-up resistance movement that gave so much trouble to the Nazis. Of course, Tito was not a democratic leader, but as a nationalist, he could rely on grassroots support against Stalin and the possibility of a Soviet invasion.

The second way in which the discussion of nonviolent movements needs to be strengthened is to adopt a more sophisticated approach to understanding revolutions that topple dictatorial regimes. In many cases, despite adopting a nonviolent approach, such revolutions result in the collapse of a dictatorship, but also the rise of a new dictatorship from the ashes of the last one. As Gene Sharp (1928–2018) pointed out in his insightful and practical set of ideas on how to fight dictatorship,

> the collapse of an oppressive regime will be seen by some persons and groups as merely the opportunity for them to step in as the new masters. . . . The new dictatorship may even be more cruel and total in its control than the old one."[32]

For example, in recent history, nonviolent movements brought an end to the dictatorships of Mohammad Reza Pahlavi (1919–1980) in Iran in 1979 and Hosni Mubarak (b. 1928) in Egypt in 2011. However, despite the grassroots support for these movements and their largely nonviolent nature, the fall of the existing dictatorship was followed by the rise of another one: that of Ruhollah

Khomeini and then Ali Khamenei in Iran and that of Abdel Fattah el-Sisi in Egypt. Thus, mass participation and nonviolence are not enough to ensure that a revolution will lead to the rise of democracy rather than another dictatorship after a revolution that topples an existing dictatorship.

THE OPPORTUNITY BUBBLE AFTER THE DICTATOR IS TOPPLED

The toppling of a dictatorship is only the first step, and often the easiest step, to developing a democracy. After the fall of a dictatorship, an *opportunity bubble* is created, a brief time period during which the conditions can begin to be set up for creating a democracy—or society can be dragged back to dictatorship by a strongman and his supporters, as I witnessed in Iran and has taken place after so many other revolutions. The reason it is so difficult for prodemocracy forces to take advantage of the opportunity bubble to move society toward long-term openness after the fall of a dictator has to do with the psychological characteristics of a population that develop in the context of dictatorship.

The population living in a dictatorship develops a psychological style, ways of thinking and acting, that are functional for life in dictatorship. For example, common to most dictatorships is a requirement that parents socialize their children to present themselves in radically different ways in public versus in private, to learn to present the family in such a way in public so as not to reveal how the family actually thinks and acts in the privacy of their home. As part of this training, children learn not to repeat in public the jokes their parents and family privately make about the ruling dictator and his regime stooges. Making jokes about the dictator can result in being jailed or even worse. As a rule, people learn they should not question or criticize what the dictator says, but treat the dictator's utterances as law.

Civil society action groups offer a mechanism to change the style of social relations, and specifically leader–follower relations, learned in dictatorships. The challenge is to bring these action groups into effect within the brief time period available, the opportunity bubble,[33] after a revolution. Most important, these action groups must focus on changing relations between leaders and followers, toward supporting a more open society. Because of limits to political plasticity,[34] creating and making effective civil society action groups must receive the highest priority.

Civil society action groups should take as their models successful grassroots movements.[35] The examples they select must lead to two types of activities: first, swift, short-term action to immediately deal with potential or actual dictatorship. These actions include mass marches and the mobilization of social movements. But the selected models should also lead to long-term, stable, ongoing, extended, grassroots networks, which are resilient enough to withstand the backlash that often takes place against prodemocracy social movements. For example, consider the backlash against the women's movement ongoing in the 21st century.[36]

The women's movement has made enormous advances since the early 20th century, despite still having a long way to go to achieve equality in political and financial domains. Consider that at the start of the 20th century, women still were not permitted to register as students in the vast majority of university courses.[37] At the start of the 21st century, there are more women than men enrolled at most major universities, and the discussion has shifted to "boys being left behind."[38] The women's movement has made progress in education through grassroots action and by competing directly and successfully with men. The battle is far from over, but now the number of women succeeding in the most competitive law schools, medical schools, business schools, and other professional schools is about equal to men. African American women have made particularly impressive advances compared with African American men.[39] This is an enormous advance from a century ago and provides a blueprint for how a collective movement can succeed.

Another successful movement was the antislavery mobilization that resulted in the formal end of slavery in the United States.[40] The abolition movement involved active participation on the part of slaves and freed Black people, as well as White Americans, with both women and men represented in all major abolitionist groups. The many challenges faced by African Americans in 21st-century America[41] tend to blind us to the enormous success of the abolitionist movement, as well as the civil rights movement that resulted in major legal and political reforms from the 1960s. These historic successes are long term and supportive of the larger movement toward actualized democracy.

At the same time we must be alert to the dangers posed by a strategy of emphasizing and exaggerating the distinctiveness of different groups, rather than what they have in common. I elaborate on this point in the next section.

MANAGING DIVERSITY AND THE OMNICULTURAL SOLUTION

A favorite tactic of prodictatorship forces is the targeting of minorities, displacing aggression onto minorities, encouraging ethnocentrism and xenophobia in the majority group, and using hatred against minorities to radicalize and mobilize their authoritarian supporters. This tactic is easier to use in societies characterized by ethnic, cultural, religious, and other forms of diversity, such as the United States and increasingly the European Union. However, as suggested by research using the minimal group paradigm (discussed in Chapter 6), group differences can be manufactured even when the actual differences between groups are trivial. Consequently, even when there are no objectively important differences between groups, it is still possible for minority groups to be marginalized and manipulated and to become a target of hatred based on trivial intergroup differences. Thus, psychological research suggests that prodictatorship forces have opportunities to put into effect the targeting of minorities and displacement of aggression even in societies that are relatively homogeneous and have little diversity on the basis of objective measures.

The traditional policies for managing diversity can be conceptualized as lying on a continuum, with complete assimilation at one extreme and complete multiculturalism at the other extreme (see Figure 10.1).

The most common form of assimilation is minority assimilation, which involves minority groups changing themselves to assimilate into the majority group. This change is often achieved through learning the majority language and taking on the majority culture, but where there are marked phenotypic differences between groups (e.g., skin color and other such physical differences), then there are obvious limits to how minority assimilation can take place. Despite such limits to assimilation, psychological research strongly suggests that the greater the similarity between people, the greater the attraction. On this basis, an argument in favor of assimilation is that a society composed of people who are more similar to one another will be more cohesive and less fragmented and will suffer fewer conflicts.

On the other hand, research on the minimal group paradigm suggests that no matter how similar people are on objective criteria, differences between them can be manufactured and exaggerated by those who are motivated to create conflicts between minority and majority groups. Besides, why should minorities assimilate and abandon their heritage cultures and languages? Why should majority cultures and languages be the dominant norm? Such questions and critical rethinking about the merits of different cultures eventually led to the rise of multiculturalism as a policy for managing diversity.[42]

Multiculturalism has been hailed as progressive and recognized as the "politically correct" policy for managing diversity, at least since the late 20th century. The main reason for the privileged position of multiculturalism is the recognition and support it is assumed to provide minorities and their ways of life. There are different forms and interpretations of multiculturalism, but common to most of these are two propositions: first, that group-based differences should be recognized and celebrated and, second, that the recognition and celebration of group-based differences will result in better relations between all minority and majority groups. Integral to this second proposition is the so-called multiculturalism hypothesis, which predicts that when group members feel confidence and pride in their own heritage cultures, they will be more open and accepting toward out-group members. Although the political motivation to safeguard group-based differences has widespread support in many 21st-century societies, the scientific basis for multiculturalism policy is highly questionable.

On the basis of empirical research, I will point out just three shortcomings of multiculturalism policy. First, both empirical research and historical examples raise serious questions about the multiculturalism hypothesis: Groups that are confident about and proud of their own heritage are not necessarily open and accepting toward outgroups—the Nazis, Islamic fundamentalists, radical "Whites only" nationalists in the European Union and the United States; the examples

FIGURE 10.1. The Assimilation-Multiculturalism Continuum

Extreme Assimilation -- Extreme Multiculturalism are many. Second, the celebration of group-based differences has in practice been associated with the manufacturing, exaggeration, and highlighting of such differences. From an early age in schools, children are being taught about how they are different. Third, the focus on how minorities and majorities are different has tended to be associated with how minorities and majorities have available different paths to success (unlike women, who have competed head-on with men in education). Subtle and implicit messages are given to minority children, guiding them to "their" ways to shine, which tend to be in sports and entertainment rather than in academia and traditional professional careers.

In short, the practical outcome of "celebrating differences" through multiculturalism policy has been to tell minority children from a very early age, subtly and sometimes not so subtly, that they are different and their paths to success are not the same as majority children. The outcome of this process is clear: Underperformance by minority children at just about every level of schooling (in contrast to the progress made by women in general). Clearly, an alternative path should be adopted for managing diversity.

The alternative path I believe to be far better than both assimilation and multiculturalism is one that first recognizes and celebrates human commonalities and second gives attention to differences between groups, in line with psychological research that supports the benefits of developing and giving primacy to a common identity.[43] I refer to this policy as *omniculturalism*, with *omni* meaning "all."[44] The basic idea of omniculturalism is that children are first socialized to learn about and give importance to all humans as a superordinate category; omniculturalism gives priority to what all humans have in common. This is in line with research demonstrating that when different people think of themselves as part of a common group identity, they show less intergroup bias.[45]

Thus, although multiculturalism is the politically correct and favored policy, it has led to the manufacturing and exaggeration of between-group differences. Rather than helping minority children, multiculturalism has sidetracked them by highlighting how they are different and should try to succeed along nonmainstream paths. The unintended consequence has been poor academic performance among minorities. The policy of omniculturalism is proposed as a healthy alternative, for all groups.

CONCLUDING COMMENT

The threat faced by democracies in the 21st century is serious and widespread. We must not adopt the lazy and incorrect assumption that democracies will inevitably win out over dictatorships; the future of open societies remains uncertain. Supporters of democracy have to fight to move the world away from dictatorship and away from the magnetic lure of strongmen who promise freedom and glory but in practice deliver corruption, injustice, and conflict. I have explored some solutions to overcoming dictatorship as a modest step in the larger struggle for more open societies. Many more possible solutions need to be put forward and tested.

ENDNOTES

1. Vygotsky (1978, p. 57).
2. One could argue that ideas about the social origins of cognition go back to ancient times, as reflected for example by the thinking of Marcus Aurelius (121 A.D.–180 A.D.): "The mind of the universe is social" (180/1964, p. 88).
3. Harré and Moghaddam (2012).
4. Bennett and Hacker (2003).
5. For a full discussion of the springboard to dictatorship, see Moghaddam (2013).
6. Critics have made this point for some time now; see Sampson (1977).
7. Mischel (2014).
8. Watts, Duncan, and Quan (2018).
9. For example, whereas the traditional research on memory attempted to exclude context, there is now growing awareness that to understand human memory processes, it is essential to include context (see discussions in Stone & Bietti, 2016).
10. The seminal book on education and democracy by John Dewey (1916) is well known, but Dewey turned his attention to this topic earlier (Dewey, 1903).
11. Dewey (1903, 1916).
12. Lipset (1959).
13. See Glaeser, Ponzetto, and Shleifer (2007), who referenced a series of relevant papers and also presented evidence to support a causal link between education and democracy.
14. Acemoglu, Johnson, Robinson, and Yared (2005).
15. For example, see Biesta (2016) and Parry (2015).
16. Moghaddam (2016b).
17. Wagoner, de Luna, and Glaveanu (2018).
18. For an overview of this research, see Chapters 15 and 16 in Moghaddam (2005a).
19. For a more in-depth discussion, see Moghaddam (2016b, Chapter 2; 2016a).
20. United Nations (1948).
21. Regarding human universals, also see Brown (1991).
22. For a more extensive discussion, see Moghaddam (2013).
23. See Karatnycky and Ackerman (n.d.)
24. Karatnycky and Ackerman (n.d., pp. 1–2)
25. Chenoweth and Stephan (2011).
26. This is suggested by the research of Winnifred Louis (2009) and her colleagues (e.g., Thomas & Louis, 2014).
27. Thoreau (2003).
28. Thoreau (2003, p. 266).
29. Thoreau (2003, p. 275).
30. Nepstad (2011).
31. For a fuller discussion of Tito's leadership and his confrontation with Stalin, see Piotrow (1958) and Banac (1988).
32. Sharp (2010, p. 74).
33. Moghaddam and Breckenridge (2011).
34. Moghaddam (2018b, 2018c).
35. Staples (2016).
36. The backlash against the women's movement is prominent in social media; for example, see Fallon (2018).
37. For a history of American higher education, see Thelin (2011). For a more critical discussion of the progress of women in education, see Unterhalter and North (2010).

38. Fortin, Oreopoulos, and Phipps (2015).
39. Bush, Chambers, and Walpole (2009).
40. Sinha (2017).
41. There is extensive research demonstrating that the problem of racial bias persists and the practical implications are important (Swencionis & Goff, 2017).
42. Moghaddam (2008b, 2016a).
43. For example, see Gaertner and Dovidio (2012).
44. Moghaddam (2009).
45. See the research on the common group identity model by Gaertner and Dovidio (2012).

AFTERWORD

Imagine you are trapped in a raging fire and are feeling terrified, running through the winding corridors of an enormous skyscraper.[1] You are having a dream, but the emotions you experience during your sleep are intense and seem painfully real. Your heart is racing, as you dream you are running faster and faster through one long, smoke-filled corridor after another. You can hear screams and cries for help—there are other people somewhere out there still fighting to stay alive in the midst of the flames, but you do not come across anyone else as you gasp for air and rush through another corridor. It is difficult to see more than a few feet away, and you can hardly breathe, but fear drives you on through what seem like endless corridors.

You feel completely lost. Did you just double back and retrace your steps? Are you running in circles? The fire is getting more intense, and now flames shoot across the corridors, blocking your movement. There is no way out. The flames singe your clothes and lick your body. Then, miraculously, a door bursts open, sunshine floods through, and a firefighter grabs your hand and leads you to safety. You are out in the street, in sunlight, safe, breathing fresh air. You calm down. You are saved.

This move from the burning building to the safety outside is *first-order change*. You are still in a dream, but now you do not experience intense fear. You feel safe and calm. Your breathing is back to normal. You sleep restfully. There has been change, but the change has taken place while you continue to sleep.

http://dx.doi.org/10.1037/0000142-012
Threat to Democracy: The Appeal of Authoritarianism in an Age of Uncertainty,
by F. M. Moghaddam

Next, imagine you are in the middle of the same dream, stuck in a skyscraper, with a raging fire sweeping through the building. You rush from corridor to corridor, trying to find a way out, away from the smoke and spreading flames. You know there are other people somewhere in the building, you can hear them screaming for help, but the thick smoke prevents you from seeing anyone else or any exits to escape. You try to call out for help, but the smoke chokes you, and the loud crashing sounds all around drown out your feeble voice. You can hardly hear yourself cry for help. You fall to your knees, breathless, about to pass out. You feel so terrified that you scream and jump awake. You are sitting up in your own bed, awake, and relieved. It was only a dream. After a few minutes you feel safe and calm. You reassure yourself, it was only a dream.

Moving from being asleep to being awake is *second-order change*. This is change from one system to another, from one kind of consciousness to another. Second-order change involves not just a change in material circumstances but also a change in psychological state.

In supporting the strongman, people seek to achieve second-order change, a change promised by the strongman. The rhetoric of the strongman launches people to imagine a different kind of world, one in which their sacred group—whether it is America, or Islam, or Christian Europe, or Hindus, or some other group—is "great again."

The promise of the strongman is not only that "you will have a better standard of living" but also that "we will be great and free again. I am the only one who can bring about the change—the real change—you want. I am the only one who can give you the freedom and security you need. Our group was great, and I will lead us to greatness again." But of course the strongman's promise is false, and the people who follow him remain stuck in a sleeping state; they only experience first-order change. The strongman leads them from one dream to another but never to second-order change; never from sleep to being awake.

ENDNOTE

1. For a more in-depth discussion of the sources of ideas in this section, see Moghaddam (2002), Moghaddam (2013), Taylor and de la Sablonnière (2014), and also the work of the "Palo Alto group," Watzlawick, Weakland, and Fisch (1974).

REFERENCES

Abdel-Samad, H. (2016). *Islamic fascism*. New York, NY: Prometheus Books. (Original work published 2014)

Acemoglu, D., Johnson, S., Robinson, J. A., & Yared, P. (2005). From education to democracy? *The American Economic Review, 95*, 44–49. http://dx.doi.org/10.1257/000282805774669916

Adorno, T. W., Frenkel-Brunswik, E., Levinson, D. J., & Sanford, B. W. (1950). *The authoritarian personality*. New York, NY: Harper & Row.

Al-Rasheed, M. (2018). *Salman's legacy: The dilemmas of a new era in Saudi Arabia*. New York, NY: Oxford University Press.

Albertazzi, D., & McDonnell, D. (Eds.). (2008). *21st century populism: The spectre of Western European democracy*. New York, NY: Palgrave Macmillan. http://dx.doi.org/10.1057/9780230592100

Albright, M. (2018). *Fascism: A warning*. New York, NY: Harper.

Allison, L. (2000). Sport and nationalism. In J. J. Coakley & E. Dunning (Eds.), *Handbook of sports studies* (pp. 344–355). London, England: Sage.

Allport, G. (1954). *The nature of prejudice*. Reading, MA: Addison-Wesley.

American Institute for Research. (2014). *Is "admin bloat" behind the high cost of college?* Retrieved from https://www.air.org/resource/admin-bloat-behind-high-cost-college

Anderson, B. (2016). *Imagined communities: Reflections on the origin and spread of nationalism* (rev. ed.). New York, NY: Verso.

Andrews, K. T. (1997). The impacts of social movements on the political process: The civil rights movement and Black electoral politics in Mississippi. *American Sociological Review, 62*, 800–819. http://dx.doi.org/10.2307/2657361

Annunziata, M., & Bourgois, H. (2018). *The future of work: How G20 countries can leverage digital-industrial innovations into stronger high-quality job growth* (Economic Discussion Papers, No. 2018-28). Retrieved from http://hdl.handle.net/10419/176570

Appenzeller, T. (2017). An unprecedented march for science. *Science, 356*, 356–357. http://dx.doi.org/10.1126/science.356.6336.356

Arendt, H. (1970). *On violence*. New York, NY: Harcourt Brace Jovanovich.

Aronson, E. (2011). *The social animal* (11th ed.). New York, NY: Worth.

Asongu, S. A. (2012). *Globalization, (fighting) corruption and development: How are these phenomena linearly or nonlinearly related in wealth effects?* (AGDI Working Paper No. WP/12/024). Retrieved from http://hdl.handle.net/10419/123557

Atkinson, A. (2015). *Inequality: What can be done?* Cambridge, MA: Harvard University Press. http://dx.doi.org/10.4159/9780674287013

Aurelius, M. (1964). *Meditations*. Harmondsworth, England: Penguin. (Original work published 180 AD)

Autor, D., Dorn, D., & Hanson, G. H. (2016). *The China shock: Learning from labor market adjustment to large changes in trade* (IZA Discussion Papers No. 9748). Retrieved from http://hdl.handle.net/10419/141507

Axworthy, M. (2016). *Revolutionary Iran: A history of the Islamic Republic*. New York, NY: Oxford University Press.

Aysan, A. F., Babacan, M., Gur, N., & Karahan, H. (Eds.). (2018). *Turkish economy: Between middle income trap and high income status*. New York, NY: Palgrave Macmillan. http://dx.doi.org/10.1007/978-3-319-70380-0

Baban, F., & Rygiel, K. (2017). Syrian refugees in Turkey: Pathways to precarity, differential inclusion, and negotiated citizenship rights. *Journal of Ethnic and Migration Studies, 43*, 41–57. http://dx.doi.org/10.1080/1369183X.2016.1192996

Baena, V. (2016). Online and mobile marketing strategies as drivers of brand love in sports teams: Findings from Real Madrid. *International Journal of Sports Marketing & Sponsorship, 17*, 202–218. http://dx.doi.org/10.1108/IJSMS-08-2016-015

Balaghi, S. (2006). *Saddam Hussein: A biography*. Westport, CT: Greenwood.

Banac, I. (1988). *With Stalin against Tito: Cominformist splits in Yugoslav communism*. Ithaca, NY: Cornell University Press.

Banks, J. A. (2015). Failed citizenship, civil engagement, and education. *Kappa Delta Pi Record, 51*, 151–154. http://dx.doi.org/10.1080/00228958.2015.1089616

Bar-Tal, D., & Staub, E. (Eds.). (1997). *Patriotism in the lives of individuals and nations*. Chicago, IL: Nelson-Hall.

Baskin, Y. (2002). *A plague of rats and rubber vines*. Washington, DC: Island Press.

Baumeister, R. F., Ainsworth, S. E., & Vohs, K. D. (2016). Are groups more or less than the sum of their members? The moderating role of individual identification. *Behavioral and Brain Sciences, 39*, e137.

BBC News. (2018, January 26). *Turkey's Erdogan vows to fight Kurdish forces as far as Iraq*. Retrieved from http://www.bbc.com/news/world-middle-east-42831296

BBC News. (2018, March 11). *China's Xi allowed to remain "president for life" as term limits removed*. Retrieved from http://www.bbc.com/news/world-asia-china-43361276

Bekdil, B. (2017, Winter). Turkey's slide into authoritarianism. *Middle East Quarterly*. Retrieved from http://www.meforum.org/6398/turkey-slide-into-authoritarianism

Beeler, C. (2018, January 18). Fewer international students coming to U.S. for graduate work in science and engineering. *PRI's The World*. Retrieved from https://www.pri.org/stories/2018-01-18/fewer-international-students-coming-us-grad-school-science-and-engineering

Benjamin, M. (2018). *Inside Iran: The real history and politics of the Islamic Republic of Iran*. New York, NY: OR Books. http://dx.doi.org/10.2307/j.ctv62hfzm

Benner, K., & Spencer, H. (2018, October 2). Four California men accused of inciting riots in Charlottesville violence. *The New York Times*. Retrieved from https://www.nytimes.com/2018/10/02/us/politics/charlottesville-california-riot-charges.html?emc=edit_th_181003&nl=todaysheadlines&nlid=420592531003

Bennett, M. R., & Hacker, P. M. S. (2003). *Philosophical foundations of neuroscience*. Malden, MA: Wiley-Blackwell.

Berlin, I. (1969). Two concepts of liberty. In *Four essays on liberty* (pp. 121–154). Oxford, England: Clarendon Press.

Berlin, I. (1980). Nationalism: Past neglect and present power. In H. Hardy (Ed.), *Against the current: Essays in the history of ideas, Isaiah Berlin* (pp. 333–355). New York, NY: Viking Press.

Berliner, D. C., & Biddle, B. J. (1996). *The manufactured crisis: Myths, fraud, and the attack on America's public schools*. New York, NY: Basic Books.

Biderman, N., & Mudrik, L. (2018). Evidence for implicit—but not unconscious—processing of object-scene relations. *Psychological Science, 29*, 266–277. http://dx.doi.org/10.1177/0956797617735745

Bielefeldt, H. (1997). Autonomy and republicanism: Immanuel Kant's philosophy of freedom. *Political Theory, 25*, 524–558. http://dx.doi.org/10.1177/0090591797025004003

Bieler, D. (2018, February 14). Shaun White wins gold but catches heat for letting American flag drag on the ground. *The Washington Post*. Retrieved from https://www.washingtonpost.com/news/early-lead/wp/2018/02/14/shaun-white-wins-gold-but-catches-heat-for-letting-american-flag-drag-on-the-ground/?utm_term=.95560d7a3671

Biesta, G. J. J. (2016). *Good education in an age of measurement: Ethics, politics, democracy*. Oxford, England: Routledge.

Billig, M. (1992). *Talking of the Royal Family*. London, England: Sage.

Billig, M. (1995). *Banal nationalism*. London, England: Sage.

Blum, G. P. (1998). *The rise of fascism in Europe*. Westport, CT: Greenwood Press.

Bremmer, I. (2018). *Us vs. them: The failure of globalization*. New York, NY: Portfolio.

Brown, D. (1991). *Human universals*. Boston, MA: McGraw-Hill.

Brownell, K. C. (2014). *Showbiz politics: Hollywood in American political life*. Chapel Hill: The University of North Carolina Press.

Bullock, A. (1993). *Hitler and Stalin: Parallel lives*. New York, NY: Vintage Books.

Burger, J. M. (2009). Replicating Milgram: Would people still obey today? *American Psychologist, 64*, 1–11. http://dx.doi.org/10.1037/a0010932

Bush, V. B., Chambers, C. R., & Walpole, M. (Eds.). (2009). *From diplomas to doctorates: The success of Black women in higher education and its implications for equal education opportunities for all*. Sterling, VA: Stylus.

Butz, D. A. (2009). National symbols as agents of psychological and social change. *Political Psychology, 30*, 779–804. http://dx.doi.org/10.1111/j.1467-9221.2009.00725.x

Butz, D. A., Plant, D. A., & Doerr, C. E. (2007). Liberty and justice for all? Implications of exposure to the U.S. flag for intergroup relations. *Personality and Social Psychology Bulletin, 33*, 396–408. http://dx.doi.org/10.1177/0146167206296299

Bychowski, G. (1969). *Dictators and disciples from Caesar to Stalin: A psychoanalytic interpretation of history*. New York, NY: International Universities Press.

Cagaptay, S. (2017). *The new sultan: Erdogan and the crisis of modern Turkey*. New York, NY: I. B. Tauris.

Cain, W. E. (Ed.). (2000). *A historical guide to Henry David Thoreau*. New York, NY: Oxford University Press.

Calabresi, M. (2017, July 31). The secret history of election 2016. *Time, 190*(5), pp. 32–39.

Campos, C. (2003). Beating the bounds: The Tour de France and national identity. *The International Journal of the History of Sport, 20*, 149–174. http://dx.doi.org/10.1080/09523360412331305673

Cardoza, A. (2010). "Making Italians?" Cycling and national identity in Italy: 1900–1950. *Journal of Modern Italian Studies, 15*, 354–377. http://dx.doi.org/10.1080/13545711003768576

Carretero, M. (Ed.). (2011). *Constructing patriotism: Teaching history and memories in global worlds*. Charlotte, NC: Information Age.

Carter, T. J., Ferguson, M. J., & Hassin, R. R. (2011). A single exposure to the American flag shifts support toward Republicanism up to 8 months later. *Psychological Science, 22*, 1011–1018. http://dx.doi.org/10.1177/0956797611414726

Catney, G. (2016). Exploring a decade of small area ethnic (de-)segregation in England and Wales. *Urban Studies, 53*, 1691–1709. http://dx.doi.org/10.1177/0042098015576855

Cech, E. A. (2017). Rugged meritocratists: The role of overt bias and meritocratic ideology in Trump supporters' opposition to social justice efforts. *Socius: Sociological Research for a Dynamic World, 3*, 1–20.

Census Briefs. (2010). *The White population 2010*. Retrieved from https://www.census.gov/prod/cen2010/briefs/c2010br-05.pdf

Cha, V. D., & Kang, D. C. (2018). *Nuclear North Korea: A debate on engagement strategies* (2nd ed.). New York, NY: Columbia University Press. http://dx.doi.org/10.7312/cha-18922

Charnysh, V., Lucas, C., & Singh, P. (2014). The ties that bind: National identity salience and pro-social behavior toward the ethnic other. *Comparative Political Studies, 48*, 267–300. http://dx.doi.org/10.1177/0010414014543103

Chenoweth, E., & Stephan, M. J. (2011). *Why civil resistance works: The strategic logic of nonviolent conflict*. New York, NY: Columbia University press.

Chesnais, J. C. (1998). Below replacement fertility in the European Union (EU-15): Facts and policies, 1960–1997. *Review of Population and Social Policy, 7*, 83–101.

Chester, J. (2016). *Status reproduction in an egalitarian society: The effect of family wealth on educational attainment, occupational status and wealth in Australia* (No. 2016-16). Retrieved from The Australian Research Council Life Course Centre website: http://www.lifecoursecentre.org.au/wp-content/uploads/2016/08/2016-16-LCC-Working-Paper-Chesters.pdf

Choma, B. L., & Hanoch, Y. (2017). Cognitive ability and authoritarianism: Understanding support for Trump and Clinton. *Personality and Individual Differences, 106*, 287–291. http://dx.doi.org/10.1016/j.paid.2016.10.054

Christiano, K. J., Swatos, W. H., & Kivisto, P. (2015). *Sociology of religion: Contemporary developments* (3rd ed.). Lanham, MD: Rowman & Littlefield.

Christie, R., & Geise, F. L. (1970). *Studies in Machiavellianism*. New York, NY: Academic Press.

Cohen, H., & Lefebvre, C. (Eds.). (2017). *Handbook of categorization in cognitive science* (2nd ed.). Amsterdam, The Netherlands: Elsevier.

Cohrs, J. C., Kielmann, S., Maes, J., & Moschner, B. (2005). Effects of right-wing authoritarianism and threat from terrorism on restriction of civil liberties. *Analyses of Social Issues and Public Policy, 5*, 263–276. http://dx.doi.org/10.1111/j.1530-2415.2005.00071.x

Colby, S. L., & Ortman, J. M. (2015). *Projections of the size and composition of the U.S. population: 2014 to 2060* (Current Population Reports P25-1143). U.S. Census Bureau, Washington, DC. Retrieved from http://wedocs.unep.org/bitstream/handle/20.500.11822/20152/colby_population.pdf?sequence=1

Coley, R. J., & Sum, A. (2012). *Fault lines in our democracy: Civic knowledge, voting behavior, and civic engagement in the United States*. ETS Center for Research on Human Capital and Education. Retrieved from http://www.ets.org/s/research/19386/rsc/pdf/18719_fault_lines_report.pdf

Constable, P., & Valenzuela, A. (1991). *A nation of enemies: Chile under Pinochet*. New York, NY: Norton.

Cook, A. C. (Ed.). (2014). *Mao's little red book: A global history*. Cambridge, England: Cambridge University Press. http://dx.doi.org/10.1017/CBO9781107298576

Cooke, L., & Xiao, Y. (2014). Gender roles and organizational HR practices: The case of women's careers in accountancy and consultancy firms in China. *Human Resource Management, 53*, 23–44. http://dx.doi.org/10.1002/hrm.21566

Cornell, S. (2017). A religious party takes hold: Turkey. *SAIS Review, 37*, S-21–S-38.

Corner, P., & Lim, J. H. (2016). *The Pelgrave handbook of mass dictatorship*. London, England: Pelgrave Macmillan. http://dx.doi.org/10.1057/978-1-137-43763-1

Coşkun, G. B. (2017). Does corruption end the dominant party system? A comparative analysis of the Italian and Turkish cases. *European Review, 25*, 320–336. http://dx.doi.org/10.1017/S1062798716000612

Crane, J. K. (Ed.). (2016). *Beastly morality: Animals as ethical agents*. New York, NY: Columbia University Press.

Crew, D. E. (1994). *Nazism and German society*. London, England: Routledge.

Crist, D. (2013). *The twilight war: The secret history of America's thirty-year conflict with Iran*. New York, NY: Penguin Books.

Cronin, M. (1999). *Sport and nationalism in Ireland: Gaelic games, soccer and Irish identity since 1884*. Dublin, Ireland: Four Courts Press.

Crystal, D. (2000). *Language death*. Cambridge, England: Cambridge University Press.

Crystal, D. (2003). *English as a global language*. Cambridge, England: Cambridge University Press. http://dx.doi.org/10.1017/CBO9780511486999

Cunningham, E., & Zakaria, Z. (2018, April 10). Turkey, once a haven for Syrian refugees, grows weary of their presence. *The Washington Post*. Retrieved from https://www.washingtonpost.com/world/turkey-to-syrian-refugees-you-dont-have-to-go-home-but-dont-stay-here/2018/04/04/d1b17d8c-222a-11e8-946c-9420060cb7bd_story.html?utm_term=.165b75d58622

Curry, O. S. (2016). Morality as cooperation: A problem-centered approach. In T. K. Shackelford & R. D. Hansen (Eds.), *The evolution of morality* (pp. 27–52). New York, NY: Springer. http://dx.doi.org/10.1007/978-3-319-19671-8_2

Curtin, S. C., Warner, M., & Hedegaard, H. (2016). *Increase in suicide in the United States, 1999–2014* (NCHS Data Brief No. 241). Retrieved from https://www.cdc.gov/nchs/products/databriefs/db241.htm

Das, E., Bushman, B. J., Bezemer, M. D., Kerkhof, P., & Vermeulen, I. E. (2009). How terrorism news reports increase prejudice against outgroups: A terror management account. *Journal of Experimental Social Psychology, 45*, 453–459. http://dx.doi.org/10.1016/j.jesp.2008.12.001

Davis, D. W., & Silver, B. D. (2004). Civil liberties vs. security: Public opinion in the context of the terrorist attacks on America. *American Journal of Political Science, 48,* 28–46. http://dx.doi.org/10.1111/j.0092-5853.2004.00054.x

de la Sablonnière, R., Taylor, D. M., Perozzo, C., & Sadykova, N. (2009). Reconceptualizing relative deprivation in the context of dramatic social change: The challenge confronting the people of Kyrgyztan. *European Journal of Social Psychology, 39,* 325–345. http://dx.doi.org/10.1002/ejsp.519

de Waal, F. B. M. (2016). Animal empathy as moral building block. In J. K. Crane (Ed.), *Beastly morality: Animals as ethical agents* (pp. 81–89). New York, NY: Columbia University Press.

Deer, P., & Schrecker, E. (2016). *The age of McCarthyism: A brief history with documents* (3rd ed.). Boston, MA: Bedford/St. Martin.

Delli Carpini, M. X., & Keeter, S. (1996). *What Americans know about politics and why it matters.* New Haven, CT: Yale University Press.

Demertzis, N. (Ed.). (2013). *Emotions in politics: The affect dimension in political tension.* New York, NY: Palgrave Macmillan. http://dx.doi.org/10.1057/9781137025661

Dershowitz, A. (2004). *Rights from wrongs: A secular theory of the origins of rights.* New York, NY: Basic Books.

Dewey, J. (1903). Democracy in education. *The Elementary School Teacher, 4,* 193–204. http://dx.doi.org/10.1086/453309

Dewey, J. (1916). *Democracy and education: An introduction to the philosophy of education.* New York, NY: Macmillan.

Diamond, J. (2016). *Trump: I could "shoot somebody and I wouldn't lose voters."* CNN., Retrieved from https://www.cnn.com/2016/01/23/politics/donald-trump-shoot-somebody-support/index.html

Do social media threaten democracy? (2017, November 4). *The Economist,* p. 11.

Dóczi, T. (2012). Gold fever (?): Sport and national identity, the Hungarian case. *International Review for the Sociology of Sport, 47,* 165–182. http://dx.doi.org/10.1177/1012690210393828

Doherty, C. (2016). *5 facts about Trump supporters' views on immigration.* Retrieved from Pew Research Center website: http://www.pewresearch.org/fact-tank/2016/08/25/5-facts-about-trump-supporters-views-of-immigration

Donnelly, J., & Whelan, D. J. (2017). *International human rights: Dilemmas in world politics.* New York, NY: Westview Press.

Dordevic, I. (2012). Twenty years later: The war did (not) begin at Maksimir: An anthropological analysis of the media narratives about a never ending football game. *Glasnik Etnografskog Instituta SANU, 60,* 210–216.

Dorling, D. (2014). *Inequality and the 1%.* London, England: Verso.

Drury, A. C., Krieckhaus, J., & Lusztig, M. (2006). Corruption, democracy, and economic growth. *International Political Science Review, 27,* 121–136. http://dx.doi.org/10.1177/0192512106061423

Duckitt, J., & Fisher, K. (2003). The impact of social threat on worldview and ideological attitudes. *Political Psychology, 24,* 199–222. http://dx.doi.org/10.1111/0162-895X.00322

Dunbar, R. I. M. (1998). The social brain hypothesis. *Evolutionary Anthropology, 6,* 178–190. http://dx.doi.org/10.1002/(SICI)1520-6505(1998)6:5<178::AID-EVAN5>3.0.CO;2-8

Dunbar, R. I. M. (2009). The social brain hypothesis and its implications for social evolution. *Annals of Human Biology, 36,* 562–572. http://dx.doi.org/10.1080/03014460902960289

Elkin, S. K., & Soltan, K. E. (Eds.). (1999). *Citizen competence and democratic institutions*. University Park: Pennsylvania State University Press.

Ellison, N. B., Steinfield, C., & Lampe, C. (2007). The benefits of Facebook "Friends": Social capital and college students' use of online social network sites. *Journal of Computer-Mediated Communication, 12*, 1143–1168. http://dx.doi.org/10.1111/j.1083-6101.2007.00367.x

Ellison, N. B., Vitak, J., Gray, R., & Lampe, C. (2014). Cultivating social resources on social network sites: Facebook relationship maintenance behaviors and their role in social capital processes. *Journal of Computer-Mediated Communication, 19*, 855–870. http://dx.doi.org/10.1111/jcc4.12078

Emerson, M. O., & Hartman, D. (2006). The rise of religious fundamentalism. *Annual Review of Sociology, 32*, 127–144. http://dx.doi.org/10.1146/annurev.soc.32.061604.123141

Encarnacion, O. G. (2018, April 16). The Trumpification of the Latin American right. *Foreign Policy*. Retrieved form https://foreignpolicy.com/2018/04/16/the-trumpification-of-the-latin-american-right

Erdbrink, T., Kirkpatrick, D. D., & Tabrizy, N. (2018, January 20). How corruption and cronyism in banking fueled Iran's protests. *The New York Times*. Retrieved from https://www.nytimes.com/2018/01/20/world/middleeast/iran-protests-corruption-banks.html

Esen, B., & Gumuscu, S. (2017). Turkey: How the coup failed. *Journal of Democracy, 28*, 59–73. http://dx.doi.org/10.1353/jod.2017.0006

Eubanks, V. (2017). *Automating inequality: How high-tech tools profile, police, and punish the poor*. New York, NY: St. Martin's Press.

European Commission. (2016). *Commission staff working document: Turkey 2016 report*. Retrieved from https://ec.europa.eu/neighbourhood-enlargement/sites/near/files/pdf/key_documents/2016/20161109_report_turkey.pdf

Evans, G. (2016). *Educational failure and working class White children in Britain*. New York, NY: Springer.

Fallon, C. (2018, January 31). The fake feminism of the #MeToo backlash. *Huffington Post*. Retrieved October 12, 2018 from https://www.huffingtonpost.com/entry/metoo-backlash-feminism_us_5a621cf7e4b01d91b2552f26

Fan, W., Zhang, Y., Wang, X., Wang, X., Zhang, X., & Zhong, Y. (2011). The temporal features of self-referential processing evoked by national flag. *Neuroscience Letters, 505*, 233–237. http://dx.doi.org/10.1016/j.neulet.2011.10.017

Finchelstein, F. (2017). *From fascism to populism in history*. Berkeley: University of California Press.

Finkel, N., & Moghaddam, F. M. (Eds.). (2005). *The psychology of rights and duties: Empirical contributions and normative commentaries*. Washington, DC: American Psychological Association. http://dx.doi.org/10.1037/10872-000

Fischer, M. E. (1989). *Nicolae Ceaşescu: A study in political leadership*. Boulder, CO: Lynne Rienner.

Fish, I. S. (2017, June 13). Emperor Trump's sycophantic cabinet meeting stinks of Beijing-like obeisance. *The Guardian*. Retrieved form https://www.theguardian.com/commentisfree/2017/jun/13/emperor-trumps-sycophantic-cabinet-meeting-stinks-beijing-obeisance

Foley, E. (2018, May 16). Trump refers to immigrants as "animals," again. *Huffington Post*. Retrieved from https://www.huffingtonpost.com/entry/trump-calls-immigrants-animals-again_us_5afca15fe4b0779345d59e2a

Fortin, N. M., Oreopoulos, P., & Phipps, S. (2015). Leaving boys behind: Gender disparities in high academic achievement. *The Journal of Human Resources, 50,* 549–579. http://dx.doi.org/10.3368/jhr.50.3.549

Fox, J. E. (2006). Consuming the nation: Holidays, sports, and the production of collective belonging. *Ethnic and Racial Studies, 29,* 217–236. http://dx.doi.org/10.1080/01419870500465207

Fox populi: Attitudes towards the mainstream media take an unconstitutional turn. (2017, August 5). *The Economist,* p. 22.

Frances, A. (2017). *Twilight of American sanity: A psychiatrist analyzes the age of Trump*. New York, NY: HarperCollins.

French, P. (2005). *Westerns: Aspects of a movie genre* (Rev. ed.). Manchester, England: Narcanet Press.

Freud, S. (1953–1974). *The standard edition of the complete psychological works of Sigmund Freud* (J. Strachey, Ed. & Trans., Vols. 1–24). London, England: Hogarth Press.

Freud, S. (1955). Group psychology and the analysis of the ego. In J. Strachey (Ed. & Trans.), *The standard edition of the complete psychological works of Sigmund Freud* (Vol. 18, pp. 67–143). London, England: Hogarth Press. (Original work published 1921)

Friedman, M. (2002). *Capitalism and freedom: Fortieth anniversary edition*. Chicago, IL: University of Chicago Press. http://dx.doi.org/10.7208/chicago/9780226264189.001.0001. (Original work published 1962)

Friedman, S. J. (2015). *Silenced no more: Voices of comfort women*. New York, NY: Freeman.

Fromm, E. (1941). *Escape from freedom*. New York, NY: Rinehart.

Fromm, E. (1970). *The anatomy of human destructiveness*. New York, NY: Holt.

Fu, Z. (1993). *Autocratic tradition and Chinese politics*. Cambridge, England: Cambridge University Press.

Fukuyama, F. (1992). *The end of history and the last man*. New York, NY: Free Press.

Fukuyama, F. (2012). The future of history: Can liberal democracy survive the decline of the middle class? *Foreign Affairs, 91,* 53–61.

Fulu, E., & Miedema, S. (2016). Globalization and changing family relations: Family violence and women's resistance in Asian Muslim societies. *Sex Roles, 74,* 480–494. http://dx.doi.org/10.1007/s11199-015-0540-7

Gaddafi, M. (2005). *The green book*. Reading, England: Ithaca Press. [Author is given as M. Al Gathafi]

Gaertner, S. L., & Dovidio, J. F. (2012). *Reducing intergroup bias: The common group identity model*. London, England: Routledge.

Gall, C. (2018, April 2). Sermons and shouted insults: How Erdogan keeps Turkey spellbound. *The New York Times*. Retrieved from https://www.nytimes.com/2018/04/02/world/middleeast/erdogan-turkey.html

Gallaher, C. (2015). Contemporary domestic terrorism in the United States. In R. D. Law (Ed.), *The Routledge history of terrorism* (pp. 317–332). London, England: Routledge.

Gallup/Knight Foundation. (2017). *American views: Trust, media and democracy*. Retrieved from https://knightfoundation.org/reports/american-views-trust-media-and-democracy

Galston, W. A. (2001). Political knowledge, political engagement, and civic education. *Annual Review of Political Science, 4,* 217–234. http://dx.doi.org/10.1146/annurev.polisci.4.1.217

Galston, W. A. (2004). Civic education and political participation. *PS: Political Science & Politics, 37*, 263–266. http://dx.doi.org/10.1017/S1049096504004202

Gatto, J. T. (2017). *The underground history of American education: Vol. I. An intimate investigation into the prison of modern schooling*. Oxford, England: Oxford Scholars Press.

Gazzaniga, M. S., & Ivry, R. B. (2013). *Cognitive neuroscience: The biology of the mind* (4th ed.). New York, NY: Norton.

Ge, S., & Yang, D. T. (2012). *Changes in China's wage structure* (Discussion Paper Series Forschungsinstitut zur Zukunft der Arbeit No. 6492). Retrieved from http://hdl.handle.net/10419/58445

Gelles, D., Thomas, L., Jr., Sorkin, A. R., & Kelly, K. (2017, August 16). Inside the C.E.O. rebellion against Trump's advisory councils. *The New York Times*. Retrieved from https://www.nytimes.com/2017/08/16/business/trumps-council-ceos.html?emc=edit_th_20170817&nl=todaysheadlines&nlid=42059253

Gel'Man, V. (2015). *Authoritarian Russia: Analyzing post-Soviet regime changes*. Pittsburgh, PA: University of Pittsburgh Press. http://dx.doi.org/10.2307/j.ctt155jmv1

Gerson, M. (2017, August 21). Trump is delighting dictators everywhere. *The Washington Post*. Retrieved from https://www.washingtonpost.com/opinions/trump-is-delighting-dictators-everywhere/2017/08/21/4cacebfe-86a2-11e7-961d-2f373b3977ee_story.html?utm_term=.e640fb54a56d

Gilens, M., & Page, B. I. (2014). Testing theories of American politics: Elites, interest groups, and average citizens. *Perspectives on Politics, 12*, 564–581. http://dx.doi.org/10.1017/S1537592714001595

Glaeser, E. L., Ponzetto, G. A. M., & Shleifer, A. (2007). Why does democracy need education? *Journal of Economic Growth, 12*, 77–99. http://dx.doi.org/10.1007/s10887-007-9015-1

Goldie, D., Linick, M., Jabbar, H., & Lubienski, C. (2014). Using biometric and social media analysis to explore the "echo chamber" hypothesis. *Educational Policy, 28*, 281–305. http://dx.doi.org/10.1177/0895904813515330

Göle, N. (2017). *The daily lives of Muslims: Islam and public confrontation in contemporary Europe* (J. Lerescu, Trans.). London, England: Zed Books.

Gordon, R. J. (2016). *The rise and fall of American growth*. Princeton, NJ: Princeton University Press. http://dx.doi.org/10.1515/9781400873302

Gormley, W. T., & Balla, S. J. (2013). *Bureaucracy and democracy: Accountability and performance* (3rd ed.). Los Angeles, CA: Sage.

Greene, J. (2015). *Administrative bloat at American universities: The real reason for high costs in higher education*. Retrieved from the Goldwater Institute website: https://goldwaterinstitute.org/article/administrative-bloat-at-american-universities-the/

Greenleaf, R. K. (2002). *Servant leadership: A journey into the nature of legitimate power and greatness*. Mahwah, NJ: Paulist Press. (Original work published 1977)

Grinshteyn, E., & Hemenway, D. (2016). Violent death rates: The U.S. compared with other high-income ORCD countries, 2010. *The American Journal of Medicine, 129*, 266–273. http://dx.doi.org/10.1016/j.amjmed.2015.10.025

Gurtov, M. (2018). At home and abroad, Trump tramples human rights. *The Asia-Pacific Journal: Japan Focus, 16*(14). Retrieved from https://apjjf.org/2018/14/Gurtov.html

Haas, I. J., & Cunningham, W. A. (2014). The uncertainty paradox: Perceived threat moderates the effect of uncertainty on political tolerance. *Political Psychology, 35,* 291–302. http://dx.doi.org/10.1111/pops.12035

Haidt, J., Koller, S., & Dias, M. (1993). Affect, culture, and morality, or is it wrong to eat your dog? *Journal of Personality and Social Psychology, 65,* 613–628. http://dx.doi.org/10.1037/0022-3514.65.4.613

Handy, S. L., Boarnet, M. G., Ewing, R., & Killingworth, R. E. (2002). How the built environment affects physical activity. *American Journal of Preventive Medicine, 23,* 64–73. http://dx.doi.org/10.1016/S0749-3797(02)00475-0

Hanif, M. (2012, November 4). The Taliban's main fear is not drones but educated girls. *The Guardian.* Retrieved from https://www.theguardian.com/commentisfree/2012/nov/04/pakistan-extremists-girls-education

Harré, R. (2018). Foreword. In B. Wagoner, F. M. Moghaddam, & J. Vaalsiner (Eds.), *The psychology of radical social change: From rage to revolution* (pp. xi–xiv). Cambridge, England: Cambridge University Press. http://dx.doi.org/10.1017/9781108377461.001

Harré, R., & Moghaddam, F. M. (Eds.). (2012). *Psychology for the third millennium: Integrating cultural and neuroscience perspectives.* London, England; Thousand Oaks, CA: Sage.

Harré, R., & Moghaddam, F. M. (Eds.). (2016). *Questioning causality: Scientific explorations of cause and consequence across social contexts.* Santa Barbara, CA: Praeger.

Hartman, A. (2002). "The red template": US policy in Soviet-occupied Afghanistan. *Third World Quarterly, 23,* 467–489. http://dx.doi.org/10.1080/01436590220138439

Hassin, R. R., Ferguson, M. J., Shidlovski, D., & Gross, L. (2007). Subliminal exposure to national flags affects political thought and behavior. *Proceedings of the National Academy of Sciences of the United States of America, 104,* 19757–19761. http://dx.doi.org/10.1073/pnas.0704679104

Helwig, C. C., & Prencipe, A. (1999). Children's judgements of flags and flag burning. *Child Development, 70,* 132–143. http://dx.doi.org/10.1111/1467-8624.00010

Hernad, S. (2017). To cognize is to categorize: Cognition is categorization. In H. Cohen & C. Lefebvre (Eds.), *Handbook of categorization in cognitive science* (2nd ed., pp. 21–54). Amsterdam, The Netherlands: Elsevier.

Hernstein, R. J., & Murray, C. (1996). *The bell curve: Intelligence and class structure in American life.* New York, NY: Free Press.

Heslam, P. S. (2016). The rise of religion and the future of capitalism. *De Ethica: A Journal of Philosophical, Theological and Applied Ethics, 2,* 53–72. http://dx.doi.org/10.3384/de-ethica.2001-8819.152353

Hing, B. O. (2004). *Defining America through immigration policy.* Philadelphia, PA: Temple University Press.

Hitler, A. (1960). Hitler's speech to the people of Danzig. In K. Snyder & R. K. Snyder (Eds.), *Readings in Western civilization* (3rd ed., pp. 827–829). New York, NY: J. B. Lippincott. (Original work published 1939)

Hobsbawm, E. J. (1992). *Nations and nationalism since 1780* (2nd ed.). Cambridge, England: Cambridge University Press.

Hogg, M. A. (2001). Social identity and the sovereignty of the group: A psychology of belonging. In C. Sedekides & M. B. Brewer (Eds.), *Individual self, relational self, collective self* (pp. 123–143). New York, NY: Psychology Press.

Holmes, D. R. (1989). *Stalking the academic communist: Intellectual freedom and the firing of Alex Novikoff*. Hanover, NH: University Press of New England.

Horowitz, J. (2018, September 7). Steve Bannon's "movement" enlists Italy's most powerful politician. *The New York Times*. Retrieved from https://www.nytimes.com/2018/09/07/world/europe/italy-steve-bannon-matteo-salvini.html

Huang, F. (2015). Building the world-class research universities: A case study of China. *Higher Education, 70*, 203–215. http://dx.doi.org/10.1007/s10734-015-9876-8

Huddy, L., Feldman, S., Taber, C., & Lahav, G. (2005). Threat, anxiety, and support for antiterrorist policies. *American Journal of Political Science, 49*, 593–608. http://dx.doi.org/10.1111/j.1540-5907.2005.00144.x

Huddy, L., Feldman, S., & Weber, C. (2007). The political consequences of perceived threat and felt insecurity. *The ANNALS of the American Academy of Political and Social Science, 614*, 131–153. http://dx.doi.org/10.1177/0002716207305951

Human Rights Watch. (2017, October 24). *Eroding checks and balances: Rule of law and human rights under attack in Poland*. Retrieved from https://www.hrw.org/report/2017/10/24/eroding-checks-and-balances/rule-law-and-human-rights-under-attack-poland

Huntington, S. P. (1991). Democracy's third wave. *Journal of Democracy, 2*, 12–34. http://dx.doi.org/10.1353/jod.1991.0016

Hutchison, M. L. (2014). Tolerating threat? The independent effects of civil conflict on domestic political tolerance. *The Journal of Conflict Resolution, 58*, 796–824. http://dx.doi.org/10.1177/0022002713478566

Illich, I. (1970). *Deschooling society*. New York, NY: Harper & Row.

Ismer, S. (2011). Embodying the nation: Football, emotions, and the construction of collective identity. *Nationalities Papers, 39*, 547–565. http://dx.doi.org/10.1080/00905992.2011.582864

Ito, T. A., & Urland, G. R. (2003). Race and gender on the brain: Electrocortical measures of attention to the race and gender of multiply categorizable individuals. *Journal of Personality and Social Psychology, 85*, 616–626. http://dx.doi.org/10.1037/0022-3514.85.4.616

Jacobs, B., & Murray, W. (2017, August 13). Donald Trump under fire after failing to denounce Virginia White supremacists. *The Guardian*. Retrieved from https://www.theguardian.com/us-news/2017/aug/12/charlottesville-protest-trump-condemns-violence-many-sides

Jacobs, P. (2014). *The 10 highest-paid college presidents*. Retrieved from http://www.businessinsider.com/highest-paid-college-presidents-2014-12

Jivraj, S., & Simpson, L. (Eds.). (2015). *Ethnic identity and inequalities in Britain: The dynamics of diversity*. Bristol, England: Policy Press. http://dx.doi.org/10.2307/j.ctt1t89504

Johnson, G. R. (1997). The evolutionary roots of patriotism. In D. Bar-Tal & E. Staub (Eds.), *Patriotism in the lives of individuals and nations* (pp. 45–90). Chicago, IL: Nelson-Hall.

Johnson, K. L., Lick, D. J., & Carpinella, C. M. (2015). Emergent research in social vision: An integrated approach to the determinants and consequences of social categorization. *Social and Personality Psychology Compass, 9*, 15–30. http://dx.doi.org/10.1111/spc3.12147

Johnstone, B. (1986). Arguments with Khomeini: Rhetorical situation and persuasive style in cross-cultural perspective. *Text: An Interdisciplinary Journal for the Study of Discourse, 6*, 171–187. http://dx.doi.org/10.1515/text.1.1986.6.2.171

Jones, T. (2018, February 22). The fascist movement that has brought Mussolini back to the mainstream. *The Guardian*. Retrieved from https://www.theguardian.com/news/2018/feb/22/casapound-italy-mussolini-fascism-mainstream

Judis, J. B. (2016). *The populist explosion: How the great recession transformed American and European politics*. New York, NY: Columbia Global Reports.

Kahne, J. S., & Sporte, S. E. (2008). Developing citizens: The impact of civic learning opportunities on students' commitment to civic participation. *American Educational Research Journal, 45*, 738–766. http://dx.doi.org/10.3102/0002831208316951

Kahneman, D. (2011). *Thinking, fast and slow*. New York, NY: Farrar, Strauss & Giroux.

Kant, I. (2016). *Fundamental principles of the metaphysics of morals* (T. K. Abbott, Trans.). South Valley, CA: CreateSpace Independent Publishing Platform. (Original work published 1785)

Kapuściński, R. (1989). *The emperor: Downfall of an autocrat* (W. R. Brand & K. Mroczkowska-Brand, Trans.). New York, NY: Vintage Books. (Original work published 1978)

Karatnycky, A., & Ackerman, P. (n.d.). *How freedom is won: From civil resistance to durable democracy*. Freedom House. Retrieved from Archive.kubatana.net/docs/cact/freedomhouse_overview_050524.pdf

Katz, J. E. (Ed.). (2017). *Machines that become us: The social context of personal communications technology*. London, England: Routledge. http://dx.doi.org/10.4324/9780203786826

Kemmelmeier, M., & Winter, D. G. (2008). Sowing patriotism, but reaping nationalism? Consequences of exposure to the American flag. *Political Psychology, 29*, 859–879. http://dx.doi.org/10.1111/j.1467-9221.2008.00670.x

Kershaw, I. (1998). *Hitler: A biography*. New York, NY: Norton.

Kersten, R. (1996). *Democracy in postwar Japan: Maruyama Masao and the search for autonomy*. Abingdon, England: Routledge.

Kersting, N. (2007). Sport and national identity: A comparison of 2006 and 2010 FIFA World Cups. *Politikon, 34*, 277–293. http://dx.doi.org/10.1080/02589340801962551

Kezer, Z. (2015). *Building modern Turkey: State, space, and ideology in the early republic*. Pittsburgh, PA: University of Pittsburgh Press.

Khomeini, R. (1979). *Islamic government*. New York, NY: Manor Books.

Kim, B. Y. (2017). *Unveiling the North Korean economy: Collapse and transition*. New York, NY: Cambridge University Press. http://dx.doi.org/10.1017/9781316874882

Kinnvall, C. (2004). Globalization and religious nationalism: Self, identity, and the search for ontological security. *Political Psychology, 25*, 741–767. http://dx.doi.org/10.1111/j.1467-9221.2004.00396.x

Kittrie, O. (2016). *Lawfare: Law as a weapon of war*. New York, NY: Oxford University Press. http://dx.doi.org/10.1093/acprof:oso/9780190263577.001.0001

Klein, J. (2011, June). The failure of American schools. *The Atlantic*. Retrieved from https://www.theatlantic.com/magazine/archive/2011/06/the-failure-of-american-schools/308497

Kornai, J. (2015). Hungary's u-turn: Retreating from democracy. *Journal of Democracy, 26*, 34–48. http://dx.doi.org/10.1353/jod.2015.0046

Kruglanski, A. W., & Orehek, E. (2012). The need for certainty as a psychological nexus for individuals and society. In M. A. Hogg & D. L. Blaylock (Eds.),

Extremism and the psychology of uncertainty (pp. 1–18). Oxford, England: Wiley-Blackwell.

Kuran, T., & Sunstein, C. R. (1999). Availability cascades and risk regulation. *Stanford Law Review, 51*, 683–768. http://dx.doi.org/10.2307/1229439

Kurlantzick, J. (2013). *Democracy in retreat: The revolt of the middle class and the worldwide decline of representative government*. New Haven, CT: Yale University Press.

Kuttner, R. (2018). *Can democracy survive global capitalism?* New York, NY: Norton.

Ladd, J. M., & Lenz, G. S. (2008). Reassessing the role of anxiety in vote choice. *Political Psychology, 29*, 275–296. http://dx.doi.org/10.1111/j.1467-9221.2008.00626.x

LaFree, G., Dugan, L., & Miller, E. (2015). *Putting terrorism in context: Lessons from the global terrorism database*. London, England: Routledge.

Laker, J., Naval, C., & Mrnjaus, K. (Eds.). (2014). *Civic pedagogies in higher education: Teaching for democracy in Europe, Canada and the USA*. New York, NY: Palgrave Macmillan. http://dx.doi.org/10.1057/9781137355591

Lampton, D. M. (2014). *Following the leader: Ruling China, from Deng Xiaoping to Xi Jinping*. Berkeley: University of California Press.

Laqueur, W. (2015). *Putinism: Russia and its future with the west*. New York, NY: St. Martin's Press.

Laustsen, L., & Petersen, M. B. (2017). Perceived conflict and leader dominance: Individual and contextual factors behind preferences for dominant leaders. *Political Psychology, 38*, 1083–1101. http://dx.doi.org/10.1111/pops.12403

Lenihan, J. H. (1980). *Showdown: Confronting modern America in the Western film*. Urbana: University of Illinois Press.

Leslie, L. L., & Rhoades, G. (1995). Rising administrative costs: Seeking explanations. *The Journal of Higher Education, 66*, 187–212.

Lexington: The coming collision. (2018, April 14–20). *The Economist*, p. 26.

Li, Q., & Brewer, M. B. (2004). What does it mean to be an American? Patriotism, nationalism, and American identity after 9/11. *Political Psychology, 25*, 727–739. http://dx.doi.org/10.1111/j.1467-9221.2004.00395.x

Lieberman, A. F. (2018). *The emotional life of the toddler* (2nd ed.). New York, NY: Simon & Schuster.

Lim, L. (2015). *The People's Republic of Amnesia: Tiananmen revisited*. New York, NY: Oxford University Press.

Lipset, S. M. (1959). Some social requisites of democracy: Economic development and political legitimacy. *The American Political Science Review, 53*, 69–105. http://dx.doi.org/10.2307/1951731

Louis, W. (2009). Collective action: And then what? *Journal of Social Issues, 65*, 727–748. http://dx.doi.org/10.1111/j.1540-4560.2009.01623.x

Lozano, A. M. (2011). Harnessing plasticity to reset dysfunctional neurons. *The New England Journal of Medicine, 364*, 1367–1368. http://dx.doi.org/10.1056/NEJMcibr1100496

Machiavelli, N. (1950). *The prince and the discourses* (L. Ricci, Trans.). New York, NY: Modern Library. (Original work published 1532)

Macrae, C. N., Quinn, K. A., Mason, M. F., & Quadflieg, S. (2005). Understanding others: The face and person construal. *Journal of Personality and Social Psychology, 89*, 686–695. http://dx.doi.org/10.1037/0022-3514.89.5.686

Malinowski, B. (1947). *Freedom and civilization*. London, England: Allen & Unwin.

Mango, A. (2000). *Ataturk: The biography of the founder of modern Turkey*. Woodstock, NY: Overlook Press.

Mann, C. C. (2006). *1491: New revelations of the Americas before Columbus*. New York, NY: Knopf.

Manza, J., & Crowley, N. (2017). Working class hero? Interrogating the social bases of the rise of Donald Trump. *The Forum, 15*, 3–28. http://dx.doi.org/10.1515/for-2017-0002

Marcus, G. E., MacKuen, M., & Neuman, W. R. (2011). Parsimony and complexity: Developing and testing theories of affective intelligence. *Political Psychology, 32*, 323–336. http://dx.doi.org/10.1111/j.1467-9221.2010.00806.x

Marguleas, O. (2017). *Freedom under watch: Under the veil of Saudi cyberspace*. Retrieved from the Henry M. Jackson School of International Studies website: https://jsis.washington.edu/news/freedom-watch-veil-saudi-cyberspace

Marples, D. R. (2000). *Lenin's revolution, Russia 1917–1921*. New York, NY: Pearson Education Limited.

Marx, K. (1976). *Capital: Vol. 1. A critique of political economy*. (B. Fowkes, Trans.). Harmondsworth, England: Penguin. (Original work published 1867)

Marx, K. (1979). The eighteenth brumaire of Louis Bonaparte. In *Collected works of Karl Marx and Frederick Engels* (Vol. 11, pp. 99–197). London, England: Lawrence and Wishard. (Original work published 1852)

Marx, K., & Engels, F. (1967). *Communist manifesto*. New York, NY: Pantheon. (Original work published 1848)

McGurn, W. (2018, April 24). The elitists' Trump excuse. *The Wall Street Journal*, p. A15.

McLaughlin, N. (1996). Nazism, nationalism, and the sociology of emotions: Escape from freedom revisited. *Sociological Theory, 14*, 241–261. http://dx.doi.org/10.2307/3045388

McMullen, R. (1968). *Art, affluence and alienation: The fine arts today*. London, England: Pall Mall.

Meir, R., & Scott, D. (2007). Tribalism: Definition, identification and relevance to the marketing of professional sports franchises. *Journal of Sports Marketing and Sponsorship, 8*, 43–59. http://dx.doi.org/10.1108/IJSMS-08-04-2007-B006

Meloni, M. (2016). *Political biology: Science and social values in human heredity from eugenics to epigenetics*. New York, NY: Palgrave Macmillan. http://dx.doi.org/10.1057/9781137377722

Memisoglu, F. (2017). Syrian refugees in Turkey: Multifaceted challenges, diverse players and ambiguous policies. *Mediterranean Politics, 22*, 317–338. http://dx.doi.org/10.1080/13629395.2016.1189479

Miklian, J., & Carney, S. (2013). Corruption, justice and violence in democratic India. *SAIS Review, 33*, 37–49.

Mikulincer, M., & Shaver, P. R. (Eds.). (2014). *Mechanisms of social connection: From brain to group*. Washington, DC: American Psychological Association. http://dx.doi.org/10.1037/14250-000

Milani, A. (2011). *The shah*. New York, NY: Palgrave Macmillan.

Milbank, D. (2017, December 18). Trump's ticket to survival: Ban all the words. *The Washington Post*. Retrieved from https://www.washingtonpost.com/opinions/trumps-ticket-to-survival-ban-all-the-words/2017/12/18/0d9e3e66-e437-11e7-a65d-1ac0fd7f097e_story.html?utm_term=.32ef42fe673f

Milgram, S. (1974). *Obedience to authority: An experimental view*. New York, NY: Harper & Row.

Miller, N., Pederson, W. C., Earlywine, M., & Pollock, V. E. (2003). A theoretical model of triggered displaced aggression. *Personality and Social Psychology Review, 7*, 75–97. http://dx.doi.org/10.1207/S15327957PSPR0701_5

Miller, T., Lawrence, G., McKay, J., & Rowe, D. (2001). *Globalization and sport*. London, England: Sage.

Mischel, W. (2014). *The marshmallow test: Why self-control is the engine of success*. New York, NY: Little, Brown.

Moghaddam, F. M. (1997). *The specialized society: The plight of the individual in an age of individualism*. Westport, CT: Praeger.

Moghaddam, F. M. (2002). *The individual and society: A cultural integration*. New York, NY: Worth.

Moghaddam, F. M. (2005a). *Great ideas in psychology: A cultural and historical introduction*. Oxford, England: Oneworld.

Moghaddam, F. M. (2005b). The staircase to terrorism: A psychological exploration. *American Psychologist, 60*, 161–169. http://dx.doi.org/10.1037/0003-066X.60.2.161

Moghaddam, F. M. (2006a). Catastrophic evolution, culture, and diversity management policy. *Culture and Psychology, 12*, 415–434. http://dx.doi.org/10.1177/1354067X06067145

Moghaddam, F. M. (2006b). Interobjectivity: The collective roots of individual consciousness and social identity. In T. Postmes & J. Jetten (Eds.), *Individuality and the group: Advances in social identity* (pp. 155–174). London, England: Sage.

Moghaddam, F. M. (2008a). *How globalization spurs terrorism: The lopsided benefits of one world and why that fuels violence*. Westport, CT: Praeger.

Moghaddam, F. M. (2008b). *Multiculturalism and intergroup relations: Implications for democracy in global context*. Washington, DC: American Psychological Association. http://dx.doi.org/10.1037/11682-000

Moghaddam, F. M. (2009). Omniculturalism: Policy solutions to fundamentalism in the era of fractured globalization. *Culture and Psychology, 15*, 337–347. http://dx.doi.org/10.1177/1354067X09337867

Moghaddam, F. M. (2010). *The new global insecurity: How terrorism, environmental collapse, economic inequalities, and resource shortages are changing our world*. Santa Barbara, CA: Praeger.

Moghaddam, F. M. (2013). *The psychology of dictatorship*. Washington, DC: American Psychological Association. http://dx.doi.org/10.1037/14138-000

Moghaddam, F. M. (2016a). Omniculturalism and our human path. *Journal of Oriental Studies, 26*, 77–97.

Moghaddam, F. M. (2016b). *The psychology of democracy*. Washington, DC: American Psychological Association. http://dx.doi.org/10.1037/14806-000

Moghaddam, F. M. (2018a). *Mutual radicalization: How groups and nations drive each other to extremes*. Washington, DC: American Psychological Association. http://dx.doi.org/10.1037/0000089-000

Moghaddam, F. M. (2018b). Political plasticity and revolution: The case of Iran. In B. Wagoner, F. M. Moghaddam, & J. Valsiner (Eds.), *The psychology of radical social change* (pp. 122–139). Cambridge, England: Cambridge University Press. http://dx.doi.org/10.1017/9781108377461.008

Moghaddam, F. M. (2018c). Psychology as the science of human plasticity. In B. Wagoner, I. B. de Luna, & V. Glaveanu (Eds.), *The road to actualized society: A psychological exploration* (pp. 285–301). Charlotte, NC: Information Age.

Moghaddam, F. M. (2018d). The shark and the octopus: Two revolutionary styles. In B. Wagoner, F. M. Moghaddam, & J. Valsiner (Eds.), *The psychology of radical social change* (pp. 275–290). Cambridge, England: Cambridge University Press. http://dx.doi.org/10.1017/9781108377461.015

Moghaddam, F. M., & Breckenridge, J. (2011). The post-tragedy "opportunity-bubble" and the prospect of citizen engagement. *Homeland Security Affairs, 7,* 1–4.

Moghaddam, F. M., Harré, R., & Lee, N. (Eds.). (2008). *Global conflict resolution through positioning analysis.* New York, NY: Springer.

Moghaddam, F. M., & Howard, C. (2017). Political plasticity. In F. M. Moghaddam (Ed.), *The Sage encyclopedia of political behavior* (Vol. 2, pp. 625–627). London, England; Thousand Oaks, CA: Sage.

Moghaddam, F. M., & Riley, C. J. (2005). Toward a cultural theory of human rights and duties in human development. In N. J. Finkel & F. M. Moghaddam (Eds.), *Human rights and duties: Empirical contributions and normative commentaries* (pp. 75–104). Washington, DC: American Psychological Association. http://dx.doi.org/10.1037/10872-004

Moghaddam, F. M., & Studer, C. (1998). *Illusions of control: Striving for control in personal and professional lives.* Westport, CT: Praeger.

Morris, E. (2018, June 11). Why Donald Trump can't kill the truth. *Time, 191*(22), p. 24.

Mosca, G. (1939). *The ruling class.* New York, NY: McGraw-Hill.

Mudde, C. (2004). The populist zeitgeist. *Government and Opposition, 39,* 541–563. http://dx.doi.org/10.1111/j.1477-7053.2004.00135.x

Mudde, C. (2007). *Populist radical right parties in Europe.* Cambridge, England: Cambridge University Press. http://dx.doi.org/10.1017/CBO9780511492037

Mullen, B., & Hu, L. T. (1989). Perceptions of ingroup and outgroup variability: A meta-analytic integration. *Journal of Basic and Applied Social Psychology, 10,* 233–252. http://dx.doi.org/10.1207/s15324834basp1003_3

Müller, J. W. (2016). *What is populism?* Philadelphia: University of Pennsylvania Press. http://dx.doi.org/10.9783/9780812293784

Nail, P. R., McGregor, I., Drinkwater, A. E., Steele, G. M., & Thompson, A. W. (2009). Threat causes liberals to think like conservatives. *Journal of Experimental Social Psychology, 45,* 901–907. http://dx.doi.org/10.1016/j.jesp.2009.04.013

Nakamura, D. (2017). Trump recycles discredited Islamic pigs' blood tale after terrorist attack in Barcelona. *The Washington Post.* Retrieved from https://www.washingtonpost.com/news/post-politics/wp/2017/08/17/trump-recycles-discredited-islamic-pigs-blood-tale-after-terrorist-attack-in-barcelona/?hpid=hp_hp-top-table-main_trump-pigsblood-430pm%3Ahomepage%2Fstory&utm_term=.370a1a6795a7

Nepstad, S. E. (2011). *Nonviolent revolutions: Civil resistance in the late 20th century.* New York, NY: Oxford University Press. http://dx.doi.org/10.1093/acprof:oso/9780199778201.001.0001

Neuberg, S. L., Kenrick, D. T., & Schaller, M. (2011). Human threat management systems: Self-protection and disease avoidance. *Neuroscience and Biobehavioral Reviews, 35,* 1042–1051. http://dx.doi.org/10.1016/j.neubiorev.2010.08.011

Ngai, M. M. (2014). *Impossible subjects: Illegal aliens and the making of modern America.* Princeton, NJ: Princeton University Press. http://dx.doi.org/10.1515/9781400850235

Nietzsche, F. (1956). Live dangerously. In W. Kaufmann (Ed.), *Existentialism from Dostoevsky to Sartre* (pp. 100–112). Cleveland, OH: Meridian Books.

Nili, M., & Rastad, M. (2007). Addressing the growth failure of the oil economies: The role of financial development. *The Quarterly Review of Economics and Finance, 46*, 726–740. http://dx.doi.org/10.1016/j.qref.2006.08.007

Nisbet, R. (1980). *History of the idea of progress*. New York, NY: Basic Books.

Noble, S. U. (2018). *The algorithms of oppression: How search engines reinforce racism*. New York, NY: New York University Press.

O'Donnell, G. (2004). The quality of democracy: Why the rule of law matters. *Journal of Democracy, 15*, 32–46. http://dx.doi.org/10.1353/jod.2004.0076

Ojo, S., Nwankwo, S., & Ghadamosi, A. (2015). The landscape of ethnic marketing in the England. In A. Jamal, L. Peñaloza, & M. Laroche (Eds.), *The Routledge companion to ethnic marketing* (pp. 97–116). London, England: Routledge.

Oliver, J. E., & Rahn, W. M. (2016). Rise of the *Trumpenvolk*: Populism in the 2016 election. *The Annals of the American Academy of Political and Social Science, 667*, 189–206. http://dx.doi.org/10.1177/0002716216662639

Oliver, P. (2012). *New religious movements: A guide for the perplexed*. London, England: Bloomsbury.

Öniş, Z. (2016). Democracy in uncertain times: Inequality and democratic development in the global North and global South. *ODTÜ Gelisme Dergisi, 43*, 317–336.

Osbeck, L., Perreault, S., & Moghaddam, F. M. (1997). Similarity and intergroup relations. *International Journal of Intercultural Relations, 21*, 113–123. http://dx.doi.org/10.1016/S0147-1767(96)00016-8

Osnos, E. (2018, May 21). Only the best people: Donald Trump's war on the "deep state." *The New Yorker*, pp. 56–65.

Ott, J. (2018). Measuring economic freedom: Better without size of government. *Social Indicators Research, 135*, 479–498. http://dx.doi.org/10.1007/s11205-016-1508-x

Özkirimli, U. (2017). *Theories of nationalism: A critical introduction* (3rd ed.). London, England: Palgrave.

Pacepa, I. M. (1987). *Red horizons: The true story of Nicolae and Elena Ceausescus' crimes, lifestyle, and corruption*. Washington, DC: Regnery Gateway.

Panayırcı, U. C., Işeri, E., & Şekercioğlu, E. (2016). Political agency of news outlets in a polarized media system: Framing the corruption probe in Turkey. *European Journal of Communication, 31*, 551–567. http://dx.doi.org/10.1177/0267323116669455

Pappas, T. S. (2014). Populist democracies: Post-authoritarian Greece and post-communist Hungary. *Government and Opposition, 49*, 1–23. http://dx.doi.org/10.1017/gov.2013.21

Pareto, V. (1935). *The mind and society: A treatise in general sociology* (Vols. 1–4). New York, NY: Dover.

Pareto, V. (1971). *Manual of political economy*. New York, NY: Augustus M. Kelley.

Parry, G. (2015). Making democrats: Education and democracy. In G. Parry & M. Moran (Eds.), *Democracy and democratization* (pp. 88–108). London, England: Routledge.

Paul, A., & Seyreck, D. M. (2017). *Constitutional changes in Turkey: A presidential system, or the president's system?* European Policy Centre. Retrieved from http://aei.pitt.edu/83866/1/pub_7374_conschangesinturkey.pdf

Pavlikova, M. (2015). Despair and alienation of modern man in society. *European Journal of Science and Theology, 11*, 191–200.

Percy, W. (1961). *The moviegoer*. New York, NY: Knopf.

Petty, R. E., & Cacioppo, J. T. (1986). *Communication and persuasion: Central and peripheral routes to attitude change.* New York, NY: Springer-Verlag. http://dx.doi.org/10.1007/978-1-4612-4964-1

Petty, R. E., Cacioppo, J. T., & Kasmer, J. A. (2015). The role of affect in the elaboration likelihood model. In L. Donohew, H. E. Sypher, & E. T. Higgins (Eds.), *Communication, social cognition, and affect* (pp. 117–146). New York, NY: Psychology Press.

Petty, R. E., Cacioppo, J. T., & Schumann, D. (1983). Central and peripheral routes to advertising effectiveness: The moderating role of involvement. *The Journal of Consumer Research, 10,* 135–146. http://dx.doi.org/10.1086/208954

Pew Research Center. (2017, May 24). *Majorities in Europe, North America worried about Islamic extremism.* Retrieved from http://www.pewforum.org/2017/05/24/majorities-in-europe-north-america-worried-about-islamic-extremism

Pew Research Center. (2017, July 26). *How the U.S. general public views Muslims and Islam.* Retrieved from http://www.pewforum.org/2017/07/26/how-the-u-s-general-public-views-muslims-and-islam

Pew Research Center. (2017, November 29). *Europe's growing Muslim population.* Retrieved from http://www.pewforum.org/2017/11/29/europes-growing-muslim-population

Phillips, D. L. (2017). *An uncertain ally: Turkey under Erdogan's dictatorship.* New York, NY: Routledge.

Piketty, T. (2014). *Capital in the 21st century* (A. Goldhammer, Trans.). Cambridge, MA: Belknap Press.

Piotrow, P. (1958). Tito and the Soviets. *Editorial research reports 1958* (Vol. II). Washington, DC: CQ Press. Retrieved from http://library.cqpress.com/cqresearcher/cqresrre1958071600

Plato. (1987). *The republic* (D. Lee, Trans.). Harmondsworth, England: Penguin.

Polyani, K. (1944). *The great transformation: The political and economic origins of our time.* Boston, MA: Beacon Press.

Pool, J., & Pool, S. (1979). *Who financed Hitler: The secret funding of Hitler's rise to power, 1919–1933.* New York, NY: Dial Press.

Pope, M., Rolf, J. N., & Siklodi, N. (2017). Special affects? Nationalist and cosmopolitan discourses through the transmission of emotions: Empirical evidence from London 2012. *British Politics, 12,* 409–431. http://dx.doi.org/10.1057/s41293-016-0042-4

Premack, D., & Woodruff, G. (1978). Does the chimpanzee have a theory of mind? *Behavioral and Brain Sciences, 1,* 515–526. http://dx.doi.org/10.1017/S0140525X00076512

Putnam, R. D. (2000). *Bowling alone: The collapse and revival of American community.* New York, NY: Simon & Schuster.

Putnam, R. D. (2016). *Our kids: The American Dream in crisis.* New York, NY: Simon & Schuster.

PwC Press Room. (2017). *UBS/PwC Billionaires Report 2017: Return to growth for billionaires globally, with Asia outpacing the US for the first time.* Retrieved from https://press.pwc.com/News-releases/ubs-pwc-billionaires-report-2017—return-to-growth-for-billionaires-globally—with-asia-outpacing-th/s/3269623a-1a6b-40c4-9bf4-6eb8b4cf15d1.

Pye, L. W. (1963). *Communications and political development* (SPD-1). Princeton, NJ: Princeton University Press. http://dx.doi.org/10.1515/9781400875214

Pyszczynski, T., Greenberg, J., & Solomon, S. (1997). Why do we need what we need? A terror management perspective on the roots of human social motivation. *Psychological Inquiry, 8*, 1–20. http://dx.doi.org/10.1207/s15327965pli0801_1

Rancour-Laferriere, D. (1988). *The mind of Stalin: A psychoanalytic study*. Ann Arbor, MI: Ardis.

Read, H. (1967). *Art and alienation: The role of the artist in society*. New York, NY: Horizon Press.

Rechel, B., Grundy, E., Rabine, J. M., Cylus, J., Mackenbach, J. P., Knai, C., & McKee, M. (2013). Ageing in the European Union. *The Lancet, 381*, 1257–1259.

Rennels, J. L., Kayl, A. J., Langlois, J. H., Davis, R. E., & Orlewicz, M. (2016). Asymmetries in infants' attention toward and categorization of male faces: The potential role of experience. *Journal of Experimental Child Psychology, 142*, 137–157. http://dx.doi.org/10.1016/j.jecp.2015.09.026

Rhodes, M., Leslie, S. J., Bianchi, L., & Chalik, L. (2018). The role of generic language in the early development of social categorization. *Child Development, 89*, 148–155. http://dx.doi.org/10.1111/cdev.12714

Ritzer, G. (1998). *The McDonaldization thesis: Explorations and extensions*. Thousand Oaks, CA: Pine Forge Press.

Robelen, E. W. (2011). Most students lack civics proficiency on NAEP. *Education Week*. Retrieved from https://www.edweek.org/ew/articles/2011/05/04/30naep.h30.html

Robeyns, I. (2005). The capability approach: A theoretical survey. *Journal of Human Development, 6*, 93–117. http://dx.doi.org/10.1080/146498805200034266

Roblain, A., Azzi, A., & Licata, L. (2016). Why do majority members prefer immigrants who adopt the host culture? The role of perceived identification with the host culture. *International Journal of Intercultural Relations, 55*, 44–54. http://dx.doi.org/10.1016/j.ijintrel.2016.08.001

Rodrick, D. (2011). *The globalization paradox: Why global markets, states, and democracy can't coexist*. New York, NY: Oxford University Press.

Rogan, T. (2017, December 12). Why Turkey's Erdogan is threatening Israel. *Washington Examiner*. Retrieved form https://www.washingtonexaminer.com/why-turkeys-erdogan-is-threatening-israel

Rose, S. O. (1992). *Limited livelihoods: Gender and class in 19th century England*. London, England: Routledge.

Rupnik, J. (2016). Surging illiberalism in the East. *Journal of Democracy, 27*, 77–87. http://dx.doi.org/10.1353/jod.2016.0064

Ryan, L. (1981). *The aboriginal Tasmanians*. St. Lucia, Australia: The University of Queensland Press.

Saab, R., Tausch, N., & Cheung, W. Y. (2015). Acting in solidarity: Testing an extended dual pathway model of collective action by bystander group members. *British Journal of Social Psychology, 54*, 539–560. http://dx.doi.org/10.1111/bjso.12095

Sakwa, R. (2014). *Putin redux: Power and contradiction in contemporary Russia*. London, England: Routledge.

Sakwa, R. (2016). Political leadership. In S. K. Wegren (Ed.), *Putin's Russia: Past imperfect, future uncertain* (6th ed., pp. 23–42). New York, NY: Rowman & Littlefield.

Salehi-Isfahani, D. (2008, March 5). *Are Iranian women overeducated?* Retrieved from https://www.brookings.edu/opinions/are-iranian-women-overeducated/

Sampson, E. E. (1977). Psychology and the American ideal. *Journal of Personality and Social Psychology, 35*, 767–782. http://dx.doi.org/10.1037/0022-3514.35.11.767

Sandholtz, W., & Koetzle, W. (2000). Accounting for corruption: Economic structure, democracy, and trade. *International Studies Quarterly, 44*, 31–50. http://dx.doi.org/10.1111/0020-8833.00147

Sanger, D. E., Sullivan, E., & Kirkpatrick, D. D. (2018, October 4). Russia targeted investigators trying to expose its misdeeds, Western allies say. *The New York Times*. Retrieved from https://www.nytimes.com/2018/10/04/us/politics/russia-hacks-doping-poisoning.html

Santos, H. C., Varnum, M. E. W., & Grossman, I. (2017). Global increases in individualism. *Psychological Science, 28*, 1228–1239. http://dx.doi.org/10.1177/0956797617700622

Sartre, J.-P. (1956). Existentialism. In W. Kaufmann (Ed.), *Existentialism from Dostoevsky to Sartre* (pp. 222–311). Cleveland, OH: Meridian Books.

Scheidel, W. (2017). *The great leveler: Violence and the history of inequality from the Stone Age to the 21st century*. Princeton, NJ: Princeton University Press. http://dx.doi.org/10.1515/9781400884605

Scher, A. (2018, June 9). LGBTQ Russians are fleeing to NYC, but they still face hostility. *Huffington Post*. Retrieved from https://www.huffingtonpost.com/entry/lgbtq-russians-are-fleeing-to-nyc_us_5b17ebeae4b0734a9939b2a3

Schrecker, E. W. (1998). *Many are the crimes: McCarthyism in America*. Princeton, NJ: Princeton University Press.

Schulman, B. J., & Zelizer, J. E. (Eds.). (2017). *Media nation: The political history of news in modern America*. Philadelphia: University of Pennsylvania Press. http://dx.doi.org/10.9783/9780812293746

Searle-White, J. (2001). *The psychology of nationalism*. New York, NY: Palgrave. http://dx.doi.org/10.1057/9780312299057

Sen, A. (1990a). *Development as freedom*. Oxford, England: Oxford University Press.

Sen, A. (1990b). Justice: Means versus freedoms. *Philosophy & Public Affairs, 19*, 111–121.

Shamir, B., Pillai, R., & Bligh, M. (Eds.). (2007). *Follower centered perspectives on leadership: A tribute to the memory of James R. Meindl*. Charlotte, NC: Information Age.

Shapiro, R. J. (2018, September 30). Don't be fooled: Working Americans are worse off under Trump. *The Washington Post*. Retrieved from https://www.washingtonpost.com/opinions/dont-be-fooled-working-americans-are-worse-off-under-trump/2018/09/30/f789f198-be82-11e8-be70-52bd-11fe18af_story.html?utm_term=.3daa6b97610c

Shapiro, S., & Brown, C. (2018). *The state of civic education*. Retrieved from Center for American Progress website: https://www.americanprogress.org/issues/education-k-12/reports/2018/02/21/446857/state-civics-education/

Sharp, G. (2010). *From dictatorship to democracy* (4th ed.). East Boston, MA: The Albert Einstein Institute.

Sherrod, L. R., Torney-Purta, J., & Flanagan, C. A. (Eds.). (2010). *Handbook of research on civic engagement in youth*. New York, NY: Wiley. http://dx.doi.org/10.1002/9780470767603

Shipman, A., Edmunds, J., & Turner, B. S. (2018). *The new power elite: Inequality, politics and greed*. New York, NY: Anthem Press. http://dx.doi.org/10.2307/j.ctt22h6qjp

Shukri, S. F. M., & Hossain, I. (2017). Strategic shifts in discourse by the AKP in Turkey, 2002–2015. *Mediterranean Quarterly, 28,* 5–26. http://dx.doi.org/10.1215/10474552-4216388

Silver, N. (2018, May 8). President Trump's approval rating has been steady. Richard Nixon's once was too. *FiveThirtyEight.* Retrieved from https://fivethirtyeight.com/features/president-trumps-approval-rating-has-been-steady-richard-nixons-once-was-too/

Sinclair, B., Smith, S. S., & Tucker, P. D. (2018). "It's largely a rigged system": Voter confidence and the winner effect in 2016. *Political Research Quarterly, 71,* pp. 854–868.

Singer, S. (2017, February 13). U.S. public schools are not failing: They're among the best in the world. *Huffington Post.* Retrieved from https://www.huffingtonpost.com/entry/us-public-schools-are-not-failing-theyre-among_us_5894e819e4b061551b3dfe51

Sinha, M. (2017). *The slave's cause: A history of abolition.* New Haven, CT: Yale University press.

Smith, A. (2017). *The wealth of nations.* CreateSpace Independent Publishing Platform. (Original work published 1776)

Smith, D. N., & Hanley, E. (2018). The anger games: Who voted for Donald Trump in the 2016 election, and why? *Critical Sociology, 44,* 195–212. http://dx.doi.org/10.1177/0896920517740615

Smith, S. A. (Ed.). (2014). *The Oxford handbook of the history of communism.* Oxford, England: Oxford University Press.

Sorkin, A. R. (2017, December 18). Tax cuts benefit the ultra rich, but not the merely rich. *The New York Times.* Retrieved from https://www.nytimes.com/2017/12/18/business/dealbook/tax-bill-wealthy.html

Spooner, M. H. (1994). *Soldiers in a narrow land: The Pinochet regime in Chile.* Berkeley: University of California Press.

Stagner, R. (1936). Fascist attitudes: An exploratory study. *The Journal of Social Psychology, 7,* 309–319. http://dx.doi.org/10.1080/00224545.1936.9919882

Staples, L. (2016). *Roots to power: A manual for grassroots organization.* Santa Barbara, CA: Praeger.

Steg, L., Van den Berg, A. E., & De Groot, J. I. M. (Eds.). (2013). *Environmental psychology: An introduction.* Chichester, England: Wiley.

Stockholm Center for Freedom. (2018). *"I am here despite assassination threats," Erdoğan claims in visit to Bosnia.* Retrieved from https://stockholmcf.org/i-am-here-despite-assassination-threats-erdogan-claims-in-visit-to-bosnia

Stone, C. B., & Bietti, L. M. (Eds.). (2016). *Contextualizing human memory: An interdisciplinary approach to understanding how individuals and groups remember the past.* London, England: Routledge.

Stone, J. (2018, June 4). The right-wing populists doing well across Europe, from Marine Le Pen to Viktor Orban. *The Independent.* Retrieved from https://www.independent.co.uk/news/world/europe/europe-populists-right-wing-success-marine-le-pen-viktor-orban-italy-slovenia-a8382766.html

Storm, I., Sobolewska, M., & Ford, R. (2017). Is ethnic prejudice declining in Britain? Change in social distance attitudes among ethnic majority and minority Britons. *The British Journal of Sociology, 68,* 410–434. http://dx.doi.org/10.1111/1468-4446.12250

Streeck, W. (2017). *How will capitalism end?* New York, NY: Verso.

Stroessinger, J. G. (2007). *Why nations go to war* (10th ed.). Belmont, CA: Thomson-Wadsworth.

Stroup, M. D. (2007). Economic freedom, democracy, and the quality of life. *World Development, 35,* 52–66. http://dx.doi.org/10.1016/j.worlddev.2006.09.003

Sveiby, K. E. (2011). Collective leadership with power symmetry: Lessons from Aboriginal prehistory. *Leadership, 7,* 385–414. http://dx.doi.org/10.1177/1742715011416892

Swencionis, J. K., & Goff, P. A. (2017). The psychological science of racial bias and policing. *Psychology, Public Policy, and Law, 23,* 398–409. http://dx.doi.org/10.1037/law0000130

Swinford, S. (2018, April 12). Russia "must give answers" after watchdog confirms spy and daughter poisoned with "high purity" Novichok. *The Telegraph.* Retrieved from https://www.telegraph.co.uk/news/2018/04/12/russian-spy-daughter-poisoned-high-purity-strain-novichok-chemical

Tajfel, H., Billig, M. G., Bundy, R. P., & Flament, C. (1971). Social categorization and intergroup behaviour. *European Journal of Social Psychology, 1,* 149–178. http://dx.doi.org/10.1002/ejsp.2420010202

Tajfel, H., & Wilkes, A. L. (1963). Classification and quantitative judgment. *British Journal of Psychology, 54,* 101–113. http://dx.doi.org/10.1111/j.2044-8295.1963.tb00865.x

Taylor, D. M., & de la Sablonnière, R. (2014). *Toward constructive change in Aboriginal communities: A social psychology perspective.* Montreal, Canada: McGill-Queens University Press.

Teixeira, R. (1992). *The disappearing American voter.* Washington, DC: Brookings Institution.

Thelin, J. R. (2011). *A history of American higher education.* Baltimore, MD: Johns Hopkins University Press.

Thomas, E. F., & Louis, W. R. (2014). When will collective action be effective? Violent and non-violent protests differentially influence perceptions of legitimacy and efficacy among sympathizers. *Personality and Social Psychology Bulletin, 40,* 263–276. http://dx.doi.org/10.1177/0146167213510525

Thoreau, H. D. (2003). *Walden and civil disobedience.* New York, NY: Barnes & Noble Classics. (*Walden* originally published 1854; *Civil disobedience* originally published 1849)

Tolstoy, L. (1957). *War and peace* (Vols. 1–2). (R. Edmonds, Trans.). Harmondsworth, England: Penguin. (Original work published 1869)

Toobin, J. (2018, January 6). Donald Trump and the rule of law. *The New Yorker.* Retrieved from https://www.newyorker.com/news/daily-comment/donald-trump-and-the-rule-of-law

Tsygankov, A. P. (2016). Foreign policy and relations with the United States. In S. K. Wegren (Ed.), *Putin's Russia: Past imperfect, future uncertain* (pp. 233–255). New York, NY: Rowman & Littlefield.

Turner, B. S. (Ed.). (2010). *The new Blackwell companion to the sociology of religion.* Chichester, England: Wiley/Blackwell. http://dx.doi.org/10.1002/9781444320787

Turner, F. J. (1920). *The frontier in American history.* New York, NY: Holt.

United Nations. (1948). *Universal declaration of human rights.* Retrieved from http://www.un.org/en/documents/udhr

United Nations Development Programme. (1990). *Human development report.* New York, NY: Oxford University Press.

Unterhalter, E., & North, A. (2010). Assessing gender mainstreaming in the education sector: Depoliticised technique or a step towards women's rights and gender equality? *Compare: A Journal of Comparative Education, 40,* 389–404. http://dx.doi.org/10.1080/03057925.2010.490358

U.S. Department of Education. (2012). *Advancing civic learning and engagement in democracy: A road map and call to action.*

Van Herpen, M. H. (2013). *Putinism: The slow rise of a radical right regime in Russia.* New York, NY: Palgrave Macmillan. http://dx.doi.org/10.1057/9781137282811

Van Herpen, M. H. (2014). *Putin's wars: The rise of Russia's new imperialism.* New York, NY: Rowman & Littlefield.

Van Vugt, M., Hogan, R., & Kaiser, R. B. (2008). Leadership, followership, and evolution: Some lessons from the past. *American Psychologist, 63,* 182–196. http://dx.doi.org/10.1037/0003-066X.63.3.182

Vance-Cheng, R., Rooney, I. C., Moghaddam, F. M., & Harré, R. (2013). Waging war, talking peace: A positioning analysis of storylines used to interpret "war for peace" rhetoric. In R. Harré & F. M. Moghaddam (Eds.), *The psychology of friendship and enmity: Relationships in love, work, politics, and war: Vol. 2. Group and intergroup understanding* (pp. 11–36). Santa Barbara, CA: Praeger.

Voegtlin, C., Boehm, S. A., & Bruch, H. (2015). How to empower employees: Using training to enhance work units' collective empowerment. *International Journal of Manpower, 36,* 354–373. http://dx.doi.org/10.1108/IJM-10-2012-0158

Vosoughi, S., Roy, D., & Aral, S. (2018). The spread of true and false news online. *Science, 359,* 1146–1151. http://dx.doi.org/10.1126/science.aap9559

Vygotsky, L. (1978). *Thought and language.* Cambridge, MA: MIT Press.

Wagoner, B., de Luna, E. B., & Glaveanu, V. (2018). *The road to actualized democracy: A psychological exploration.* Charlotte, NC: Information Age.

Waldman, S. A., & Caliskan, E. (2017). *The new Turkey and its discontents.* New York, NY: Oxford University Press. http://dx.doi.org/10.1093/oso/9780190668372.001.0001

Warshaw, R. (1962). *The immediate experience: Movies, comics, theater and other aspects of popular culture.* New York, NY: Doubleday.

Watts, T. W., Duncan, G. J., & Quan, H. (2018). Revisiting the marshmallow test: A conceptual replication investigating links between early delay of gratification and later outcomes. *Psychological Science.* Retrieved from https://dx.doi.org/10.1177/0956797618761661

Watzlawick, P., Weakland, J. H., & Fisch, R. (1974). *Change: Principles of problem formation and problem resolution.* New York, NY: Norton.

Weeks, B. E. (2015). Emotions, partisanship, and misperceptions: How anger and anxiety moderate the effect of partisanship bias on susceptibility to political misinformation. *Journal of Communication, 65,* 699–719. http://dx.doi.org/10.1111/jcom.12164

Wegren, S. K. (2016). *Putin's Russia: Past imperfect, future uncertain* (6th ed.). New York, NY: Rowman & Littlefield.

Weingast, B. R. (1998). Political stability and Civil War: Institutions, commitment, and American democracy. In R. H. Bates, A. Greif, M. Levi, J. L. Rosenthal, & B. R. Weingast (Eds.), *Analytic narratives* (pp. 149–193). Princeton, NJ: Princeton University Press.

What has become of the Republican Party? (2018, April 21–27). *The Economist,* p. 9.

Wike, R., Simmons, K., & Fetterolf, J. (2017). *Globally, broad support for representative and direct democracy.* Retrieved from Pew Research Center website: http://www.pewglobal.org/2017/10/16/globally-broad-support-for-representative-and-direct-democracy

Wilcox, Q. (2017). The trickle down theory of corruption. *Huffington Post.* Retrieved from http://www.huffingtonpost.com/quenby-wilcox-/the-trickle-down-theory-o_b_11071892.html

Witte, G., & Birnbaum, M. (2018, April 6). E.U. faces a rebellion tougher than Brexit. *The Washington Post,* pp. A1, A9.

Woessmann, L. (2016). The importance of school systems: Evidence from international differences in student achievement. *The Journal of Economic Perspectives, 30,* 3–32. http://dx.doi.org/10.1257/jep.30.3.3

Wood, J. C., & McLure, M. (Eds.). (1999). *Vilfredo Pareto: Critical assessments of leading economists.* London, England: Routledge.

World Economic Forum. (2018). *The global risks report 2018* (13th ed.). Retrieved from http://www3.weforum.org/docs/WEF_GRR18_Report.pdf

World Health Organization. (2018, January 31). *Suicide, key facts.* Retrieved from http://www.who.int/en/news-room/fact-sheets/detail/suicide

Wright, W. (1975). *Six guns and society: A structured study of the Western.* Berkeley: University of California Press.

Xue, L., Kerstetter, D., & Hunt, C. (2017). Tourism development and changing rural identity in China. *Annals of Tourism Research, 66,* 170–182. http://dx.doi.org/10.1016/j.annals.2017.07.016

Yadav, V., & Mukherjee, B. (2016). *The politics of corruption in dictatorships.* New York, NY: Cambridge University Press. http://dx.doi.org/10.1017/CBO9781316014950

Yardi, S., & Boyd, D. (2010). Dynamic debates: An analysis of group polarization over time on Twitter. *Bulletin of Science, Technology & Society, 30,* 316–327. http://dx.doi.org/10.1177/0270467610380011

Yavuz, M. H. (2018). Postscript: How credible are alternative coup scenarios? In M. H. Yavuz & B. Balci (Eds.), *Turkey's 15th coup: What happened and why* (eBook). Salt Lake City: University of Utah Press.

Yeo, A., & Chubb, D. (Eds.). (2018). *North Korean human rights: Activists and networks.* New York, NY: Cambridge University Press. http://dx.doi.org/10.1017/9781108589543

Zimbardo, P. (2008). *The Lucifer effect: Understanding how good people turn evil.* New York, NY: Random House.

Zoega, G. (2016). *On the causes of Brexit: Regional differences in economic prosperity and voting behavior.* Retrieved from https://voxeu.org/article/brexit-economic-prosperity-and-voting-behavior

Zywicki, T., & Koopman, C. (2017). *The changing of the guard: The political economy of administrative bloat in American higher education* (George Mason Law & Economic Research Paper No. 17-12). Retrieved from https://papers.ssrn.com/sol3/papers.cfm?abstract_id=2939915

INDEX

A

J

K

T

X

Y

ABOUT THE AUTHOR

Fathali M. Moghaddam, PhD, is a professor in the Department of Psychology and director of the Interdisciplinary Program in Cognitive Science at Georgetown University. He is the editor of *Peace and Conflict: Journal of Peace Psychology* (a quarterly journal published by the American Psychological Association). Dr. Moghaddam was born in Iran, educated from an early age in England, and worked for the United Nations and for McGill University before joining Georgetown in 1990. He returned to Iran in the "Spring of Revolution" in 1979 and was researching there during the hostage-taking crisis and the early years of the Iran–Iraq war. He has conducted experimental and field research in numerous cultural contexts and published extensively on radicalization, intergroup conflict, human rights and duties, and the psychology of dictatorship and democracy. His most recent books include *The Psychology of Dictatorship* (2013), *The Psychology of Democracy* (2016), *The SAGE Encyclopedia of Political Behavior* (2017), and *Mutual Radicalization: How Groups and Nations Drive Each Other to Extremes* (2018). Dr. Moghaddam has received numerous recognitions for his scholarly contributions, including the Outstanding International Psychologist Award for 2012 from the American Psychological Association, Division of International Psychology. More about his research can be found on his website (http://www.fathalimoghaddam.com).